More Praise for Rick Webb's
Agency: Starting a Creative Firm in the Age of Digital Marketing

"A compendium of everything that all the smartest people in agencies have ever told me, but that I'd long forgotten. This is less of a book, more of a call to action. I found myself plotting my own start-up well before the halfway mark."

—Ben Malbon, Marketing Director, Creative Partnerships, Google

"*Agency* is the unvarnished truth about starting and running an agency. Its thoroughness will change the lives of many agency owners. But its transparency might have a larger impact—asking 'why are you doing this?' and possibly even rescuing some from going down a path that is not for the faint of heart."

—Michael Lebowitz, Founder and CEO, Big Spaceship

"Webb's *Agency* dives deep into all the things you could, should, and will probably end up doing when you build your own agency. Webb shares invaluable lessons from the advertising/marketing world and beyond. This is necessary reading for anyone who has dreamt of building their own company."

—Doug Jaeger, Partner, JaegerSloan, Former President, Art Directors Club

"This is the book I wish I was able to read before I started my agency. It's filled with lessons I learned the hard way. If you're even considering starting an agency, read this book before you do. It will either scare you out of doing it, or inspire and lead you toward building the next great shop. *Agency* will be your *Hitchhiker's Guide to the Galaxy*."

—Ian Schafer, CEO, Deep Focus

"When I sat down to take a look at Webb's book, I grabbed a pen in case there were a few gems worth underlining. Webb is bright and brutally honest. Turns out I underlined, exclamation-pointed, and asterisked almost the entire book. Anyone in business would benefit from giving *Agency* a read."

—Susan Credle, Chief Creative Officer, Leo Burnett, USA

"There aren't many tools out there for folks building modern creative firms, because so much has changed in terms of what clients and consumers want. Webb has done an excellent job of ripping the bedsheet off of the old agency model and making us all stare at how strange it is to operate that way in today's world. He has actually been in the trenches, successfully doing the work that he is writing about, so his advice is relevant and credible, which makes it easier to get behind and put into practice."

—James Moody, Cofounder and CEO, Guerilla Suit

AGENCY

STARTING A CREATIVE FIRM IN THE AGE OF DIGITAL MARKETING

RICK WEBB

palgrave
macmillan

AGENCY

First published in 2015 by
PALGRAVE MACMILLAN®
in the United States—a division of St. Martin's Press LLC,
175 Fifth Avenue, New York, NY 10010.

Where this book is distributed in the UK, Europe and the rest of the world,
this is by Palgrave Macmillan, a division of Macmillan Publishers Limited,
registered in England, company number 785998, of Houndmills,
Basingstoke, Hampshire RG21 6XS.

Palgrave Macmillan is the global academic imprint of the above companies
and has companies and representatives throughout the world.

Palgrave® and Macmillan® are registered trademarks in the United States,
the United Kingdom, Europe and other countries.

ISBN: 978–1–137–27986–6

Library of Congress Cataloging-in-Publication Data

Webb, Rick.
    Agency : starting a creative firm in the age of digital marketing / Rick
Webb.
        pages cm.—(Advertising age)
        ISBN 978–1–137–27986–6—
        ISBN 1–137–27986–9
        1. Advertising agencies—Management. 2. Internet marketing.
    3. Marketing—Management. 4. New business enterprises—Management.
    5. Small business—Management. 6. Entrepreneurship. I. Title.

HF6178.W43 2014
659.1068′1—dc23   2014024464

A catalogue record of the book is available from the British Library.

Design by Newgen Knowledge Works (P) Ltd., Chennai, India.

First edition: January 2015

10 9 8 7 6 5 4 3 2 1

Printed in the United States of America.

For Mallory, who inspired me to write it all down.

CONTENTS

ACKNOWLEDGMENTS

Thanks first go to my partners and coworkers at The Barbarian Group. Benjamin Palmer, Keith Butters, Robert Hodgin, Aubrey Anderson, Jay Sun, Bruce Winterton, and Brian Costello were some of the best partners a man could hope to work for. Among the present and former Barbarian ranks, Rob Allen, Noah Brier, Chet Gulland, Tim Hwang, Shelby MacLeod, Frank Marquardt, Eva McCloskey, Doug McDermott, Ryan McManus, Colin Nagy, Mike Paulo, Doug Pfeffer, Kenji Ross, Mike Rubenstein, Stephanie Smeriglio, Cheryl Swirnow, and Nat Wales deserve particular recognition. Last but not least, the irreplaceable Jen Jonsson taught me a good chunk of what lies in these pages.

Thanks to those whom I interviewed for the book, who read it for me, or who offered invaluable advice, including Mallory Blair, Zac Blume, Rick Boyko, John Bragg, David Catalano, Peter Coughter, Sue Credle, Cindy Gallop, Ron Goldin, Steve Hayden, Doug Jaeger, Gareth Kay, Kevin Kearney, Diana Kimball, Lydia Kim, Michael Lebowitz, Glynnis MacNicol, Ben Malbon, Jenna Matecki, Megan McCarthy, Josh Miller, James Moody, Chris Puckett, Paul Rush, Ian Schafer, Elizabeth Spiers, Helayne Spivack and everyone at the Brandcenter, Gabriel Stuart, Baratunde Thurston, Ronen V, Sam Valenti, Alex Van Buren, and Gino Zahnd.

Thanks to everyone at *AdAge*, most notably Allison Arden, who helped me get this project off the ground. Thanks to Laurie Harting for editing the book and easing me gently into the world of publishing, Alexis Nelson, and everyone at Palgrave Macmillan. Thanks, too, to Cynthia Mason, without whose help this never would have happened.

Finally, personal thanks to go to my parents, my sister, Val, and my wife, Emma, who pops up once or twice in the book despite her grave concerns. Love.

INTRODUCTION

Agency. Services firm. Creative services. Consultancy. Studio. So many different terms that all come to the same point: you are growing your craft into something larger than you.

Are there how-to manuals for starting such a company? David Ogilvy's *Confessions of an Ad Man* comes to mind. There is none greater. It's still a wonderful read. If you haven't read it, you should go read that first. It's astonishing how much of it is still applicable today. But other than that, I have not found much useful information out there. My shop had to wing it. We had to learn as we went, and, boy, did we make a lot of mistakes. I would have killed for a book that told me concretely what the hell was going on and how to handle it.

What *are* out there are pithy books by famous ad execs talking about the work. They offer inspirational quotes, like, "I wouldn't hesitate for a second to choose the plain looking ad that is alive and vital and meaningful, over the ad that is beautiful and dumb" (Bill Bernbach).[1] Your head is filled with visions of creating great ads, of changing culture, of pounding your fists on the table and telling the clients, "Damn it, man. This ad is genius. You must run it." They look at you with a mixture of awe and fear and buy your work. You walk out the door. Your colleagues are amazed.

Sure, there are tons of great ad books written by great ad creatives. They are books about the process of making a great campaign. What's different here?

Many people starting out agencies come to me asking for advice. My old agency did some great work, but by and large, the vast majority of questions people ask me have nothing to do with coming up with a great idea, or how to sell great work. *They already know how to do great work.*

Instead, what people tend to ask is a litany of pedestrian questions about billing, about human resources (HR), about hiring people, firing people. They want to know about dealing with banks, information technology (IT) departments, and (shudder) procurement officers. People ask questions about how to make money and how to sell their agency.

Things have changed in advertising and marketing. A lot. The technology, the processes. Everything you read about in the ad press every day. But more importantly, the *people* starting agencies are different. Ad people still start big, traditional agencies, like they did in the old days. An art director, an account director, a finance officer, and a copywriter branch off from a preexisting agency and hang out their shingle. They might not know jack about the Internet or everything that's changing in the world, and you might, but they sure know how agencies are supposed to work. And most agency management books are written for these people.

Generally speaking, however, this is a rarity these days.

These days, most of the coolest, dynamic new shops launched in the last few years have been founded by outsiders. Designers, PR people, product people, developers. People who sense an opportunity to offer their services to marketers, but don't know where to start. This may well be you.

These people—your people!—need to know different things about agency life. They don't need to be told that the Internet isn't a scary place and that it's important. They need to understand what the hell weird terms like "below-the-line" mean. They need to understand the mechanics of bootstrapping, since in the beautiful tech start-up land that they read about in *TechCrunch*, everyone is funded. They need to know about making products at agencies. They need to know how to price and bill a job. They definitely need to know what a "media agency" is. And many of them don't. When I came to advertising, it took me years to figure out what a "media agency" was. No one told me. I was embarrassed to ask.

Marketing companies used to be started by marketing people. Now they are started by Internet people. They need a different education.

Finally, let's face it: most of the books on this subject are no fun. They don't tell you the truth. Well, I mean, they don't lie, but they hardly tell you how things play out on the ground. This is what has made Ogilvy's book so timeless—it's so much more than a manual. It offers proper advice, yes, but it also has a point of view. It says controversial things once in a while. It speaks from experience and isn't afraid to share it.

So that's what I'm setting out to do here. Hopefully you'll understand what it means to run one of these companies, and you'll get practical advice out of this book. But ideally it'll also help you think. It'll help you think about what you're even doing in this business. It'll cover things like billing and HR and procurement, yes, but it'll also cover such vital topics as the existential freak-out, the bum of a partner, the joys and miseries of trying to build a product inside your agency. Should you work for equity? Can I get rich out of this? Can I get really rich? Can I get really, *really* rich? (Answer: no, not really.)

A few words on terminology before we begin.

People have some baggage around the word "agency." This is not entirely unreasonable. The term is from a past time when companies such as ours operated as an *agent* of a client company. In a world that is increasingly more project-driven versus retainer driven, this is often no longer the case. While I've endeavored not to use the word too often when referring to your company, it's best to not get too hung up on this topic. The word's meaning has evolved. At points where I'm talking about your company *and* a traditional agency, I've taken additional care to avoid referring to your company as an agency, reserving the word for the larger, traditional agency.

We should also make a note on the word "advertising" versus "marketing." In this book, we will use both words, more or less interchangeably, for the world in which your company operates. We do this because on the Web, the two are starting to blend together. Advertising, of course, traditionally involved the purchase of paid media, whereas marketing was more scientific and holistic. Social media, especially, is blurring this: ad agencies often do social media marketing, for example, that involves no paid media. You may well work in both marketing and advertising right at this moment. This is a fascinating topic, but one for another book. PR agency owner Mallory Blair commented on this while reading this book, "I just honestly pretend like you're a Canadian who calls PR 'advertising' just like they call bathrooms 'washrooms' etc. and it works out." Sound advice.

A final note: I am advocating a specific approach. I am advocating an approach of making your agency grow through greatness. There will be times when reading this book, you'll find yourself saying, "Is that really true? Couldn't I win the pitch on a mediocre idea and a cheap price?" The answer is probably yes. There are agencies out there that are huge and rich and astonishingly mediocre. This is not a book to make an agency like that, for two reasons. Firstly, I don't see the point. The only reasons that agencies like that exist have to do with money, and if you're just in it to make money, why are you in advertising? You may as well go straight into banking. Secondly, those are agencies started by financiers, and not practitioners of a craft. This book is for the practitioner. If you're looking to that approach, I'm afraid this book will only be moderately helpful, if at all. But if you're looking to make a great company, and one people love to work at, this is the book for you. Let's go!

PART I

CULTURE AND VISION

WHY AM I DOING THIS?

Why do you want to start an agency?

Why, in God's name, do you want to start an ad agency or, whoops, excuse me, a creative services business? How did you arrive at this decision? What has prompted you?

This is the first thing I always ask people when they tell me they are thinking of starting a services firm, and it never ceases to amaze me how many of them can't give me an answer.

BE HONEST WITH YOURSELF AND YOUR PARTNERS

Maybe your parents were in advertising, and you just know it's your calling. Maybe you like to be around creative people, but don't feel very creative yourself, and yet don't want to spend your life in an industry devoid of creativity. I know a lot of those people. That's totally cool.

Here's the important thing: whatever your reasons for wanting to start a marketing services company, it is absolutely necessary that you are honest with yourself and your partners. It isn't necessarily a bad thing if you and your partners have different ideas of what they want to get out of the company, so long as these are frankly addressed up front. It's amazing how much two people can discuss a plan without getting to the central core of why they're doing it, and if you're not careful, you'll end up several years down the road before such things are frankly addressed, and by then it may well be too late to accommodate both of your needs and desires.

A large chunk of the disasters that happen and that ruin agencies stem from this simple problem at the beginning. Time and time again I've seen agencies that aren't quite sure why they're even doing this work. I've seen agencies in which the different founders want different things, and they have to go through tremendous restructuring and adjustment to address this, often at a critical time in the company's life when they should be focused on killing it. It's a distraction at best, a catastrophe if you're not careful.

In my agency, when we finally got around to asking each other what we wanted out of this whole enterprise and why we did it, it was an incredibly awkward conversation, and many people had trouble even expressing what they wanted to gain. The realization that dawned on all of us that we wanted different things was tough to handle. We had been heads down, doing great work, growing and becoming more famous all along the way. But eventually we got to a point where it became obvious we expected the firm to go in different directions. We got through these existential challenges, but not without a year or two of heartbreak and turmoil. It wasn't pretty.

And even if you're solo, know thyself. Stick a pin on a timeline five years out and say where you want to be. Will you be exactly there? No. But by now, hopefully, you've learned in life that the pin in the map is more than a prediction, more than an exact plan. It is a guiding light, a magic eight ball, a decision-making cypher. Answer the hard questions up front. It's easier than doing it later. Honest.

THE VISION

Before you get started running your business out in the big, cold world, you need to know what your company stands for. This is not an academic exercise. Doing this right can have a profound impact on your business as it grows. Doing it poorly—or not doing it all—can have a wildly detrimental impact on your company.

What is a vision? It is more than a tagline, although that may be part of it.

It is different from a mission statement, though that, too, is certainly related.

A vision is for internal and external use. There may be different interpretations or focuses on different parts of the vision for different audiences, but it is paramount that they are all in alignment. The same vision that drives you should be the vision that you claim drives you to your clients. Anything else breeds dishonesty, and dishonesty breeds malcontent within and without and, worse, amoral employees.

The vision of a company needs to come from the leadership of the company—that is you, or you and your partners. The more people who are involved, the more difficult it is. Doing it later is harder. Do it now, do it early, and do it quickly. It should act as your beacon for hiring employees, choosing work, and making all of your difficult decisions.

MISSION VERSUS VISION

So what is a vision? Why do we focus on this, as opposed to the "mission statement" that I hear so much about in my business books?

The main distinction between the mission and the vision is that one describes the *goal* and one describes the *tactics*. The mission of a company is inherent in what it does. That is, if you are a design firm, your mission is probably going to include delivering design to clients.

The vision, by contrast, is broader in its industry scope. The vision describes *why* you are going to do this.

Nike's mission statement is "To bring inspiration and innovation to every athlete in the world."[1] This does not describe its values, or its tactics, or its beliefs, but simply what it is aiming to achieve.

The values of a company are more important than the mission. The values are what makes it distinct. The values define who the company is and how it will operate.

YOUR VISION IS YOUR BRAND

Many people in marketing confuse a vision with a "brand." What is a brand? I stumbled upon a post on the Q&A site Quora some years ago that asked exactly this question. The Quora community voted this as the best answer: "a brand is the complete expression of an entity (company, product, person, etc.) that is being communicated creating an experience *in the public*, both rational and emotional."[2] (emphasis added).

The challenge with a brand is that it's only externally facing. This can only take a company so far, if the company's internal beliefs and values radically differ from its external brand. The challenge with this is that in the era of social media and increasing transparency, it's becoming more and more impossible to put forth a different face to the public than a company shows internally. Zappos's chief executive officer (CEO), Tony Hsieh, sums this up in his groundbreaking book *Delivering Happiness*: "With the Internet connecting everyone together, companies are becoming more and more transparent whether they like it or not. An unhappy customer or a disgruntled employee can blog about a bad experience with a company, and the story can spread like wildfire by e-mail or with tools like Twitter.[3]"

Hsieh directly attributes the success of Zappo's to having a set of core values that the company lives, both internally and externally. As Hsieh says,

> We believe that it's really important to come up with core values that you can commit to. And by commit, we mean that you're willing to hire and fire based on them. If you're willing to do that, then you're well on your way to building a company culture that is in line with the brand you want to build. You can let all of your employees be your brand ambassadors, not just the marketing or PR department. And they can be brand ambassadors both inside and outside the office.[4]

In rating The Barbarian Group's success in developing a set of core values, I would give us a B–. And even when we half-assed the whole affair of defining core values, these values were incredibly useful on innumerable occasions. They became the rules of any debate, the guideposts to making difficult decisions, to settling disagreements. "Which of these solutions best represents our core values?" They give the company something to fall back on when telling a client that it is not going to do something the client otherwise wants. "I'm sorry, but that is just not something this company believes in." Values can assist in the hiring of people. The benefits are innumerable.

And, even better, the whole thing is basically free. Not having a vision for your company is like not taking a free upgrade to first class. Why would you *not* do it?

MORE THAN A TAGLINE, THOUGH A TAGLINE HELPS

Many people—especially consumers—confuse a brand with a tagline. A tagline is a wonderful thing, and can be incredibly useful. Ours was "It's gonna be awesome," born of a phrase my partner, Benjamin, used to always say to clients as the project was getting going. People loved it. Clients called us on it when things weren't awesome. "This is not that awesome," clients would say when they were disappointed, and it would rally us, every time.

But that tagline was not our values. It was just a facet of them. Compare Nike's mission statement: "To bring inspiration and innovation to every athlete in the world" with its world-renowned tagline "Just do it."

Taglines can change through the years. "Coke is it," "The Real Thing," "Happiness." All of these are taglines for the Coca-Cola company over the past few decades, which have changed, while their core mission and values have not.

The tagline flows from the vision.

YOUR VISION IS YOUR CULTURE

It's important to note the immense influence that your company's values will have on the culture of the company. If your values are explicitly about profit, you may influence a hardworking, take-no-prisoners sort of culture, whereas if your values explicitly recognize the importance of fun and a work-life balance, you will see a more laid-back vibe. If your culture and your values are at odds, your clients and employees will sense this, and will abandon you. Says Hsieh, "if you get the culture right, most of the other stuff...will happen naturally on its own."[5] There are practical benefits of spending time on building culture. One of the great things about having a culture infused with the values of the company is that you have a substantially increased ability to trust your employees to do the right thing.

Brand. Tagline. Culture. All of these flow from the values of the company, similar to when your mind, body and spirit are aligned. It's as if you just went to the chiropractor, and nothing is out of place, everything gels, and everything operates on its own, with excellence and efficiency.

Many of the rewards for culture building through the years will be manifest. Over time, it will be obvious that the exercise has saved you millions of dollars. Many other times, things will just work. You'll never even realize a massive problem you've avoided because an HR director did not hire the wrong person, or someone didn't accidentally do something that your company found immoral, reaping untold damage that you have avoided.

DEFINING YOUR VISION

Something has driven you to start this company. Perhaps you are in it for the money—that is okay. Perhaps you've been frustrated by the way other people in your industry run their business. Perhaps they don't believe in the work, or take enough care. Perhaps there is a specific process issue you take with the way in which everyone else does their business: such as you do not believe in a separate client service department, or you see the negative toll that constant pitch work can take on a company, and you've vowed to change it.

We can take this motivation and turn it into your values. Make a list of everything you want your company to be. "No assholes." "No compromises on the work." "No interference from client service." "The best." "Rich."

Commenting on the founding of BBH, John Hegarty talks about the company's founding principles. "I explained the need for an advertising agency to stand for something. Don't just rely on your creative reputations—have some beliefs that, when articulated, would dramatize a client benefit. In other words: work out what your 'angle' is. It's a brutal yet simple way of interrogating your value. I reminded my friend of how we started BBH, with no creative pitches from day one. We did this, perverse as it may seem, to dramatize our creative credentials—to put them on a pedestal."[6]

Next take this list and turn it into positive traits. Turn "no assholes" into "we believe in kindness and professionalism in all people and projects." "No compromises" turns into "We aim to do the best work, bar none," and so on. Scott Goodson of Strawberry Frog describes the relationship between their name, culture, and their vision. "When we set out, *Advertising Age* had published an article calling the established corporate agencies 'dinosaurs.' We were Frogs. Dinosaurs were slow and had the systems of the past that weren't the systems of the future and represented all the things that lead to bad creativity and expensive costs for clients....It was Frog v Dinosaur in an epic battle along the very battle lines of evolution and fun."[7]

Think about the things that go without saying, and say them. You want to make money. You want your clients to be happy. You care about design or your trade. You have opinions about your trade.

At The Barbarian Group, early on (though not soon enough), we came up with our list of values for the company. It was a great list. We included it in every initial proposal to our clients.

But it missed a few things. Years into TBG, in 2009, I came out of my office in TriBeCa and asked the intern who sat outside my office in the intern pool what they were up to.

"Oh, I'm just leaving comments on this message board about Project X," she said.

"What do you mean?" I asked. I was the engagement partner on this project, and hadn't heard of any message board component.

"Oh, you know. I am pretending to be a teenage girl in these message boards and talking about how cool Project X is and telling people to visit it," the intern replied. You could tell the woman was not especially psyched about this assignment.

Furthermore, this activity was also expressly against everything TBG had believed in, as we absolutely believed in the authenticity of our work, never being fake, and never deceiving the end customer.

"How did this come about?" I asked.

"Oh, the client asked for it."

I dug a little more, finding the client service exec on the project and asking her what gives. You could tell that she, too, wasn't super excited about the assignment, but she told me, "Oh, you know, the client didn't really budget for any marketing, and wants more people to see the project, and asked us to do this as a favor. It's not the greatest, but I figured we'd do them a solid."

It occurred to me that the client service executive's heart was in the right place: she wanted to serve the client. And it also occurred to me that, while the partners believed passionately that we should not deceive customers, we didn't do a great job making this value completely clear to all of the employees. We had been growing fast, and we could no longer rely on word of mouth.

On that day, I stopped everything, and set up a process to speak to every single new employee myself, for 15 minutes, as a stopgap. I would tell them that if they ever, ever felt like they were doing something deceitful or unethical, to immediately come to me and let me know. They were seeing these words come out of my mouth, and I meant them—we, the whole company and all the partners—meant them. I addressed this explicitly in the next company meeting.

We updated our values. Hsieh says in *Delivering Happiness* that it took him a few years to nail down the perfect list of values. It will take time. But start now.

WRITE IT DOWN, DO IT NOW.

This is not to say we didn't, as individuals, have values. This was, more than anything, a process error. We didn't make them easily findable. We thought that it would be manifestly obvious that we should only hire nice people, until one day an asshole accidentally got hired whom we didn't know about. We thought it was obvious we shouldn't deceive the customer, until one day, an intern was hard at work deceiving the customer without our knowing about it.

It is important that you write these values down and spread them throughout the company.

THE VALUE PROPOSITION OF CULTURE

Your company is going to have a culture one way or another. Your company may develop a culture of fear, paranoia, and political infighting, or it may develop a culture of mutual trust, productivity, and fulfillment. While you cannot dictate the culture of your company, you have massive influence over the direction in which it progresses.

Of all the things that you may get right or wrong when you start your company, the culture is the one that is most important to get right at the beginning. It is painfully difficult to change a company's culture after it takes root. Some would say it is impossible. Not winning any work? You can try something else. Got your billing processes or production processes wrong? You can fix them. This is not the case with culture. It can take years to change a company's culture. It is vital that you tend to it from the start.

Culture starts forming from day one. We have a fondness for talking about "the old days." Everything we do early on has the potential to become an enshrined process, tradition, or legend. We must always be conscious of this.

I have seen many companies fail because they didn't think about culture when starting their company. By the time the founders finally pinned down what the problem was with their company, it was too late. They did not have the resources or time to fix it.

You're going to be spending a large part of your life at this company. You're just like everyone else: you don't want to work at a place that sucks. Make sure your company doesn't suck, not just for your sake but for all your employees' sake.

Building a great culture is one of the few "win-win" scenarios when you're starting your own business. For relatively little money, you not only get to build something totally rewarding but you reap productivity benefits as well. *Culture is not a waste of money*

When we founded the Barbarian Group, the world was conscious of "dot com excess." One giant, industry-wide hangover was taking place. People all over tech were asking, "What were we thinking?" People who blew a million bucks, or even $50,000 on a party, were now rueing the day, and there was a new tone of austerity in the air.

Did we really need tetherball courts at work? Five-thousand-dollar pool tables? Free meals? Turns out, they are not necessary. And in fact, the vast majority of the perks you see at America's celebrated workplaces, such as Google, are both well beyond your means and unnecessary.

Culture is not bought. A company such as yours can build a great culture without spending thousands of dollars.

Then, of course, there is the conundrum of creativity. It's well known that in order to think creatively and to come up with a truly great idea, you need an environment that fosters this. This can look, to the outsider, like the creative thinker isn't doing anything. Get a whole group of creative thinkers in one agency, and there are times when all of them might look like they're doing nothing. It's easy to take potshots at this. "What does a pool table have to do with building ROI [return on investment]?"

The benefits of culture can be broken down into two concrete areas: competition and productivity.

CULTURE KEEPS YOU COMPETITIVE

First, culture directly benefits the bottom line. David Ogilvy put it bluntly: "If you have a gentle, kind, human agency, you won't have to pay so much. And it attracts the best employees, and it attracts the most attractive clients. It will also give you a happier time through life."[1] People want to work for great companies. They will work at great companies for less money than they will work for at less great companies. A fun, creative workplace with like-minded professionals can be equal to pay. We know this when we think about our own job, but it's easy to forget when you're responsible for it for others.

There is nothing wrong with making a company a great place for employees to work, and if that costs a little money, it makes perfect sense. This can then be reflected in your costs—a great company where people love working can charge less than a competitor that has to pay people more in order to retain them. It's imperative that you use this to your advantage.

This is true at all sizes of companies. One of the great things about culture is that it *never stops working*. A company with 10,000, or even 100,000, employees can still be one of the best places to work in the world, and so can a company of 10. If your company infuses itself with culture, and you take care to not kill it, it will offer a permanent competitive advantage.

CULTURE MAKES EMPLOYEES BETTER

Culture improves performance. Employees will work *harder* and *smarter* for great companies. Professor James L. Heskett wrote in his latest book, *The Culture Cycle*, that "Organization culture is not a soft concept," and that "its impact on profit can be measured and quantified." Citing such factors as employee loyalty, referrals, reduced turnover, customer loyalty, and increased productivity, he finds that as much as half of the profitability difference between competing companies can be attributed to workplace culture.[2]

Research from the Hay Group finds that highly engaged employees are, on average, 50 percent more likely to exceed expectations than the least-engaged workers. And companies with highly engaged people outperform firms with the most disengaged folks—by 54 percent in employee retention, by 89 percent in customer satisfaction, and by fourfold in revenue growth.[3]

Finally, in creative companies such as yours, culture will bring forth better ideas. Famed ad man Leo Burnett noted that "Creative ideas flourish best in a shop which preserves some spirit of fun. Nobody is in business for fun, but that does not mean there cannot be fun in business."[4] It is a fact that, as often as we may find ourselves wishing it were untrue, creative ideas require creative environments. A rewarding workplace culture will make our ideas better. And while better ideas are not the only thing that wins us business, it's nearly impossible to win business without great ideas.

CULTURE AND VISION

Great culture springs, logically and seamlessly, from your company's vision. The vision and the culture of your company need to exist in harmony. The importance of this cannot be overstated. A culture that's at odds with the vision of the company is one that is more expensive and less effective. Employees question why they are at work. In a seminal *Harvard Business Review* article, Rob Goffee and Gareth Jones extensively researched what makes some companies more ideal for employees to work at than others. They find, unsurprisingly, that workers need purpose. Your company needs to give your employees compelling, powerful motivators for why they give you their energy.[1] We've talked about the importance of establishing a unique and compelling vision for your company. That vision will be the wellspring of your culture, which is one of the reasons why it is important to shape that vision as early as possible, preferably before you go into business. Let us consider the multiple levels at which the simple question "Why?" can work. A coherent explanation can answer multiple levels of "Why?" without contradicting itself.

"Why did you throw away that milk?" "Because it was spoiled." "Why did it spoil?" "Because we didn't drink it all before it went bad." "Why?" "Because we've been eating out too much." "Why?" "Because we've been too busy lately." "Why?" "Because your grandma is sick, and we've been taking care of her." The mundane flows to the more profound, the more important, in a seamless way. Multiple levels of "Why?" give the questioner perspective.

This is what we must achieve with our culture. The culture of the company needs to be lurking in the back of the head of all employees, in a coherent and inspiring way, when they are faced with tasks that may otherwise seem mundane or useless. Believing you need to spend three hours cleaning up an Excel spreadsheet because it is a small piece in a larger puzzle of achieving a vision is much more powerful than your doing it for a paycheck. An employee can do many things for a paycheck. She needs to believe that working for you, at this company, is the best thing she could be doing.

Great culture can take on several forms—some companies pride themselves on their hardworking, heads-down attitude. Some pride themselves on their propensity for giving back to society through charitable and nonprofit work. Some cultures believe in a work-life balance. Some cultures strive for a fun environment. The exact shape and identity of your culture will spring from you and your vision of the company.

You won't control the culture, however. Over time, your company culture will take on a life of its own. You are the gardener, laying the seeds for a great culture. Your job is to foster a great culture, nourish it, and eliminate the troublesome weeds. You cannot fully control the culture of your company, nor should it be built around the cult of you.

EXPRESSING THE VISION AND THE CULTURE

It's vitally important that you find ways to express the vision behind your company and encourage every employee to develop culture around that vision. The vision of your company may be obvious to you, but it is not necessarily obvious to everyone else. You must tell them about your vision, over and over. Unrelentingly. Forever. If you don't, employees will imprint upon themselves, and then others, their own interpretation of the vision of your company. People will come to work for your company without understanding what it believes in. You will then attract people who do not necessarily agree with your vision. This leads to a company that is not at one with itself and is not working toward one vision. This is death.

Says entrepreneur Brett Martin, "Think of culture as a cofounder that is present when you are not. You are decisive, communicative, and respectful but it's your culture that helps everyone know how to act when you are out of the room. Give that voice clarity and authority."[2] It's vital that you write down what your company holds dear. Develop a vision statement and a set of core beliefs. Make sure everyone understands them and can repeat them. Reinforce upon them the importance of applying the core beliefs to any decision-making process. Any and every employee should be able to say what the company stands for.

GROWING CULTURE ORGANICALLY

Culture is one of the great levelers in corporate America, just as working stupid hours is. Rich people and poor people can both work stupid hours.

Likewise, rich companies and poor companies can both build solid corporate cultures. You don't need an inside advantage to build a strong corporate culture. Even better, a great corporate culture can give you an inside advantage for almost no money. Culture is, in short, a force multiplier for the companies that choose to embrace it. Culture does not need to be expensive.

Yet, it has to be acknowledged that culture is not completely free.

The goal is to create as rewarding a culture as possible for as little money as possible. Economic theory comes into play here. You are looking for the greatest amount of *marginal* culture —the biggest bang for each buck—not the most amazing culture that can be bought for any amount of money.

Not all culturally improving purchases are created the same, and often a $300 game console can bring as much or more entertainment as a $2,000 pool table. Pretend you are a cash-strapped parent on Christmas Day: shoot for the biggest bang for the buck when it comes to buying culturally enhancing items, not the biggest bang. The most effective purchases are those that encourage together time between employees and team bonding. Pizza parties are cheap and good. So is beer after work. Not so much during the day.

When the company is bootstrapping and money is tight, try to work it so that new, cheap, incremental culture-enhancing purchases appear in the office often rather than making one big purchase a year. This will foster the sense that the workplace is always an adventure.

At The Barbarian Group, we did what we could with our limited funds and an increasingly austere economic environment regarding fun and games in the office. We never bought a pool table, and the first Ping-Pong table at TBG didn't appear for something like six years after the company's founding. But we did encourage camaraderie through numerous company outings— bar outings, dinners, movies, concerts.

Bean bags. Bean bags helped greatly. And they're cheap.

SUPPORTING SPONTANEOUS CULTURE

A planned process and approach to culture do not preclude organic cultural growth. As the cultural gardener, you need to plant a few seeds. Think of a few things—events, traditions, processes, and so forth—that represent the vision of your company and engender some culture. Get a few of them off the ground. You do not need to think of them all—indeed, one of the most important hallmarks of a successful culture is that it happens spontaneously. A culture that springs entirely from you will not scale. But you do need to set some examples and get the party started.

At The Barbarian Group, I liked birthdays, so we made a point of celebrating everyone's birthday from the beginning. When we set up the first employee database and wiki, we threw a field into it for favorite type of birthday cake. I didn't start organizing the birthday parties myself, but because other people could see that birthdays mattered, and there was this fun field in the employee database around birthday cakes, from there it took on a life of its own. The first office manager trained all the other ones who followed, and ten years later, every birthday was still celebrated with the employee's preferred birthday cake. All I did was plant the seeds.

The email introduction evolved in this way as well. The first pass of the employee manual that the early studio manager and keeper of culture, Mike Rubenstein, and I cooked up, walked a new employee through setting up their calendar and mail. Mike made a passing comment in there, saying, "Once you've got all this set up, send an email to everyone@ and introduce yourself. Include a photo. Preferably an embarrassing one." He wrote it as a quick passing joke, but it has become, today, a rite of passage and a hallowed tradition in the company. You have to get your introduction email right, and the picture has to be embarrassing. People are ranked on their photos. If the photo's not embarrassing enough, another photo will be requested. This practice helps all the employees learn something about the new employee, and those who have some hobbies or interests in common will pipe up and perhaps invite the new employee to an extracurricular event or share an album or something. One or two enterprising employees who want to start a club are super useful in supporting spontaneous culture. You may even want to give them some sort of designation, or at least encouragement. If you support them a little, others will come forward. We've had softball teams, kickball, Ping-Pong, bowling, and Dungeons & Dragons tournaments, *Twin Peaks* nights, Magic: The Gathering nights, sci-fi movie nights, cooking events, wine tastings, and an infinite number of other club events, all started by enthusiastic employees.

As a manager, you're looking for these opportunities. Seek out places where there is employee enthusiasm or a good idea. Focus primarily on the ones that don't cost a whole lot. Then throw in a little bit of money to support them. Cultural traditions that spring from the employees are exponentially more powerful than those that are imposed upon them from the top down. They are also far less expensive.

GARDENING AND UMPIRING

The temperature and dogs can seem like ridiculous things to worry about when you're focused on the fast growth of your company. But these are the types of issues you will need to keep your eye on. Don't let disagreements fester—come down quickly and fairly on potential areas of employee disagreement. And keep an eye out for opportunities to elevate traditions and practices that the employees have built on their own. Offer to support after-hours clubs, for example, or pay for an outing.

5

COMMUNICATION

There is no culture without communication. You will need to communicate with your employees regularly, and they will need to communicate with one another. While in an early stage company the tendency is to rely primarily on quick emails and oral communication, this is problematic. First off, it does not scale, and secondly, it does not create an archive of cultural communication for new employees to rapidly get up to speed. Before too long, your company's communication will need to be something that scales.

But first, we need to develop a strategy for how, what, and when to communicate with our employees. What you tell your employees when you have 2 people will be different from when you have 20 or 200. And the early decisions have long-term consequences. When you tell an employee, for example, how much profit the company made, are you comfortable with 20 more people knowing that? 200?

ON TRANSPARENCY

As you develop the culture of your company, you are going to have to develop a perspective and opinion on the notion of transparency. Like it or not, you're going to have to tell your employees things, often.

You'll hear a lot about the word transparency. Employees will constantly clamor for more information. I find that what they are really clamoring for is not more transparency, but rather a consistent level of transparency. A company that is highly communicative toward its employees but that clams up one day is a company that will have a lot of worried employees. The inverse is true as well.

Transparency is not a binary adjective. You don't either have transparency or you don't. It is a sliding scale. Transparency also has a vision component. If your company's vision is based on a highly communicative, collaborative environment, the level of transparency at the company will need to be commensurately open. If your company's vision is more based around efficiency and hard work, this may prove to be less so. Brett Martin comments that "The trick is to avoid hollow words. Since a startup's culture mirrors that of its founder, maybe the best thing that you can do is work hard to get clear on who you are. Write that down and share it with your team. If you've been honest, every action you take will reinforce your values."[1]

It is most useful to start in the early days with a subtractive view of transparency. Write out a list of things that you DON'T believe everyone should be allowed to know. I find that this list often includes things like the health conditions of employees, HR infractions, and the salaries of employees. Other things may also be on the list. Is it okay for everyone in the company to know about every new business pitch? Will this distract employees from their work? Is it okay for everyone to know when and why you fired someone? These are things you will need to answer. Work it out in advance, and make sure the basis for your decisions flow from your vision.

Fast growth places additional challenges on transparency. When you are a small company, it is easier to allow all the employees to know almost everything about the company. As you grow, this will become both logistically more difficult as well as more difficult to justify. Be prepared for this and have a plan.

At whatever level you find that you are comfortable, it will involve regular communication with the employees. Find a process for this: an email list, a regular company meeting. Also be aware of the historical nature of these forms of communication—do you want them archived? And, finally, make sure the process accounts for new employees. They need to be rapidly brought up to speed on past events. If your entire transparency initiative is oral, this can be hard.

COMPANY MEETING

Nearly every company needs at least one regular company meeting. You'll need to develop a plan for this.

Take care not to use the company meeting solely for propaganda or talking AT the employees. A brief management update is certainly merited in company meetings, especially in times of flux. But the goal should be that either the employees themselves are talking or you are answering questions directly asked by the employees. Our most effective company meeting format was exactly that: ten minutes for a brief update from management, then updates on departments or individual projects from various employees, ending with a series of answers to questions anonymously submitted from the employees.

I cannot overemphasize the importance of answering anonymous questions from the employees. While your company is very, very small (say, fewer than five people) formally answering employee questions is unnecessary, as it's easy for them to just come to you. However, as you grow, it very rapidly becomes vital to implement this in a formal manner. Even in a company of ten employees, people begin to be less willing to walk right up to you and ask you a blunt question. If you doubt that your company needs this mechanism, I encourage you to try it once. Odds are that you will be as surprised and appalled as I was at the questions asked. The tone and content of these questions were clear indicators that we had not been communicating with our employees as well as we hoped.

These questions will often represent various levels on the scale of "whys," and your job is to try and answer them not just at the appropriate level, but slowly working the answer up the scale toward the larger vision of the company. If someone asks, for example, if you can have Red Bull available in the soda fridge, don't just say no. Explain that Red Bull is expensive, and that you keep costs down on these things to keep expenses down, to stay competitive, to win the best work, so the employees can work on the coolest stuff—tying a seemingly mundane question into the larger vision. This is vital.

Some questions will be harsh and accusatory. Answer them calmly and politely, again relating them to the larger vision. Some of them will really fluster you, so it's wise to see them in advance and prepare your answers. Don't fly off the cuff. When employees are angry or accusatory, our job is to turn them around and get them believing again, even if our pride may be hurt in the short term.

This process will last forever. It can seem that eventually you'll answer every question, but new stuff comes up constantly. Tony Hseih, CEO of Zappos, comments that even after years of having an employee question program, "We continue to receive great questions from our employees."[2]

WORKING FROM HOME AND MEETINGS

It may seem counterintuitive to tackle these two topics at the same time, but they are intimately related. You will need points of view, and policies, on both of them, and it's unwise to make those policies in a vacuum without thinking about the other topic. Having a liberal work-from-home policy, for example, in a culture that has many meetings, inherently means that the meetings will end up with lots of people calling in, and to put it bluntly, large conference calls suck.

At the same time, having a liberal work-from-home policy can be an incredibly powerful employee incentive and perk. It can also, however, be a massive area of employee abuse. You'll need to decide how you want to play this. At The Barbarian Group, we believed strongly in the ability for employees to stay home and work when they needed to get things done. A liberal work-from-home policy can be a powerful antidote to the distracting environment of today's modern, open office plans. It was important too, however, to place guidelines and rules around the work-from-home policy. If you had a meeting, you needed to come in for it. You could not rely on other team members to cover for you if you were working at home. If your job involved interacting with other people that day (work reviews, client meetings, company meetings), you needed to come to work. Your opinions on a work-from-home policy may vary, and your vision may not be one that is conducive to people working off-site. Develop a perspective for your company early on, keeping in mind how you will scale it.

Also keep in mind how the policy will affect meetings. Meetings are inevitable. You may be able to reduce the number of meetings per individual or per day, and you may be able to get the duration of meetings down, but you'll never completely eradicate them. It is therefore vital that some sort of meeting etiquette is introduced at your company. Some companies love having meetings with everyone standing up to encourage brevity. Some have a "no computers or phones" rule to keep everyone focused. Also bear in mind that meetings are more disruptive for employees in some roles than others. A single meeting may ruin a developer's entire day, whereas a client service exec may constantly live in meetings.

ELECTRONIC LISTS

There are two important components to your group communication: the official channels and the unofficial ones.

Post everything of relevance to the official channel. Minutes from company meetings. Notices about hires or departures. Information that conforms to your level of transparency. Make sure there is an archive for easy perusal by new employees. All official communication should tie back to the vision in some way if possible.

In addition to some sort of announcement email list from the managers, consider implementing an electronic group or list for the employees to chat with each other about whatever they want. It could be an email list, a message board, a chat room. This will operate as a virtual "water cooler." Give them an outlet to chat. You may also want to consider making subgroups for various departments, hobbies, and so on. Take time to think through the structure of these, ensuring that there is an "official" channel for important announcements that is differentiated from the "everyone" channel that anyone can post to.

We had an all-company email list that anyone could post anything to. That helped a lot. Endless, pointless debates would rage on the everyone@ mailing list about every topic under the sun. Photoshopped in-jokes and memes would run rampant. There was one particularly epic thread debating the various methods of sorting a music collection—whether by first name, last name, or last name, first name. What to do about bands that start with "The?" Whether you rename the tags or just let iTunes handle it.

There will be times you'll need to police the everyone channel, but, again, think about the corporate culture when developing the policy. If creativity, fun, and company bonding are a goal for your culture, the everyone list can bring your team together. This is what you should strive for. It keeps employees engaged, and allows you to quickly spot any problem areas.

PART II

THE WORK

6

WHAT IS GOOD?

We now turn to the work at hand, the work that your firm will be doing for your clients. Your *craft*.

This book assumes you know your craft. I don't purport to tell you what good work is, in your particular line of work. You know. You're already good at your craft. That's why people are trying to hire you. What we discuss here is not the finer nuances of your craft, but rather how your craft and your business intersect, how they affect one another. For very quickly, as you grow your business you'll realize that the two are inextricably entwined. Great work is a product of the environment in which it is made.

Let's start with the obvious: you always need to do good work. Your work is your marketing. It is why people will hear about you. It's why people will hire you. Later on, you'll develop a "real" marketing capability within your firm, but even then the work will matter. Good work is why we are in business. If you have some vague business plan in your head that predicates itself on not doing good work, put this book down. This is not for you. Good work should always be the aim. This whole book is about striving to set up the perfect circumstances in which to do great work as often as possible.

This is not a book about outsourcing things. This is not a book about half-assing things. This is a book about making things of quality for discerning buyers who need something of quality. Let us never forget that.

What, then, does it take to do perfect work?

We need a great client, someone who fights for us, partners with us, and gives us the space we need to do great work. That great client needs to be selling a great product, something that makes the world a better place and that we can believe in. This great client needs to give us enough time and money to do the job right. We need the right people around us to do the work. We need them to be able to do *this* work, even if the company has other clients and work.

Except this never happens.

Let us now, then, turn to reality: compromises will be made.

Our principal job—our most important job—is to manage these compromises effectively.

Consider the famous adage "the work can be good, fast, or cheap. Choose two." This is the marketing design version of what is known as the "project management triangle."

The great artist strives to create perfection without compromise. The great designer strives for perfection in the face of compromise. The great artist can achieve her aim. The great designer can never achieve hers. It is an endless quest, without success, without end.

It is a deeply human, timeless construct. Originally known as the "trilemma," the roots of this trace back to ancient Greek times.

Design is the art of doing things with constraints. We never have all of our perfect conditions fulfilled.

So, then, *in reality we can never do perfect work*. We can come close, but there is always some real-work constraint keeping us from perfection.

The art is to know how far on the scale you can slide to the other side.

In the marketing world, executives have had, for as long as anyone can remember, a very specific approach to this: you do the work that wins the awards, and you do the work that makes the money. Never the twain shall meet. More than once through the years, I was counseled to take this approach by agency lifers. It never felt particularly right to me that there were these "marquee" clients who got great work—presumably for not much money—and then many other clients who paid a lot but got boring work. This goes against what I believe in personally.

I also believe that in the digital world this is less of an option than it is (or was) in traditional advertising. There are too many moving pieces. People notice immediately. It's nearly impossible to half-ass a web development project and get away for it for very long, whether the client is paying enough or not. The site will crash, and people will stop using it. I also believe that the environment in which we live—where marketing can take myriad forms rather than just a television spot or a magazine ad—dictates that we need to exhibit our expertise across multiple marketing platforms. We will often find ourselves working on an iOS app one day, a Facebook campaign the next, a website the next. New platforms and campaign types will constantly spring up.

Why is this important? Because *we may only have one or two gigs to prove our chops in a new medium*. These days, every project has a radically increased chance of needing to perform as a case study. Fifty years ago we could make two great broadcast spots, twenty bad spots, put the two good ones on our portfolio reel for clients, and disown the twenty bad. Now the first two iPhone apps, or iAds, or animated gifs for Tumblr that we make need to be great, or we'll never get more gigs and we'll miss a whole cycle of new services we can offer to clients.

But, again: *in reality we can never do our best work.*

We need to be okay with this. We need to ride the margins. We need to know when the ends justify the means. We need to know that even if we can't make something perfect, we can make something *better*.

I cannot tell you how many times I found myself looking at a potential project, seeing all the drawbacks, and knowing, in my heart, that the only way this client was going to get anything even remotely acceptable was that if we took the project, even if by all my normal, rational criteria, it was going to suck. But this is what we do. We help our clients. We fulfill a need. When a client is sitting there begging you to do something, saying they know it's not ideal circumstances but they have faith in you, and they *know* you'll meet their needs better than anyone, it's hard to argue that not taking it is the right thing to do.

So, then, here we come to the secret truth we'll never say out loud: there will be times when we know we need to take a job for which we aren't going to do our best work. Sometimes we will need to take a job for the money. Sometimes we will need to take it for the experience. Sometimes we will need to take a crappy job to keep an otherwise good client.

This is a very hard reality for perfectionists to accept. And though they may be ever thwarted, your company needs perfectionists.

If you're a perfectionist, *you* will have a difficult time accepting this truth.

Here we need to perform a bit of mental jujitsu because you must learn to simultaneously accept this truth and completely reject it. You must learn to constantly pursue the best work you can do, but know that perfection can never be achieved. You must exist on two planes of reality simultaneously.

You can never give up your pursuit of perfection, yet you cannot let it take over. This isn't art. It's design. Constraints matter. There will be times you can push back on the constraints—get a client to accept a late delivery, or to pay more money—and there will be times you simply. Cannot. Do. This.

Conversely, you may be of the opposite ilk. You may be all too amenable to glossing over the details, to just get it done. Here, too, you must forever strive to counterbalance your natural instinct. Perfect is the enemy of the good, as they say. This is all natural. But in a tightly constrained process, the number of obstacles that arise—and the number of constraints that present themselves—is innumerable. If you gloss over each one of them, you'll have a muddled mess. Details matter. If you're not a person who is attentive to detail, make sure other makers in your company are. Work to give them breathing room, making room. You can neither accept nor let go of every constraint.

For me, it helps to view quality and constraints as yin and yang. They are the two essential components to the trade you have. Both must be respected. Both must be revered, but both must be malleable.

Speaking from a perspective of constraints, there are two principal demons that must be fought: time and money. The key to battling both is to fight as much of the battle as you can upfront. This is obvious. The place where you can have the most impact on quality is by setting up the job at the outset with enough time and enough money. Seventy-five percent of your battles should be fought before your makers begin work. Fight like hell to get your team enough time and your company enough money. Don't be afraid to walk away from jobs that are impossible.

Don't be afraid to break this rule, but do so selectively and sparingly. For us, the Subservient Chicken, our award-winning collaboration with Burger King and Crispin, Porter + Bogusky, was exactly such a job. The money was crap. The timing was tight. But the project was just too brilliant, too wonderful, and we knew we were exactly the right team for the job. We made the right call there.

There were plenty of times, however, when we made the wrong call.

We turned down a significant equity stake to do the initial web build of one of the most successful start-ups ever created in New York. Our stake would now be worth well over $40 million.

We declined to bid on the construction of Hulu, thinking it was a doomed project.

On the flip side, we took several projects that we thought were going to be world changing, and totally flopped. One comes to mind, for Red Stripe, that I still believe is one of the greatest marketing sites ever built on the Web. Virtually no one saw it.

You don't always get it right, but that is okay. Lick your wounds and move on.

And you never give up trying to do your best work.

We should talk about the 25 percent of the dealing that happens after the launch of the project. First, let's tackle head-on a popular but misguided approach to this. Several companies intentionally lowball their initial bid in order to win the work, confident that they can make it up later through add-on fees. There is a key distinction to be made between *intentionally* lowballing a bid in order to win it, and billing later for circumstances that change down the road. I strongly recommend against the former. The damnation here is that your competitors will do this. Be honest and upfront about how much the project will probably cost. Your competitors will submit a bid that is two-thirds of yours, insisting it can actually be done for that amount. Your best bet here is to tell the truth and explain exactly what your competitors are doing. If your client chooses to go the cheaper route, tell them to expect lots of additional fees, and when they are tired of working that way, to give you call.

The reason we are talking about this now is because you will experience a strong temptation to lowball on time or money to win the job. This can and will impact the quality of the work. Talk to your team before doing this. They may see this is a good opportunity, something they really want to do, and be okay with it. They may have some free cycles and welcome the chance to bang something out over a weekend. Or they may have too much work already. Rushing a job through when people are up for it can still result in something of high quality. Rushing a job through when no one's up for it suffers from radically diminished chances of delivering quality. Context matters.

There will also be times when, as the project moves along, you realize that with a little extra time or money you can make something exponentially more amazing. The key here is exponentially. Think of it in this manner. This is a necessarily fuzzy, objective plane of mathematics, but if a 10 percent increase in time or money only yields a potential improvement of 10 percent, the opportunity is not particularly special. If, however, a 10 percent increase in time or money can double the quality, you have an opportunity that should absolutely be explored. It's been my experience that clients very much welcome these opportunities being brought to their attention.

Then there are the times when you know—you just *know*—that your work is terrible and you need more resources to get it to a place that is good for everyone. This is totally okay. You need to bring this dilemma to your client. The client will make the ultimate answer. Hopefully the client will say, "I respect your opinion, and I will get you the extra resources." It is entirely likely, though, that the client will say, "We don't have a choice, I understand it doesn't meet your standards, but it's good enough for me." There will even be times your client will say, "If you didn't think you could do it up to snuff at the beginning, why did you take the job?" These are depressing clients, but they are, in reality, asking a reasonable question. Your answer is either something along the lines of "We messed up this or that," in which case you own up, apologize, and work toward fixing it. Your answer may also be something along the lines of "This was just one of those times nothing gelled." No one wants to hear this, but if it's the truth, state it. It happens sometimes. Work with the client to figure out what the right course of action is.

Finally, remember that *quality is relative*. Even among like-minded individuals, even within your team. There are two tricks here: learn to embrace each other's opinions, but also be keenly aware whether your position on the team or in the process is coloring your opinion. Be aware of your biases. In the early days, I found myself all too willing to pretend that our "good enough" work was great because it was my job to get the work out the door. My partners were often appalled by my opinions, knowing the work wasn't what it could be. We were both right, but both coming from our own positions on the team. Compromise was needed, and perspective needed to be shared. We got better at that through the years, and you will too.

7

IDEAS

In no industry will you find so much talk about ideas. The power of ideas. The importance of ideas. The *value* of ideas. But before too long, you'll realize that, at its core, an eternal debate permeates the advertising industry. Is it the idea? Or the execution. Witness the following quotes:

> There's just a tremendous amount of craftsmanship in between a great idea and a great product. —Steve Jobs

> But the truth is, it's not the idea, it's never the idea, it's always what you do with it. —Neil Gaiman

> A really great talent finds its happiness in execution. —Johann Wolfgang von Goethe

> Genius is one percent inspiration, ninety-nine percent perspiration. —Thomas Edison

> Originality is nothing but judicious imitation. —Voltaire

> Good artists borrow. Great artists steal. —T.S. Elliot, Pablo Picasso, Igor Stravinsky, and God knows who else.

> The secret to creativity is knowing how to hide your sources. —Albert Einstein (apocryphal)[1]

So many quotes. But this barrage of quotes serves a purpose. So many viewpoints. Ideas. Creativity. Everyone has an opinion.

We like to say our industry is the industry of ideas. Many industries are the industries of ideas. Is engineering *not* the industry of ideas? The law? Literature? Science?

Yet it seems to be our industry that is obsessed with ideas and value. You can patent a new idea in science. You can patent a new idea in engineering.

You can copyright, to some extent, a new idea in literature. It's much harder in advertising. This has ramifications.

Advertising has an increased focus on ideas because it is not only charged with coming up with big ideas but it has to *insert those ideas into our heads and into the national conversation.* This leads to an environment of cutthroat meme warfare. In this industry, the best ideas are, by definition, the ones that stick in people's heads. They *have* to stick in people's heads. It is true, that at the center of any effective marketing campaign, there needs to be a core idea that resonates with the consumer. An insight. A truth. "Just do it." "Think different." All great advertising has this as a component. This is why advertising is so obsessed with ideas.

This is why people in marketing endlessly talk about "the power of the big idea." Creativity. Innovation. Tons of shops trumpet these words in their own marketing and on their home page. Here's a funny exercise: Google the phrase "idea factory." You'll see six marketing companies, a game designer, and two video production companies, all on the first page of search results.[2] You'll have to endure ad execs and marketing gurus waxing philosophical about the power of an idea throughout your career.

Ideas come at all levels. A big idea is nothing without thousands of smaller ideas underneath it. The top-level creative shop is primarily concerned about being known in the client world for a great big idea and stellar execution. They're less concerned with being known for "holy smokes" graphic design or amazing animation or illustration, whereas you might be. You're also concerned with being known among other marketing companies, and maybe small and local brands. Your "audiences" of potential clients may well be different. Think of the Oscars. The actors are not competing against the score composers, or the visual effects wizards. They are all looking for recognition, yes, but often they are looking for recognition from different groups of people. Indeed, different groups of people even vote for the acting awards and the visual effects awards. But they are all competing for an Oscar, even when they've worked on the same film.

I would also note that opposing parties often have different ideas of what the "idea" is. For the longest time, my cofounder and TBG's faithful CEO Benjamin Palmer had a dream. He had it in his head that he really wanted to do something with puppets. We would endlessly pitch different ideas to different clients involving puppets. Did TBG sign a few forms giving "our ideas" to a few different potential clients through the years? Yes. Did some of them include puppets? Yes. Would a client *really* go sue us if we used puppets one day? Hardly. Would they sue us if we used puppets for a direct competitor, in the exact same type of campaign that we pitched them, with a positioning similar to theirs? More likely. But all we wanted to do was use puppets.

Think of a great billboard creative team. There exists a campaign within which they are working, such as "Just do it" or "Think different." But the great billboard creative team must take that larger insight and think of a way to make it resonate with the consumer as they drive by at 60 miles per hour. They may take into consideration a photograph, an illustration, copy, perhaps even the shape of the billboard, or a digital component. Is this "idea" or "execution" at this point? It is both.

This is the level at which most of us will be playing for much of our career. Whole careers can be made out of taking a great brand insight and running with it on the ill-named "executional" level. Great ideas abound at all levels. It is to our detriment that, in advertising, we focus on the one large brand positioning as "the idea."

BEING KNOWN FOR GOOD IDEAS VERSUS BEING PAID FOR GOOD IDEAS

There is, in short, a halo around good ideas, or a secondary, ancillary value on top of the idea itself. The value of a good idea is priceless, as we all know. It has immense value. But it also has *incalculable* value. Is a good idea for a big brand worth a million dollars? A hundred million? Perhaps. We can never know for sure. And because it cannot be calculated, any business that is known for good ideas has a value that is inherently higher than it would be otherwise, by a seemingly arbitrary amount. It is good for a business to be known for generating good ideas.

And here we come to a key point: from a business perspective, *being known for a good idea is more valuable than being paid for good idea*. It's easy to confuse the two. It's easy to calculate the value you got paid for a good idea: "I thought up the Post-it Note, sold the patent, and now I am worth $100 million." It's not so easy to calculate the value of being known for a good idea. And, in many cases, it can be worth much, much more. TBG did many, many jobs where we weren't paid for the idea, or paid much, that ended up being hugely successful, and our renown for doing this work reaped rewards well in excess of whatever we might have been originally paid for the work.

To be perfectly clear: *your company has to have good ideas*. You need them. It's vital that you harness this economic reality: *there is immense value in being known for good ideas, whether you get paid for them in the short term or not.* Your company is more valuable when it's known for having good ideas.

You just don't necessarily need to get paid for them.

OWNERSHIP VERSUS CREDIT VERSUS PAY

This brings us to the timeless debate in advertising about the ownership of ideas. When pitching work, you often give away 10 percent of that work to win the rest. When that 10 percent is the *idea*, the incalculable value of the good idea skews this formula. When you do $10,000 of production work to win $100,000 of production work, it's a clear-cut win. When you do $X of idea conception work to win $100,000 of production work, the economics are not so clear.

It's easy to get wrapped up in this, to focus on how your ideas should be worth more than your production, or how once your potential client has your great idea, they steal it, run with it, and don't need you. In a 2005 *AdWeek* article, BBDO's chairman, David Lubars, concurs. "This is not about getting a stipend to cover our out-of-pocket costs and expenses. Ideas are the currency of our business. They're worth millions of dollars. I'm not going to hand over ideas that could be huge in exchange for out-of-pocket costs. It's incumbent on us to take a stand or we're doomed to be a commodity."[3]

Viewed through this new insight that *being known for a good idea is more valuable than being paid for good idea*, this calculus changes somewhat. If there is a long-term value in being known for the good idea that outweighs the short-term payment, it is okay to give that idea away, provided you can still be known for it. This is key. *Focus on the credit for the idea, not the ownership or payment.*

We did this to spectacular results in our early years. We expended extraordinary effort negotiating with our clients to be sure that we got credit for our work. Some agencies were great about this. Goodby, Silverstein & Partners, and head of digital production, Mike Geiger, in particular, were exemplary about this. Others were not so good. When the agency was less than helpful, we often made our case in the press. Actually, we always worked to make our case in the press. We did this because we knew it was vitally important for our company to be known for our good ideas.

But honestly, "stealing ideas" is a pretty rare occurrence in the ad industry. I suspect it's more institutional. The client organization is not, typically, set up to steal ideas. Steal credit? Yes. Outright theft of ideas? Not so much. A person within the client organization who does so may well have a shadow cast on their accomplishments with their peers. Or perhaps they know that a good idea is nothing without execution, and they can't execute, so they may as well have the idea person execute. Either way, this reinforces the approach to focus on the credit, not the ownership.

Two people with the very same idea will execute it radically differently. There were a couple times when someone in our company would come up to me and show me some campaign and say, "They stole our idea." Perhaps it was something we had already put out in the world. Perhaps a brand was now doing something that bore some glancing resemblance to something we had pitched years ago. But in reality, in both cases, it was quite different, and often no good. Or at least not what we would have done. If anything, this served to reinforce my belief that the idea is only a small part of the equation. Give two people the homework assignment "Write a book about lasers, Styrofoam and a despairing, newly divorced scientist," and you will get back two radically different stories, even with a high-level of specificity in the assignment.

ORGANIZATION AND IDEAS

This is not a book about personal creativity. You will need to blaze your own path here.

What I can say is that we can increase the number of great ideas our company generates through the harnessing of the best resource we have in the company: the rest of the team.

Luckily for you, you are building a company. There will be additional people around you. It is imperative that you learn to empower the people in your company to come up with great ideas. Do not try and be the guru.

This will not fly in the long term, which is why it is vitally important that the company grows beyond being a company of you. Let go of the ego. Take steps to empower the rest of the company to come up with great ideas.

As fun as it is to imagine being Don Draper and waltzing into a room and wowing clients with your genius, it doesn't usually work that way. You can still waltz in, but the ideas will more often than not come from the team. The team is there to help the company consistently deliver, even when an individual— you—cannot. That's half the point.

This is done through culture and process. Embrace the notion that the whole company is a tool to use in pursuit of great ideas. They shouldn't all come from you. Indeed, if they still are, your company is failing.

THE POWER OF MANY IDEAS

Early in my career, I used to worry about people stealing one of our ideas. I was focused on many of these negative scenarios. Pitches. Giving the ideas away for free. Getting paid *now.* While wrestling with the legal terms of one particular pitch, I took my concerns to my partner, Benjamin. He brushed off my concerns and said something that struck me as profound, and a completely different way of looking at this:

> Whatever. I have tons of ideas. I'm happy to get them out of my head. It's better to see one of them make it into the real world than sit in my head doing nothing.

Set free your mind from the shackles of clinging to ownership of any one idea. Focus instead on developing the ability—in yourself and in your organization—to be constantly generating as many ideas as possible. Once you start looking at the sum of all your ideas, and not any single one, you can be set free of the pesky bonds that hold us back from becoming a truly great creator.

8

PROCESS

Before you get too far along in your company, you're going to have to think about process.

How much process, whether we need process, hating process, useful process, overly processed, resetting process, implementing process.

Process is the collection of policies, habits, rules, guidelines, and documentation by which the employees of your company work together to get things done.

When you were just one person, process may have all been in your head, and that would have been just fine. But now that there are more people than just you, this will get progressively more difficult. When there are two, three, or even ten of you, you can probably get away with having a process that is entirely verbal.

As you get to 20, 30, or 100 people, this will become increasingly impossible. You'll have to *write the process down*.

There will be no process at your company until you and your colleagues make one. If you've never started a company before, this can be a bit confusing. You may have worked at other agencies, and the process just existed. You got your job there, learned some rules, saw some forms, and people came to you and told you what to do and you did it. You might not have thought about the process at all. When I was working at one of my first agencies, I never gave any thought to process. Every day or so a nice woman came over and told me what I needed to do, and asked me how long it would take, and told me to whom to talk when I was done. It just worked. I never once thought about all the work that went into making that happen: defining a process, identifying job roles—hers and mine—writing job descriptions, placing job ads, hiring recruiters, interviewing, hiring us, making schedules, knowing to whom I should go to get approval on my work, that person getting approval from someone above them. I didn't think about it at all, except maybe when it didn't work and suddenly I had to do something in half the time I regularly needed. But, boy, then I was upset about how messed up the process was.

At your company, no one is going to just magically make a process for you. You'll have to craft the process with your colleagues, carving valuable time out of your work schedule to get everyone on the same page. This means you can't be a complete dysfunctional wasteland waiting for salvation. The team members are going to have to make this happen. You're going to have to work together to make it happen.

And the whole time you're working on it, someone is going to tell you how unnecessary it is, how much it sucks, how there should be more of it, how there should be less of it.

And, to be fair, they may have a point. Process requires constant vigilance, the constant addition of important procedures and, just as importantly, the bold removal of some antiquated or stifling ones. Process isn't something you will get to set up and then forget about. It's a garden, requiring constant care. A garden that half of your team will hate. A whole book could be written about process. Many books *have* been written about process. Process exists in almost every industry. Many industries draw inspiration for their process from other industries. Eric Reis's *Lean Startup* methodologies are explicitly heavily indebted to his fascination with "The Toyota Way," a manufacturing process for cars pioneered by the Japanese carmaker. Additionally, there is a whole body of work involving the extension of process to creative-driven industries, in which some of the assembly line thinking of the manufacturing world may not be applicable.

The marketing industry draws inspiration in crafting its processes from several places. But for all of this, this is just an overview. These are just the basics. There is an amazing amount to learn and think about when it comes to process. Our goal here is to point you to several areas of exploration and consideration. This book's overview of agency processes is by no means exhaustive.

WHY PROCESS MATTERS

Process can help protect you from bad mistakes. It can also protect you from mistakes that you *want* to make. A nonexistent process will let the company take a crappy, money-losing job and not even know it. A mediocre process will keep the company from taking an awesome, money-losing job that also might make you famous. A good process will help you learn whether a job is going to be awesome or not, whether it will lose money or help you not lose money, will tell you whether this job might make you famous, and then take all that information, wrap it up in a bow, and let you make the best, fully informed decision. A great process will radically improve the quality of ideas and the creativity of your employees.

GROWTH DEMANDS PROCESS

First and foremost, *there can be no growth without process*. Process is how you keep quality up when your company extends beyond one person. At the beginning, it will be quite likely that all of the processes of the company are in the heads of the employees. This works great when you're small, but it is a recipe for disaster as you get bigger. If you are going to grow, then process matters. Growth without solid processes is a sure-fire path to waste, poor ideas, and upset clients.

MONEY

Have you ever done a project that you were ridiculously proud of, only to learn that it didn't make a penny? It's happened to us more than once. The *Subservient Chicken* that we did with Crispin and Burger King was one of those examples. Sometimes you know that a project is going to pay off in a manner other than cash money upfront. Remember that *being known for a good idea is more valuable than being paid for good ideas*. But in order for this to work, you have to know how much money the project *should* have cost. Otherwise, you are making decisions blind.

And there are, of course, those times when it was a good, solid project that you were proud of and happy to put your name on, but wasn't necessarily designed to be a "showcase" piece. It was supposed to be moneymaking work, except things went out of control, and in the end, you didn't make any money on it. This happened to us with our worldwide redesign of the Red Bull websites. To this day, it's one of the projects I am most proud of. And to this day, it irks me that I'm still not sure we made any money on it, and am pretty sure we *lost* money on it. But I'm not 100 percent sure either way because our processes were not up to snuff.

And this story, as sad as it is, only scratches the surface. I have known companies to go out of business because they did not have a handle on their money and how it related to their individual projects.

It should go without saying that keeping your company in business is a vital requirement. And distasteful as it may be to some creatives' mentality, money keeps your company in business. Process is how you make sure you make money on jobs. And making money on jobs is how you stay in business.

The little things add up. The difference in costs between any two shops today is nominal. The pitch process is incredibly competitive. There will often be very little difference in cost between multiple companies. Some firms may undercut intentionally. Some may overbid because they do not have a handle on their costs. But in the end, in the long run, among well-run shops, these all balance out, and by and large the shops get roughly the same amount of revenue for the same amount of work. The ones who underbid either go out of business or make it up on add-on costs to the project. The ones who overbid go out of business or adapt.

This means that the way your company stands out in the crowd is through the careful, expert management of the money you do have. This does not mean penny-pinching. It means efficient and intelligent allocation of your money and rigorous waste management. This is what will have an impact on your bottom line in the form of your profit margin. And this is one of the most important criteria by which you will be measured if and when an acquisition opportunity comes along. It is one thing to say, "Our margins are about 10 percent." It is another to say, "Our margins are about 30 percent, but from that we spend about 10 percent on training and cultural enhancements to retain the best employees at a lower salary."

WORK QUALITY

Those in the technical profession tend to be more aware of process's merits in ensuring that their work is free of mistakes. Anyone who's ever launched a site that hasn't gone through the quality assurance (QA) process on the browser that the client uses, and had the client think that the whole site is broken and freak out about how the company doesn't know what it is doing—all because the client is using Internet Explorer 4—understands that quality assurance can be vital. Ditto for anyone who's ever launched a site to a million people, only to have it crash.

The value of QA is also apparent to anyone who's run an ad on television with a typo. For while technical types may be hyperaware of the QA aspects of a good process, QA processes are not confined to the coding arts. As your company grows, the process by which you implement creative approvals will be of vital importance in not only maintaining the quality of work in your company but also fostering growth in talent and independence in your employees. It's one thing for a partner to approve every piece of creative when there are two or three pieces a day. It's another when there are two or three hundred. Process is what separates the companies that maintain their quality while growing and those that turn mediocre.

CREATIVITY

Finally, as much as creative thinkers like to carp about process, the fact is that good processes can radically improve the quality of work and that merit of the ideas that your employees generate. This is, without a doubt, the most difficult aspect of crafting a process—drafting one that does not stifle creativity, but rather fosters it. It is also a slightly different approach to thinking about process. Most process theory, historically, has been about the process of an *organization*. When thinking about creativity, we must also begin to delve into the *personal* creative process: how we think, the environments most suitable for creative ideas.

Growth. Money. Quality. Creativity. Those are four pretty valid reasons why you should be thinking about process.

PROCESS IN MARKETING SERVICES FIRMS

There have been two broad areas of process interest for advertising and marketing consultancies when it comes to process: creativity and production.

CREATIVE PROCESS

The art and science of creative process is a relatively new one. In the modern world, perhaps one of the earliest thinkers on the process of creativity was the English economist Graham Wallas. Although primarily interested in politics and economics, in 1926 he indulged his interest in human nature and society and wrote the book, *The Art of Thought*—still an invaluable work in our field. *The Art of Thought* spelled out Wallas's concept of four steps to creation: preparation, incubation, illumination, and verification. Though the exact steps have varied in innumerable theories since, this multiple-step approach has been a guidepost in the various theories of creativity that followed. Read it.

In his classic on creative thought in the advertising industry, *A Technique for Producing New Ideas*, early J Walter Thompson copywriter, and first chairman of the Ad Council, James Webb Young (no relation), explicitly linked his techniques to those of Wallas, and held firmly that there can be a process to great ideas. Young outlined a process of gathering raw materials, working over the materials in your mind, incubating, birthing the idea, and shipping the idea.[1] It remains one of the must-read works for anyone interested in creativity and this business.

In 1953, BBDO Co-founder and ad legend Alex Osborn published the bestseller *Applied Imagination,* which introduced the technique known as brainstorming. Its influence has been massive, if controversial, and many people are familiar with its basic tenets: defer judgment, reach for quantity, reduce social inhibitions among group members, stimulate idea generation. The goal was for a group to work together efficiently. More current research questions Osborn's central tenet that a group working together can come up with more ideas than individuals, but the technique remains a staple of creative companies to this day. We at TBG had some success with group brainstorming, though often our experience corroborated more recent research—the individual can be mightily creative on their own. We found that a group discussion of ideas, individually arrived at previously, was a powerful combination of these two methods.

It was in the mid-twentieth century that the advertising industry really began to dwell on "the creativity problem"—where ideas came from and how the organization of the agency and the industry helped or hindered the quest. The debates at the time would ring familiar to anyone in business today: brainstorming versus individual ideation. Research supporting creativity or hindering it. Too many roles—copywriters, art directors, researchers—or not enough specialization. Various shops and famous ad men took different approaches and made different stands. Just like today. The song remains the same.[2]

In 1967, American psychologist J. P. Guilford created the structure of intellect model, which attempted to outline the various facets of intellect and human intelligence. He proposed three broad areas of human intelligence: operations, content, and product. Within the operations component, he categorized creativity, under the rubric "divergent production," as the ability to generate multiple solutions to a problem. He also laid out the strategies for creative problem solving. Glenn Griffin and Deborah Morrison in *The*

Creative Process Illustrated commented on Guilford's model that "the 'operations' referenced in SI include 'thinking strategies' which can be learned and practiced, providing more evidence that people can develop their creative ability if they are motivated to do so. Most of the advertising creatives we know have their own favorite techniques for finding ideas. For example, some are list makers (e.g., lists of product characteristics, lists of alternative uses for a product, lists of places where the product could be used), and others enjoy sketching mind maps."[3]

Other recent trends and concepts worth exploring are Edward De Bono's concept of lateral thinking, which tackles the problem indirectly rather than head-on, and Tony Buzan's technique of mind mapping, using a roughly drawn diagram of circles connoting concepts connected by lines, with the size indicating their relative importance. Also worth a quick read, as painful as it can be at times, is Malcom Gladwell's *Outliers*, which explores the 10,000-hour rule: that we can achieve expert proficiency in something after 10,000 hours of practice. In terms of creativity, this supports the earlier theories of Walls and Young that creativity is a skill that can be improved upon with practice.

This is all very fascinating, and many of the businesses that readers of this book may be considering starting would do well to explore the various models and theories of creativity. Others may be intensely process driven, such as user experience design or software engineering. There may be a facet of creative problem solving that you will want to work concretely into your process, but in general, many of these techniques are best explored at the individual level. Griffin and Morrison's *The Creative Process Illustrated* looks extensively at the various creative techniques used by individual practitioners of the various marketing crafts. While some of them are implemented at the company level, many of them are more the personal tricks that an individual can harness. When considering crafting a process around creativity, tread with caution. It would be wiser to foster an environment conducive to individual creativity, exploration, and learning, than to attempt to apply the personal techniques that work for you on the individual level.

MAKE CREATIVTY A CENTRAL PART OF YOUR CULTURE

The place where you can have the most profound effect on creativity in your company is in its culture. It cannot be stated emphatically enough: never stop striving to make your company's culture support creativity.

Creativity has been key to everything we do at the Barbarian Group. That sounds trite, but it really means something to us. Digital advertising is something of a paradox when it comes to creativity. On the one hand, the Web is one of the most profound, transformative, and rewarding creative media that humanity has ever invented. On the other hand, this amazing creative environment is astonishingly cutthroat, and infinite amounts of excellent work go unseen. The Web is replete with an infinite number of hilarious, amazing, awe-inspiring, moving, and brilliant types of content. It can be a full-time job just to keep up. Most people don't even try. They look at a few of the most interesting creative things on the Web each day, and move on. It's a brutally competitive medium.

At The Barbarian Group, we viewed ourselves as the spiritual successor to DDB's philosophy of advertising: driven more by great, moving creative than by metrics. It was our belief that a great piece of advertising on the Web would only work for the same reason any other great thing on the Web made by a 16-year-old kid works: because it is insanely creative. The metrics and strategy can only follow the creativity. This helped us place creativity at the forefront of what we do.

Journalist David Kiley has said, "One of the mantras of good creative agencies in the late 1990s would be, 'Don't let your strategy show.' That means, especially when it comes to targeting young consumers, that ads mustn't be too obvious. Ads shouldn't try too hard to be cool and hip. If they are, the very people being targeted will reject them."[4] This is doubly true on the Web. Why would anyone spend two minutes of their lunch break on a brand site if they were feeling targeted and unappreciated, when they could kill that time on Facebook or looking at LOLCats?

This meant that we always called BS when a campaign was coming from a place that was too client driven, and was tone deaf to the zeitgeist of the Web. If it didn't play with the web audience, we wouldn't do it. We always reminded ourselves, "The Internet is our audience." That is, we were competing, every day, against every single other website or video on the Web. We had to be just as good. Regardless of the client's goal, the strategy, or the budget—the creative had to be worthy of the Internet's attention. If it wasn't, every penny was wasted. On television, even a poor ad is seen millions of times. This is not the case on the Web.

DISTRIBUTED IDEATION

One night, while my partner Benjamin and I were traipsing around Tokyo, after hanging out at a World Economic Forum conference, we conceived a new idea that could help the creativity of all our employees—we called it: BEARD (a fake acronym—we secretly just named it after the bearded men who would have to build it). BEARD was an application, written by The Barbarian Group, that allowed everyone in the company to participate in the development of every idea that the company had. A new, media-agnostic role—the creative lead—would be selected from the team assigned to the project by the partner in charge, taking into account the brief and generally which team member was probably best able to shepherd the most likely creative execution. That creative lead would then post the brief and the challenge at hand to BEARD, and the whole company would offer ideas. The creative lead's job was to take those ideas and weed out the impractical and the inappropriate, identify the best, and flesh them out for presentation and approval by the client.

We realized that we could draw from the world of the Web to solve our problem. That is, we could encourage everyone in the company to participate.

It was a revelation, and a great success. It unleashed the creative potential of the entire company on every single project: the impact of this was profound. Through the history of advertising, you hear stories of the art director up against the deadline, suffering from a lack of ideas, racking her brains and freaking the hell out. But with BEARD, such creative blocks were rare. You might be out of ideas, but with the whole company backing you up, the vast majority of the time you got something to work with enough that you could get your own juices flowing and flesh it out.

It also allowed for the whole company to keep every creative lead up to speed on whatever was hot on the Internet at the time. A developer might post "have you seen this new app" and post a link, and that might get a designer to comment about how that app would be great if it were just slightly different, and then the whole team was off to the races.

The creation of BEARD was a boon for the company. It eliminated the need for the "creative technologist," a sort of tech Sherpa buddy to traditional art directors that had been in vogue at large agencies. It eliminated our company's inability to keep up with the rapidly changing Internet culture. It assisted every creative lead in coming up with ideas. It brought the company together across the offices. We still used traditional brainstorming methods, but BEARD often gave better results. Quiet people were more likely to post in BEARD, and with BEARD it was harder for the extroverted to subsume the quieter individuals.

The use of BEARD and the implementation of the creative lead allowed the Barbarian Group to maintain creative excellence at all times. It got the right person on the right project, and armed them with the company's full knowledge of the Internet culture at that moment. It transcended the legacy roles of a traditional advertising agency and embraced the notion that a great idea on the Internet could come from anywhere.

WHAT YOU CAN DO

I have found that, when evaluating the various theories of creativity and what you, as a manager/owner, can do to foster it in your company, it really comes down to two things:

First, find a balance between the group and the individual. Leverage the advantages of both, and mitigate the disadvantages of both. Bring a group together when it makes sense, and let individuals go off and do some good thinking on their own when it makes sense. Change things up, cater to the strengths of the individual creatives, and don't force it too much.

Secondly, never stop working to help your company's culture support creativity.

We can't get into the heads of our workers. But we can shape the environment around them.

PRODUCTION PROCESS

The other component of process within a marketing service firm generally falls under the rubric of production processes.

Firstly, *how* a creative shop does its work has been impacted by the networked office of the modern era. We've seen echoes of this in the process concepts such as business process re-engineering, and IT's impact on marketing is no exception.

Secondly, with the rise of the influence of the Web on marketing in general, traditional agencies, since the late 1990s, have been bringing coders, technologists, and developers into their workplace to create some of this new work. These developers have brought along their attendant process traditions, and those traditions have rubbed off on the agency world.

Even today, some rough version of a traffic process is still necessary. When your firm is small, this is easy to do. Everyone knows to come and darken your doorway and get approval on a piece of work. As you grow, however, you'll need to make this into a more formalized affair. While much of the job of traffic can now be done by tools such as Basecamp, it's still important to implement some codified guidelines in your company. Additionally, the complexity of today's work may demand approvals from many different parties. Along with the usual creative approvals at one or more levels in the organization, client approvals, and the like, you may now have technical approvals, both from the client IT department as well as internally from a tech director. Take care to set these up early on, and, again, embrace principles, not rules.

Process points that are common throughout any company such as yours include the following:

- proposals
- pricing and scoping
- the brief
- traffic
- producers and PMs
- creative approvals
- technical reviews
- client reviews
- actualization
- discounts

Whatever process you create will probably need to touch upon each of these. Now, a word of caution. I am not advocating a detailed, rigorous process around each and every one of these items. For years, TBG operated without formal briefs. I know many companies that operate without ever making formalized proposals.

And our discount process was pretty much as simple as "talk to Rick to get an approval on a discount." But even that, right there, which is a ridiculously simple process to implement and describe, was incredibly useful. Prior to that process point, no one in the company had a full picture of the finances of the company, and discounts were being handed out willy-nilly.

THE EXPANDING NUMBER OF ROLES

When advertising started, the only role was media buyer. Then we added the copywriter sometime in the early 1920s, and account execs and the art director in the 1930s and 1940s. The planner came along in the 1960s, and since then roles have proliferated even more. We have information architects, developers, engagement planners, user experience designers, cultural anthropologists, graphic designers, content creators, strategists, digital strategists, and the list goes on. Many of them are indeed necessary, given the complexities of developing a comprehensive campaign across all media, worldwide. However, the sheer size of the team is getting unwieldy. If your business is one that travels in these realms, much of the application of process will involve the art of keeping everyone on the team whom you need, without suffering from team bloat and paralysis.

THE JOB OF CREATIVE IDEATION

Creating great work on the Web is like asymmetrical warfare: the organization of your forces can hold you back. Ad agencies have been traditionally organized in a very clear way: a team consisting of an art director and a copywriter came up with the concept, which was created against a brief developed by the account executive and the planner, and the rest of the team was there to support it. On the Internet, however, this structure doesn't always apply. This is a massively important point: great creative on the Web almost never comes from an art director/copywriter team. The hilarious memes, viral videos, weird data visualization charts, hilarious Venn diagrams, highly addictive games, and genius blogs that millions of people produce every day are what we are competing against. They are what people love on the Internet.

This presents a conundrum. At traditional agencies, we are taking our conventional army up against the insurgents and guerrillas of the Web, and they are better organized for effectiveness than we are. We, like a military fighting insurgents, need to adapt and bite their style.

Somewhere around 2006 at The Barbarian Group, we decided that the art director/copywriter combination was no longer guaranteed to be responsible for the creative idea. We needed to adapt to the reality of how great creative on the Web was made, and empower whichever team member was most appropriate for the challenge at hand. We would then designate her the "Creative Lead," regardless of her traditional role, and put her in charge of the creative team. If the creative solution called for a hilarious application, then perhaps the engineer on the team would be the Creative Lead. If the idea demanded a great user interface, perhaps the User Experience designer would play the role of Creative Lead. If the idea called for a blog, with almost no pictures, then the copywriter on their own should lead the creative team. We retained all the individual roles on the team—we still had copywriters, art directors, designers, developers and ux designers—but we identified which one of these was the "Creative Lead" on each project case by case.

This approach was instrumental in differentiating TBG and making sure our creative work was appropriate to the Web, successful and groundbreaking. We did not have to shoehorn our ideas into the art director/copywriter paradigm. We didn't come to the solution with a specific execution in mind.

Most importantly, this method ensured that our process did not interfere with our most important mission: to create great work that resonated.

MANAGING TECHNOLOGICAL CHANGE

Technology is changing fast. At a traditional agency, where you have a lot of legacy art directors, the knowledge of what might be the best creative execution on the Web might not rest with the art director/copywriter combination. If the thing-of-the-week is podcasts, or iOS apps, or Tumblr blogs, or finding a way to market in Vine or Snapchat, and you're looking to hit the demographic of people who are up on the cool thing of the week on the Web, the team probably needs to know about the cool thing of the week. Traditional agencies try and surmount this by employing a "creative technologist" alongside the art director/copywriter duo. This person's job is to make sure that the creative team is up on the latest technologies and understands what's possible with them. This can work if you have, say, 200 legacy art directors. In that case, it's probably cheaper to hire 10 creative technologists to ride shotgun than it is to convince, cajole, train, and bribe 200 art directors to get with the times.

In your company, you almost certainly do not have 200 legacy, pre-Internet art directors. This is good. This means you can expect them to have a certain amount of knowledge and cultural literacy of the Web.

Even then, however, just keeping up with the technological offerings of the various start-ups is more or less a full-time job. In our case, while our young, Internet-savvy workforce was knowledgeable about Internet culture, and was empowered to pursue any great idea in any medium via the "Creative Lead" role and processes, more was needed.

Ultimately, we employed one additional person to do nothing more keep than up with the new tools, technologies, and services that Internet companies are offering and educate the rest of the company. This person liaised with new companies and explored different ways to use these new tools for brands. Her name was Shelby MacLeod. She had evolved from an account person into a social media executive at the company. In her new role, she worked with platforms such as Twitter, Facebook, Buzzfeed, and Stumbleupon, as well as ad tech tools like Kiip, Hootsuite, and Sysomos (a gaming awards platform, social media participation tool, and social consumer sentiment monitoring tool, respectively). She talked to hundreds of these companies, learning about what they could offer marketers. She then educated and disseminated this learning throughout the company, working with all clients and teams to keep the whole company up to date on the latest technological trends. Some may say Shelby's role was that of a Creative Technologist. While similar, Shelby focused more on business opportunities and deals, rather than just tech.

WATERFALL AND AGILE

One of the great mysteries of the web era when it comes to advertising is why there has been no web equivalent of the soap opera, or even Mutual of Omaha's *Wild Kingdom*. On the Web, great destination sites are made by software companies. Brands come in, after the fact, slap some ads on them, and pay the bills. Surely a clever brand ought to be able to build its own great destination site? Why are we beholden to Facebook, Twitter, Tumblr, and the like? Why can't we make our own?

One step on this path is discovering the holy philosophy of agile development, or iterative development. Agile development is a mind-set, a set of methodologies, a religion, a worldview. It's an attempt to fight back the feature bloat and blown deadlines that can plague software development. In short, agile development involves a flexible approach to software development.

WATERFALL DEVELOPMENT

Traditional, or waterfall, project planning involves setting up a long list of deadlines, deliverables, milestones, and phases. Everything is planned upfront, and project management is comprised mainly of making sure deadlines are met and milestones are hit. A waterfall development plan is called such because the graphical representation of the plan, known as a Gantt Chart, resembles a waterfall (Figure 8.1).

Since the beginning of the industry, this has been the traditional way that software is developed. It's similar to traditional project management in many industries—from manufacturing to architecture to party planning.

However, when applied to software, waterfall planning has been fraught with peril from the start, especially on long projects. If your project is going

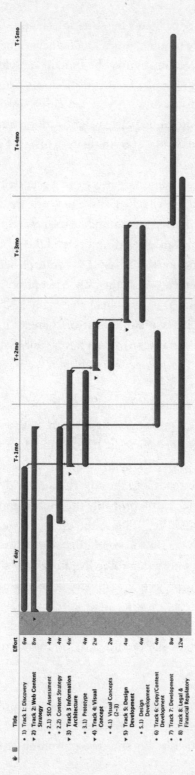

Figure 8.1 Gantt chart for Project Management Flow.

on for a year, for example, inevitably the situation changes. A competitor may put out a new version of a product. A product manager might quit, and a new one might be hired. The company may be bought or sold. New factors are introduced during the development of the project.

If you're making a house or a car you can either finish up the house or car you're working on, and immediately begin work on a new, better one, or you can stop midway and change everything up. This is, of course, timely and expensive.

The same is true with traditional software in a waterfall planning process: the whole project plan can be chucked, and a new one made. A certain phase of the project can be extended to accommodate the new requirements. Both of these, of course, invariably cause delays and extend the project. Another popular method is the much-mocked "Phase 2." If your project needs to launch on time, but new requirements arise, the only real option is to keep building what you're building, launch it, and then dive right into a Phase 2, which usually, by this time, includes a laundry list of changes, fixes, and enhancements. Phase 2 is mocked because so often it never really happens. The project launches, it's not as good as anyone was hoping for, and enthusiasm for the whole enterprise wanes.

As in the software industry through the 1990s, in digital advertising through the 2000s this was the standard approach. I experienced this countless times while at traditional agencies. It's still the dominant paradigm in digital marketing production, though, finally, after nearly 20 years, agile development is making inroads into the advertising world.

The waterfall approach is still probably the most common form of project management in our industry. It's also the one that your clients are going to be most comfortable with. In some circumstances, this is just fine. Short, quick jobs, jobs that are only going to be live for a very short time, are two common examples. Many projects that involve developing web banners, rich media, and creative concepts are still run as waterfall projects. In the PR and graphic design industry, waterfall is still the default as well—indeed, agile has made few inroads here (though I predict this, too may change).

AGILE DEVELOPMENT

Agile development seeks to replace the whole waterfall project management approach for ongoing jobs with a different paradigm. There are different agile methodologies—such as extreme programming (XP) or Scrum. For simplicity's sake, we'll use the Scrum methodology, as that is the one that we employed at TBG.

Scrum was originally conceived for controlled manufacturing in the late 1980s, but by the mid-1990s, it was being applied to software development. The word scrum comes from the procedure in rugby in which the game is restarted after a penalty or the ball goes out of play. It's a nice metaphor. Take a step back, reset, start again.

There is one other aspect of web development that lends itself nicely to Scrum: the possibility of continued deployment. A key difference between a web app and a house, a car, a party, or even a CD-ROM is that a web app can be developed again and again. You can launch new code to the Web, even after users are using your site. This opens up new possibilities.

Inherent in the theory of agile development is the acceptance and understanding that circumstances change. The second pillar of agile is that the best approach is to launch with a minimum viable product, or MVP. That is, coding and getting something, anything, launched, rather than nothing, as soon as possible, is better than coding for a long time and adding a lot of features before you even launch, because it's the Web, and you can launch again later. You launch, then add features.

This has the advantage of getting something into the hands of all the stakeholders as soon as possible, allowing for everyone to see and feel the product. Then discussions are had about which additional, or incremental, feature is most important to build next. It forces everyone to have conversations at regular intervals, therefore allowing new requirements to crop up sooner rather than later.

This is the core of the major tenet of agile: iterative development. This means that code is deployed at regular intervals—often every one, two, or four weeks. These intervals are called sprints. This is key: you don't develop willy-nilly and release a new feature when you feel like it. You are always releasing new code, in regular intervals. You are always releasing new features. Forward progress is always made.

The process works thusly: a meeting takes place with all stakeholders. Along with the development team, there are two key roles in Scrum: the product owner and the scrum master. The product owner is the voice of the customer, the voice of the people. They write user stories and define tasks, and add them to the backlog, which is an evolving list of all outstanding to-dos. The scrum master is the person who protects the developers from overcommitting and ensures that the rules are followed. The rest of the development team consists of developers, designers, user experience (UX) experts, testers, and perhaps documentation writers. Everyone at the meeting discusses which features are most important to build. Honest assessments are made of how long it would take to add any feature, and people are held to that by the scrum master. Anything that takes longer than the amount of a sprint is broken down into smaller pieces. If there are new requirements, they are discussed and added to the backlog. If new situations arise, and the product needs to adapt and change, new tasks and stories are written and added to the backlog. Then, at each meeting, the team as a whole decides what's most important, right now, to build next. To do this, they rank the backlog, and agree to tackle the top-ranked items in the backlog first. It's at this meeting that all the discussions are had, arguments are undertaken, and compromises are made. The differences are hammered out. The team then agrees on the backlog, identifying what to build in the next sprint. And off they go.

The sprint then starts, and everything on the sprint is built and deployed. The team as a whole checks it out, and a new sprint meeting, or stand-up meeting, is held, and the process starts again. This allows for the introduction of new information into the production process at regular intervals. If the project is a quick one and the situation is highly fluid, then perhaps the sprint is shortened to a week. If it's a longer project and events change slowly, a sprint may be as long as a month.

For software development, this is a revelation. Code is always launched, people are always seeing things, and there is a sane, practical, and effective process for steering the ship in a new direction if the situation arises and everyone agrees the new circumstances need to be addressed immediately.

Agile development is practically a religion in Silicon Valley. There's not a major software product that's come out of the valley in the last 20 years that doesn't embrace some form of agile development.

And it's not hard to see why this would be so useful in the marketing world. It eradicates the dreaded phase two. It keeps people on schedule and on time. It eliminates the possibility of overburdening the developers, and adding so many features to the mix that it is unrealistic to launch on time. It also can reduce the dreaded change order, where the customer is bled dry through a thousand cuts of small, additional fees for new time or new features. This whole process can be miserable and deteriorate the client-vendor relationship.

When it works, agile methodologies can be a powerful weapon for a brand. It can rapidly adjust its online marketing message to adapt to new realities. It allows brands to deploy robust online offerings for their customers. Nike+ wouldn't have happened without employing agile methodologies. It can open up a new world for brands online. For example, in the old days, if a new technology like Facebook Connect were invented, and a brand identified it as something that would be hugely beneficial for them, by increasing their email database or allowing them to connect to more customers in a new way, they could rapidly deploy and develop the new technology. In the old days, they would have to ask their digital agency (assuming they already had one they worked with routinely) to come up with a bid, get the bid approved, get it signed, get the resources assigned at the company, make a timeline, and go build it. The differences can be profound.

CRAFTING A PROCESS
ALIGN YOUR PROCESS WITH THE LARGER VISION OF YOUR COMPANY

In talking about the explicit connection between vision and company, BBH cofounder John Hegarty says, "Whatever you believe in has to be believed in from day one and implemented from day one."[5] This is a direct, simple way of explaining something of profound importance: by far the most important facet of an effective company process is that it is aligned to the larger vision of the company. A company that does not embrace its own vision in the very manner in which it completes its work is a company at war with itself. This is the single most important thing to do when crafting a process. If your company's vision stresses genius and creativity, it is probably not a super reaffirming policy to tell everyone they can't go for walks when concepting, and they all need to be at their desks at 8:30 in the morning. If your company stresses dedication and hard work, however, then maybe this is more plausible.

Writing in the *Harvard Business Review*, John Coleman clearly establishes this link. "Values are of little importance unless they are enshrined in a company's practices. If an organization professes, 'people are our greatest asset,' it should also be ready to invest in people in visible ways."[6]

Sometimes the connections between process and vision may not be readily apparent. Let us look at this quote from the Wikipedia community's guidelines for posting on the site:

Process is important on Wikipedia, and to Wikipedia. Some people minimize the importance of process by pointing to Wikipedia policies such as "Ignore all rules" and "Wikipedia is not a bureaucracy" or other

Wikipedia essays such as "Product over Process" or "Snowball clause." But process is essential to the creation of the product. Process is a fundamental tool for carrying out community consensus, and for allowing a very large number of people to work together on a collaborative project.[7]

Wikipedia's process *includes* such seemingly antiprocess koans as "ignore all rules" and "Wikipedia is not a bureaucracy." These can seem like arguments against process. But in fact, they are simply part of Wikipedia's larger ethos: many people making many changes.

We see something similar going on at Facebook. Facebook's internal motto was for a long time "move fast and break things." On the surface, this would seem like a manifest rejection of process. But that does not mean there is no process. There are still innumerable processes to comply with at Facebook. If you or I walked in there and sat down at a computer, we'd not have the slightest clue how to deploy code, because there is a rigorous process by which to do so. Deploy processes are still utilized. Facebook engineering manager Ralph Herbrich discusses the difference in a blog post on research at Facebook. "Move fast and break things" is not about negating process. *It is about speeding the process up to learn faster:*

> Before I joined Facebook I misread the motto "Move Fast and Break Things" as doing whole product development cycles in weeks rather than months, but the point of this motto is instead about iterating fast.[8]

With both Facebook and Wikipedia, tenets of their process, which at first blush seem to be the rejection of process, are in fact well-thought-out process guidelines to keep process minimized and the organizations moving as quickly as their users. These process tenets are, in fact, in line with the visions for each organization.

This is what we must strive to do. I reiterate: *A company that does not embrace its own vision in the very manner in which it completes its work is a company at war with itself.*

This is also a great means of keeping yourself honest. If secretly your vision for your company is to do work as cheaply and quickly as possible, and your process has a lot of highfalutin verbiage about the importance of creativity, the conflict will be apparent to you, your employees, and your customers. It will ring false. People will notice. And you'll hate yourself for the lie.

GROW WITH YOUR PROCESS AND ITERATE FROM THERE

The easiest way to begin crafting a process is to start when you are small, and have it be little more than a document by which you, as an individual or a small team, already operate. The odds are you and your partners have developed a fairly efficient, effective way to work together already. It may not be spoken aloud. It may not even be conscious. But it is happening if you are working together well.

By starting early, and documenting what you already do, the process of your company can capture the principles and essence of what makes your company unique, rather than changing your company, as it would if you implemented a process later, on top of something that is already working. It's never too early to begin thinking about process. This doesn't mean that it needs to be a burden. Indeed, half the advantage of describing your process early is to avoid its being a burden.

Nigel Bogle of BBH used to say, "How big can we get before we get boring?" He was drawing a direct link between growth and quality. BBH's Hegarty elaborated, "As your success feeds your growth, so your growth destroys your success."[9] As you grow, natural tensions and challenges will emerge with the ad hoc or unspoken processes you already have. Rob Goffee and Gareth Jones say their studies reinforce this. "As successful entrepreneurial businesses grow, they often come to believe that new, complicated processes will undermine their culture. But systematization need not lead to bureaucratization, not if people understand what the rules are for and view them as legitimate."[10]

If you have these down on paper, it will be easier to make small, incremental changes to the process that account for new challenges as they arise. In the early days, the first process steps may well consist of adding simple steps to make sure your projects stay on time or on budget, or your work's good enough. Early on, if you have a process principle that "no work leaves the office without all the partners agreeing it's good enough," it is easier to swap out a more scalable rule later—say "no work leaves the office without a partner's approving it," or "without at least two partners approving it." These implementations, done on their own, later, would cause more confusion than they would as a modification to an existing principle. Another example might be something along the lines of "no discounts are offered without the approval of a partner." But later, as you specialize, one partner may not have a handle on the detailed day-to-day finances anymore, and it'll be easy to say "no discounts without the approval of Jane."

It will be a challenge to make sure that your process isn't overcontrolling and stifling, but letting the process grow with the company, from as early a point as possible, will go a long way toward ensuring that the processes mirror the needs and work manner of the company from the get-go.

At least once a quarter, have everyone who is relevant sit down and talk about the process, what's working, what can be jettisoned, what new processes need to be implemented. You don't need to spend too much time on this. Remember, every minute that is spent on process is a minute someone isn't making money for the company. Keep it light.

Every few years, chuck the whole thing out the window and start again. Some of the same stuff might make it in, but the whole process will feel liberating. If you end up with the exact same processes—and you won't—then take it as evidence that your company has its act together.

Consider taking out one process step whenever you add a new one.

FOSTER CREATIVITY

While many of the important reasons for implementing process revolve around time and money, we should never forget that the processes we implement in the company impact the creative ability of each and every individual within the company. This is not confined to the "creative" department. A good process necessitates a good amount of effort to ensure that the individuals of the company are creatively empowered and have the space to think, room to breathe, and time that they need to get their creative juices flowing.

A good rule of thumb when thinking about process is that 50 percent of your processes should go toward making sure your company stays in business, and 50 percent of your processes should go toward making sure that the work your company does is the best it can be. Dedicating at least half of your process weight to the latter goal ensures that the processes of the company will not foster resentment among the rank and file, but rather they will see them as bulwarks against outside pressures—tools that help get them what they need to get the job done. This may include creatively stimulating activities within the office—game machines, music, and whatnot—spaces for people to be alone and think in quiet, schedules that respect "maker time" versus "manager time," and permissive out-of-office rules during concepting phases.

James Young, in his *A Technique for Producing Ideas,* speaks of the difference between *specific* knowledge and *general* knowledge. Both are required for a great work:

Of equal importance with the gathering of these specific materials is the continuous process of gathering general materials...

In advertising an idea results from a new combination of specific knowledge about products and people with general knowledge about life and events.[11]

W. Glenn Griffin and Deborah Morrison back this up in *The Creative Process Illustrated* by saying that "Ads (even the greatest ones) are just products. Creativity, however, is the human enterprise that brought them into being. It is a rich and wonderful process informed by culture and environment, the straightforward and the serendipitous: your education, your travel to the shoreline or to London or to a new neighborhood, that thing that happened to you in the third grade, the smell of your grandmother's perfume, what you read and watch and subscribe to, where you spend Saturday nights and Tuesday mornings."[12] Employee perks that foster these feelings are not there to coddle the employees. These are there to encourage the creativity on which your company survives. There has been some blowback during this recession, about the privileges and perks afforded to creative people in the workplace. Grumble all you want, but skimp on these at your own peril.

Finally, Hegarty makes the explicit link between a creativity-driven process and the agency business. "If you are a creative business, as opposed to a business with a creative department, then creativity has to be at the heart of your organization. It has to be seen to be at the heart of the company, and not only to drive it, but also to attract other, equally inspiring creative thinkers. I think that's called 'a virtuous circle.'"[13]

AVOID TEAM BLOAT

Whatever your process, as your company grows, your capabilities expand, and the work you do becomes more complex, there is a natural tendency for the project team to grow and grow with more people. When we started, our project team consisted of a producer, a designer, and a developer. By year ten, it consisted of an account person (or two), a creative director, an art director, a designer, a copywriter, a user experience designer, a technical director, a developer (or two, or three), a strategist, an analytics analyst, and an engagement partner. I am probably forgetting someone.

Some of these new roles were necessary to ensure quality. Some of them were necessary to ensure the client's needs were being met. And in fact, we kept this team really lean. I've seen other companies with three, four, or even five more team members beyond this—engagement planners, specialized interface designers, titles you've never heard of.

Some of this team growth is, then, necessary. But much of it is not. There is a natural tendency in an organization to specialize more and throw more bodies at any given problem as the resources become available.

Fight this urge with all your might. A larger team is a more expensive team, even if the client is paying for every hour used. Trust me on this. But more broadly, a company that keeps its teams lean keeps its overhead low, and its profits and margins higher. This is vital.

Finally, people are more empowered on small teams, where there is more of a sense of ownership. When you have ten colonels on a project, you have no leader. When you have one, your leader is manifest.

EMBRACE TRANSPARENCY

Management professor Timothy Dolan comments on the concept of adhocracy that it is characterized by a more open, transparent environment than a traditional bureaucracy. "Other significant distinctions between adhocracy and bureaucracy are that the former is oriented towards transparency and collaboration while the latter is oriented towards ascribed authority often held and maintained through secrecy, resistance to innovation and turf defense"[14] We should cotton to this characteristic of adhocracies and embrace it.

I am a firm believer in transparency, but, like all hypothetical principles applied to real life, the devil's in the details. When it comes to your process, however, transparency is absolutely your friend. Processes are living, breathing documents, and they are only as smart as the people who have made them. Transparency can encourage people within your company to offer suggestions to improve your processes.

Goffee and Jones reinforce this in their findings. "The organization of your dreams does not deceive, stonewall, distort, or spin. It recognizes that in the age of Facebook, WikiLeaks, and Twitter, you're better off telling people the truth before someone else does. It respects its employees' need to know what's really going on so that they can do their jobs, particularly in volatile environments where it's already difficult to keep everyone aligned and where workers at all levels are being asked to think more strategically."[15]

But more importantly, it can also make them feel connected to those processes, and invested in them. If the people in the company understand what drives a process, they will be more likely to embrace it. There was much grumbling about my strict rules about discounts until I explained to everyone just how tight the finances were, and what pointless financial losses we endured before we had implemented a process around approving discounts.

EMBRACE DISSENT

In his seminal history of the American advertising industry, Stephen Fox wrote, "Though overflowing with vivid individuals and opinions, the business lacked a tradition of internal dissent. Reformers in the industry risked being dismissed as heretics and gadflies, disloyal, not team players."[16] This is not what you want in your company. Do not stifle dissent, especially when it comes to process. If your team is grumbling about a process point, revisit it openly, discuss it openly, and find a solution to it together that meets all the needs. If you are finding your process too stifling, say something about it and work to solve it. Encourage people to speak up. Acknowledge their concerns about being overprocessed, and work to address them.

A process is dead if the team does not embrace it. Think of yourself as a firebrand populist politician with the team's interests at heart. Employees have many reasons to dislike process. It is labor intensive. It stifles creativity. It can limit options. It can be disruptive. These are hallmarks of a process that is not well. Watch for them. If employees are complaining about these things, take up their causes, listen to them, fight for them. Beware of developing a hardened battle line between "pro-process" management and "antiprocess" employees.

GUIDELINES NOT RULES

Perhaps the most important tenet of developing an effective but nonstifling process in your company is to remember to focus on principles and not rules. This is true for all types of organizations, but it is especially true in creative ones. One of the biggest risks of crafting a process—and one of the most frequent complaints about the process within an organization—is that it stifles individual intellect, initiative, and creativity. Our process must not do this.

In order to achieve this, the process should be principle based and not rule based. Recall the precepts of the adhocracy, versus the bureaucracy. You want to land on the former side of that scale.

I cannot stress this enough: *if your process is a guideline-based manifestation of your company's vision, it will be incredibly empowering and effective.*

You do not want to do what we did at one agency I worked at and come up with a 200-point list of procedures and rules. You want guidelines, and you want principles. This is all the more powerful when these principles are reinforced by, and in support of, the vision of your company. This can be a challenge if you are a control freak, or if you don't employ skilled people. If this is the case, work on those issues in other manners than imposing additional processes.

HIRE ACCORDINGLY

If your process is a set of guidelines supported by the larger vision of the company, it should be fairly easy to hire people who can fit into your process regimen because these will be people who mesh with your company's larger culture and vision.

There will come a time when you are tempted to hire someone who does not match the vision of your company, or who is not respectful of your ways. This is a terrible idea. Rare orchids do not transplant well to extreme climates.[17]

Additionally, as your company grows, you will need to find some people who are charged as being "keepers of the process." These will typically be two or more roles. The first is a person in the company who is the official and final arbiter and documenter of the process. I played this role at TBG in the early years, and over time ceded it to our director of production, Jen Jonsson. We handled disputes about process and facilitated conversations about what we should do when a weakness in the process was exposed. We maintained the documentation of the process (though often other people's help was enlisted). The second role you'll need is one or more people who ensure that the process is adhered to on any individual project. You are looking for managers of process—these are typically producers in the company, so we will use that term. They are not "project managers," but rather creators. Facilitators. People who can make things happen and make sure the process is followed, but who do not stifle the company with rules.

THE TYPE OF COMPANY YOU ARE MATTERS

It's entirely possible at this point that your company does only one thing, and does that one thing well. Processes in your industry may be well defined. The web design community, the tech community, the user experience community, and more all have healthy dialogues about the best practices and processes within your industry. There are trade groups you can join, discussion boards for which you can register, and meetups and conferences in which you can participate. I encourage these actions heartily.

However, many of the traditional disciplines are beginning to overlap. Things are not as clear cut as they used to be. Technology and the Web are influencing all of the creative and marketing disciplines and crafts, and the processes are beginning to bleed over. It is worth having a handle on the basics of process from related and complementary disciplines. Educate yourself.

Secondly, if you are a company on a growth trajectory, it will be almost completely inevitable that, over time, your company will begin to offer additional services. There's a good chance that one day your processes will need to grow beyond the processes of your current "core competency," or primary service offering. This will require looking at your processes in a more holistic way, across multiple disciplines. The thinking described above, then, becomes an excellent beginner's guide to crafting processes that work with many different roles.

DIFFERENT DEPARTMENTS NEED DIFFERENT ACCOMMODATIONS TO PROCESS

The tech portion of your company is often more rigorously processed than the creatives. Different levels of process for each department are often common and acceptable. Think about it from all angles—the creatives, the salespeople.

The technical department may well have rigorous processes that do not extend to the rest of the company. Many technical managers have a strong preference for implementing such processes as unit testing, lean start-up-inspired a/b testing and validating, QA procedures, version control systems, security protocols, and the like.

The finance department, too, will need more rigorous controls. Some are required by law—audits, receipts, invoices, and so forth. And some are commonsense, such as getting two partners to approve spending over a certain level or requiring multiple signatures on large checks.

The process details within a specific part of the company should be broadly overseen by the partners, and important points of principle should be agreed upon, especially those that correspond to the vision of the company: "We do not tolerate bugs," "There is no margin for error in our finances," "Shipping code quickly is more important than being perfect," "We embrace creative financing and want to push the limits of what the IRS finds legal" (hey, some people are into that sort of thing), and so on. These should be agreed upon by the entire leadership of the company and be supported by the larger vision of the company. But the details should be left to the department heads, or those that understand the inner workings of that department. Focus instead on the larger processes that bind the company together.

TECHNOLOGY PLAYS A ROLE, BUT DOES NOT DEFINE PROCESS

Technology has had an impact on the processes of creative-based organizations: most notably with the advent of project management and collaborative tools like Basecamp, as well as in the realm of distributed, remote brainstorming, such as with the tool BEARD that we made in-house at TBG. Technology has also allowed for better communication with remote coworkers, enabling teams to be spread throughout the building, city, country, or world. We've seen commensurate process innovations in other areas of the marketing enterprise: collaborative writing tools such as Google Docs for writers, royalty-free image licensing and content-development platforms like Percolate and Contently for art buyers and social media managers, advances in bookkeeping software, invoicing and payment systems, and accounting tools for the finance department.

Technology will prove invaluable in implementing your processes. New technologies will arise constantly. It will be a challenge to keep abreast of these new technologies as your company grows. The implementation of new technologies will become more and more difficult as well, as your company scales. Nonetheless, effort must be expended to stay on top of such things. This is most effective at the departmental level. Encourage your department heads in learning about the latest tools to improve the processes of the company, and support their endeavors to implement them.

For all of this, however, technology does not replace guidelines and principles. Indeed, technology has a rather rough time comprehending them. Take care to not cede too much authority to systems that do not understand nuance. We hit this snag with our project management system Pipeline at TBG. It was a highly effective system, embraced by just about everyone. But one part that never caught on was the functionality that required the users to check a box every time an approval was obtained, and at every step of the proposal pipeline. This part of the system sacrificed principles for rules, and therefore ended up not being useful.

TRAIN AND DOCUMENT

It's easy to write down "the process" in a document that no one ever sees. You may not even notice for a while that this is a problem, since the employees you have now may already know the process. It'll only become apparent over time, as many new employees join up, that the process is not widely understood. New employees will endeavor to pick up the process through trial and error, and by questioning other employees. Slowly your process will turn into one large, muddled game of Chinese telephone (God, that game needs a new name).

It is vital that the process is clearly documented and kept somewhere that everyone knows about and can revisit easily. It's also important that individual employees are taught the process, in person, when they start at the company.

As new processes are implemented, you will find yourself spending a good amount of effort making sure that they ripple through the company and that everyone understands, accepts, and abides by the new processes. Incentives, rewards, and games work well here. Highlight in company meetings examples of how the new process would have saved someone's ass on a past screwup. Offer rewards to people who exhibit good process instincts. Stay on the people who do not follow the process.

WALK THE WALK

Finally, walk the walk yourself. The era in which a leader can ignore the rules he set out for others isn't *quite* dead yet, but it is dying. You cannot be a hypocrite. You are not the "boss." This thinking will alienate the people you most need to make your company succeed. Goffee and Jones report that the best workers "are becoming more suspicious of charisma, as many charismatic leaders turn out to have feet of clay."[18]

It is certainly fun to be the Dear Leader. You'll get no argument from me there. Indeed, as your company and stature grow, some employees will even tacitly encourage it, assuming you're exempt from the rules and asking you what you want. Do not give in to this temptation. You may need an "administrative assistant" eventually, for example, but hold off until other people who also need admins can have them, or until your employees threaten you with a coup if you don't comply with their demand that you get one.

By following the process rules you've implemented, you are showing that respect for them runs through the entire company. By ignoring them, you are showing everyone they don't matter.

IN CLOSING

Many services firms are good at what they do. Process is what helps make them great. Process is what helps them keep doing their best work and grow while doing it. Your company cannot simply be good. In order to succeed, it must be great. The great company works with process, vision, and culture all operating in a virtuous cycle to ensure that the work is spectacular, and the company has the resources it needs to keep employees invested and functioning at the highest level.

It's natural to be skeptical of process, but it still must be embraced. Think of your views on process as those of a Reagan conservative—an honest, old-fashioned one and not the current bastardization of one. You are delving into process with a healthy skepticism of it, seeking to improve the parts of it that help us, and eliminating those that don't. Use your skepticism to improve the process, not kill it.

Or perhaps think of process as lighter fluid. You want a good amount of lighter fluid when you light the match, but if you put too much on there, well, you're going to get a nice fireball and some singed eyebrows.

9

WORKING FOR OTHER AGENCIES

Depending on the type of consultancy you are thinking about creating, there is a very good chance that you will find yourself working with other agencies and consultancies as your clients. Indeed, if you plan on being a specialist shop, you may *always* find yourself working with agencies as clients. But even if you're trying to build the next BBDO, you're going to be working with other agencies, with them as the vendor and you as the client. The marketing ecosystem is phenomenally interconnected. On any one large brand today, there are literally dozens of agencies working on various aspects of the business. Some have direct relationships, but more often the agencies work together in a web of contracting and subcontracting.

Working with agencies has many advantages, to be sure. There can also be some challenges. But for all but a select few consultancies, other agencies will be a significant component of your work for a long period of time.

This is, on the face of it, not necessarily an obvious notion. Many people, when starting a services shop, envision themselves working primarily—or exclusively—with brands.

Early on in your career, it's worthwhile to develop a plan and a point of view when it comes to working with agencies. Do you want to work primarily for agencies? Now? Forever? What is your ultimate goal? For us, agencies were a means to an end. My partner Benjamin said more than once, "Working with agencies allows us to work on a larger stage with larger brands. One day we will be able to do this on our own. But for now, they are necessary." This was our plan: to work with agencies for as long as it took to grow our business, establish our reputation, and hone our craft. Over time, we would wean ourselves off of them.

Other shops I know work exclusively with other agencies and love it. They love not having to deal with clients. They love working on projects they wouldn't get otherwise. They love the ease of repeat work. This is totally okay. Develop a plan.

THE ADVANTAGES OF WORKING WITH OTHER AGENCIES

LOW COST OF WINNING WORK

Perhaps the greatest advantage for the specialist shop that is working with other agencies is the low cost of winning the work. If, for example, you are a UX or a digital product consultancy, winning work directly from clients can be a time-consuming process. In many cases, the client is almost completely uneducated about your offering, the challenges in the marketplace, or the very basics of developing, say, an iOS app (these specific examples will, of course, eventually be dated, but the concept will remain). If this particular client has a lead agency, however, that agency can bear a lot of the heavy lifting on that sale, teaching the client and establishing the strategic need. This is a bunch of work you will not have to do. You will now be talking to the agency, which, comparatively speaking, knows what it is talking about.

Low project acquisition costs are also reinforced by the fact that you only have to maintain good relationships with a few key agencies, and they can then bring multiple projects to you. It's only so often that a brand needs a new website, or iOS app, or even a print ad. The agency, by contrast, often needs these things, as their whole raison d'être is to get their clients up to speed on the latest brand and marketing techniques. Many agencies excel at repeatedly selling the same marketing components to several of their brands. This can work in your favor if you develop a strong relationship across a client agency. You can end up as their go-to person for several clients. Early on, we developed a relationship like this with Goodby, becoming one of their go-to shops for minisites (hey, it was the oughts) for such clients as HP, Saturn, Discover Card, Emerald Nuts, and Comcast.

LESS PITCHING

One more low-acquisition-cost benefit: often with agency work, you don't have to pitch to win the job. That is the agency's problem. At least, you don't have to pitch in the traditional sense, with a giant presentation, a dog and pony show, comped boards, and so on. Early in our company's history, we were chasing a large job with an agency. I went all out on the pitch. The agency producer said, "This is great, but I really just need a one-pager with your price and timing." I sent it. Boom. Done. I never had to send anything OTHER than simple pricing and timing to Goodby for years, at least, until the jobs got more daring, more complex, and higher budget.

Being able to win jobs by just sending in pricing and timing, and maybe a paragraph of thinking is glorious. Wonderful. Advertising nirvana. Agencies—good agencies—can provide this.

WORK WITH PEOPLE WHO KNOW WHAT THEY'RE DOING (RELATIVELY SPEAKING)

Another concrete luxury of working with agencies as clients is that they have a robust account service corps. They are responsible for maintaining the relationship with the client. You are not. This is *great*. I cannot overemphasize how wonderful it is not to have to deal with angry clients. This is not to say you won't have to maintain *your* relationship with the agency, but by and large, this is a far less difficult undertaking. Agency people are *busy*. They want problem solvers; they want you to get things done. And they seem to have their own built-in ability to get too drunk and into too much trouble when they're visiting your city. You don't have to do it for them. This is nice.

By working with agencies, you can keep your relationships with your clients—the agencies—lightweight. One or two people should be able to maintain your relationship with five to ten agencies. This can often bring in more work than you will need for years, and do so incredibly cheaply. By contrast, maintaining relationships with five to ten brand clients, directly, can require a minimum of ten and up to thirty or forty people. The cost savings can be tremendous, especially early on. Remember: in the beginning at a high-growth services company, your goal is to bring in as many quality billings as quickly and cheaply as possible. Doing this without having to hire a robust account staff serves both of these goals.

WORK WITH MORE SOPHISTICATED CLIENTS FASTER

Here we touch on another benefit of working with agencies: the quality of the work. We are referring specifically to the sophistication of the work and the quality of the brand. Now, far be it from me to claim that agencies have a handle on the outermost realms of digital marketing, but I can say working for GM, Pepsi, Nike, or a car company will get your shop noticed faster than a bunch of work for local bars and restaurants, even if they are really, really cool. *Some* people may understand this work comes through another agency, and *some* of them may count that against you, but they are few and far between. By and large, your work will be noticed more, and your opportunities to do better work are expanded if you work for higher quality brands.

KNOWLEDGEABLE PRODUCERS

Finally, let's talk about the production corps. This cannot be understated. Agencies have *producers*. Yes, there will be times you're working on some project that is technically or conceptually beyond the ken of the agency producer. And there was a period in the early 2000s when agencies decided all of their broadcast producers should learn digital. That was a mess, but it is, more or less, over. And even in these situations, the existence of a dedicated person who grasps the concepts of timelines, deliverables, deadlines, and change management, *and is responsible for them* on the client side cannot be overemphasized. No end client has this. Yes, highly sophisticated marketing organizations such as Procter & Gamble and Coca-Cola have supremely qualified marketing managers and marketing organizations, and someone, somewhere, is responsible for timelines on their side. But it's not the same as having a dedicated producer agency side who manages the timeline. Having an agency producer between you and the client can be phenomenally effective. There are few things more satisfying than hearing the answer "Yep. Of course. Let me go fix that" when you say, "We need more time and money." Producers, especially at agencies, are passionate, skilled craftspeople, and they believe in giving creators the leeway they need. This rarely exists at brands themselves.

At The Barbarian Group, we made heavy use of agency work in our early years. I would say it wasn't until year five or six that direct-to-brand work outweighed agency work. This allowed us to keep our client service staff light and our acquisition costs low. Often, when we'd talk to other people in our line of work, they'd ask, "How do you guys get your work?" And we could say, "Oh, you know, the phone just rings." This was true, but not only for the reasons implied. It was also true because we had great relationships with several great agencies. And they would know they could count on us.

THE DISADVANTAGES OF WORKING WITH OTHER AGENCIES

This is not to say that working with agencies doesn't have its drawbacks. Excuse me for a bit of a rant here. Try to stay in a Zen mind-set. Beware of starting to hate your clients.

GROWTH CRACK

First and foremost, agencies are sort of like growth crack. It's easy to win a lot of work and grow really fast, without having developed robust capabilities in certain parts of your company that you will, eventually, need. Most notably this applies to client service, but also to finance, collections, new business, and the higher-level strategy and planning roles. Eventually you may need to grow these. Be sure to keep an eye on all of this. It's easy to get addicted to the fast, easy, new business cycle of agency work, and never build these areas.

And while it's not 100 percent necessary to *ever* strengthen these areas, the odds are you're going to want to. Your company is worth more, and it is easier to get work, if your company is known for its high-level strategic thinking along with its executional prowess. If you simply just keep taking work that the agency dreamed up, this will never happen.

A TECHNOLOGY KNOWLEDGE GAP

Agencies—large agencies, at least—are also slower to grasp the cutting edge. We'll get into the economic forces underlying this in a bit, but it's been my experience that many agencies are poorly skilled at keeping their eye on the ball of the next big thing. Or the next cool thing.

PAYMENT RISK

There can be payment issues. Some of the less-than-elite agencies often sign billing terms without thinking about it, and then later on blink at you, doe-eyed, when the payment is due and say something like, "but we don't pay you until we get paid," acting completely confused as to why you ever thought otherwise. This has happened to me more times than I can count. You will want to rip their head off, thinking, "Do you see this document here? With your signature on it? Does this mean nothing to you?" Well, no, it doesn't.

In the television production industry, there are established practices for this. Hard and fast rules, agreed to by all agencies. Payments due at certain points along the way. It's all very well defined. After nearly 25 years of digital production for advertising agencies, standardized billing and payment practices still do not exist for the Web. Beware of this when you work with agencies. Be firm. Greater trust and leeway can be granted to the agencies that have proven their worth. Many will qualify. Many will not. Know what sort of people you're dealing with, and be firm with the closefisted ones.

WHO GETS THE CREDIT?

Then there are the credit issues.

Despite years of back and forth, discussions and negotiations, many, many agencies are uncomfortable about sharing full credit, especially for the idea. We've seen why: *being known for a good idea is more valuable than being paid for good idea.* Agencies are not dumb. They know this.

We had this play out in extreme detail when working for one of the world's best-known agencies. We had done a project together. We all loved it, knew it would be a big hit. Our PR director, Eva McCloskey, called their PR department. They had, up till then, been great about sharing PR on projects. But they, too, knew this one was game changing. Suddenly the PR department went quiet. They became monumentally uninterested in sharing credit. Eventually Eva got their PR head on the phone. He was blunt: "We're not sharing PR on this one."

Eva tried to talk sense into him. She pointed out her own good relationships with the press. "Go ahead," he said. "No one will listen to you." This is not something you say to Eva. She politely hung up, worked her contacts, and got major, massive press for us for the project. His bluntness was, in a way, useful. It laid the issue bare for us. It wiped the naiveté from our eyes. It made us realize we had to work for our share of the credit. To this day, we are every bit as well known for the project as the client agency. It shouldn't have been this way. It should have been cooperative, but sometimes you have to fight fire with fire.

I should say that some agencies are wonderful about sharing credit: Goodby, in particular, was a fantastic partner as far as sharing credit. We'd go to award shows with them, walk the stage with them. Wieden + Kennedy and Arnold were also particularly good.

We won the Titanium Lion and several other awards in 2007 with Droga5 for the Tap Project for UNICEF. We won the Cyber Lion Grand Prix and several other prizes in 2004 with Crispin, Porter + Bogusky for the Subservient Chicken for Burger King, and the Grand Prix in 2005, again with Crispin, for Method. Was our name on every single award entry? Probably not. Did people know we did the work? Yes. Because we shouted it from the rooftops. You can get into arguments with your client agencies about this—and many companies have. But tactically, it may be your best bet to just make sure people know you won the work, and not bite the hand that feeds you. Letting the world know you did the work puts the onus on the client agency to shout you down, which makes them look petty and afraid. It is unlikely they'll possess the shortsightedness to get into a kerfuffle with you in the press, so long as you don't start one. Your call. Just beware that this is absolutely an issue you will encounter when working with agencies.

A CONFRONTATIONAL ECONOMIC ENVIRONMENT

In the old days, agencies were paid a commission—a percentage of a total ad spent, regardless of the work. If a brand was spending $50 million a year on advertising, the agency was paid 15 percent, or $7.5 million. This practice started to disappear in the '60s, and has since completely disappeared for "creative" work (that is, everything but the media buy itself). Since then, there has been an economic tension at the core of all advertising agencies that has been unresolved: while the concepting and idea work might pay the most per hour, the bulk of the money is spent in the production of the ideas.

A quick example: An brand spends $100 million a year. Ninety million dollars of that probably goes to the media buy—paying the actual publications, TV stations, billboard companies, and the like. Of the remaining $10 million, perhaps $2 million is spent on the idea generation, strategy, conceptualization, and account service. The balance—roughly $8 million—is spent on the "production" of all the work. This is why companies such as yours may be referred to as "production shops" by traditional agencies.

The $90 million is spent by "media agencies"—these are specialized agencies that do nothing but buy media for clients. They do not do creative.

The balance is spent on "creative agencies" and production.

In reality, these days, most agencies are creative agencies AND production shops. While it's nice to make a good margin on the $2 million you're receiving for the creative concepting, economic pressures are dictating that most shops also want to capture the remaining $8 million of production revenue, even if it is at a lower margin. Which means they may eventually want your work.

WHY AGENCIES RARELY SPECIALIZE

Large agencies have always had a bit of an identity crisis when it comes to production. In principle, it makes sense for the lead agency to be a partner with the brand on the big idea, the overall strategy, and the branding, and work with other vendors—smaller firms, more specialized companies, and production shops—on execution. The root causes come from three places. First, the pressure from shareholders for the public agency holding companies is always to show growth. Yes, production may be less profitable per hour than creative work, but there is a lot more of it. By capturing the production revenue, a creative shop can show revenue growth.

Second, all service shops are, broadly speaking, valued on a multiple of revenue, regardless of the source of the income. Again, yes, some hours (idea concepting, strategy) are more profitable than others (Photoshop work, Quality Assurance), but acquirers are generally only looking at average margins, and all shops have roughly the same average margins. By taking on more of this low-margin work, a company still becomes more valuable to a potential acquirer.

The third driver of this trend roughly falls under the parameters of Clayton Christensen's *The Innovator's Dilemma*. The most interesting trends and techniques going on in marketing are, broadly speaking, the new ones. When a new marketing vehicle is introduced—from the television spot to the iOS app to ads in the XBox—it is only a few of the more cutting-edge marketers that test the waters. I have a personal list of these: Pepsico, Coca-Cola, Procter & Gamble. There's not a lot of revenue and not a lot of activity around a new marketing technique. These can be looked at as classic disrupting innovations in *The Innovator's Dilemma*, which implies that the larger, entrenched players tend to discount them as not worth it from a point of view of market size and profit margins. Over time, however, the new innovation takes root, primarily through new entrants to the market who are comfortable with the smaller market size and profit margins. This may well be you, if you are a social shop, mobile shop, or some other shop specializing in a new offering. Eventually, the new technology threatens the entrenched player's core business, and the new market has already been won by the new players (hopefully you!). The older, larger businesses' only alternative at this point is acquisition.

This has been the ebb and flow of agency land since the dawn of time. It was like this with direct marketing. With research. With radio. With television. With digital in the dot-com boom. It's happening now with digital, social, mobile, and pr.

In 2008, hot shop Crispin, Porter Bogusky acquired a 60-person digital shop in Boulder, Colorado, called Texturemedia. Alex Bogusky, Crispin cochair at the time, called it "one of the most important steps we've taken in [building] our digital capabilities." Texturemedia CEO Andrew Davidson said the merger "allows us to further leverage our interactive expertise at the highest level."[1] Davidson stayed at Crispin for two years, nine months, before moving on.[2] What was really happening was that Crispin was purchasing a production capacity it had, in the past, farmed out to companies like yours.

I don't call out Crispin specifically. We've seen this across the board. Dentsu purchased the Romanian firm Kinecto and the Indian agency Webchutney, both in May 2013.[3] Publicis bought Indigo Consulting for Leo Burnett in April 2012, and the Middle Eastern services company Flip Media in February of that year. JWT Singapore bought Hungama Digital in June 2012. TBWA India bought Magnon in January 2013. Y&R acquired the Turkish digital shop C-Section in February 2013. Aegis acquired Roundarch in February 2012. CREATETHEGROUP acquired digital shop Morpheus Media in June 2011[4]. The list is endless.

AGENCIES WILL ULTIMATELY WANT YOUR WORK

In working with an agency, you are almost certainly working for the production dollars. The agency—your client—is attempting to a) keep the $2 million in concepting money, and b) capture some revenue on the production, but keep costs low, by hiring you and marking you up.

Eventually, however, there is a good chance the agency will turn its eye to the revenue it has been "letting go" and passing on to you.

If you work in PR, or Social, or some other ancillary field, this is still true. Everyone would love to get their hands on your revenue.

It is my strong recommendation that you never rely too heavily on any one agency client. Agencies can be filled with good people, but they are, in the end, competitors. Martin Sorrell, CEO of the WPP agency holding company, famously termed Google to be WPP's "frenemy."[5] The same principle applies here. You may have a great relationship with a client agency and its people, but there is every possibility that one day it will look at how much money it is paying you and decide it wants that money for itself.

We've seen this time and time again in marketing, and it has been one of the dominant trends through the digital evolution. At a high level, this explains holding companies' mega purchases of large digital shops such as AKQA, Digitas, R/GA, and LBi. It also explains why they are constantly snapping up small specialty shops that you've never heard of. Eventually, whatever business you're in will be big enough and interesting enough for them to muscle in on it.

THINGS THAT WORK IN YOUR FAVOR

The good news is that there areas in which you can avoid this risk. For example, this economic situation does not apply if you are, say, a world-famous graphic designer or copywriter. That is, if you are an in-demand expert on an established field, you have substantial advantages. Go ahead and hire copywriters, agency client. They won't be as good as I am, and your ads won't be as good as mine, and we both know it. I'll go work for your competitor and win the work.

Moreover, while picking up these new companies is compelling from an economic point of view, holding companies can't always buy the best people. The experts and most talented practitioners of a craft want to work on the best and most interesting projects. These are, by definition, rare. And they are rarer still for any single individual shop. This means there is a constant trend of the best people leaving large shops and starting smaller ones where they can get more of the interesting projects. Advertising is, of course, a phenomenally cutthroat, highly competitive business, with a massive premium placed on the top talent who can manifestly contribute to winning the big jobs. They have to do whatever it takes—and hire whatever it takes—to win. It is a false dichotomy to assume you can win the work just as easily with that ten-person design shop you bought in Topeka, rather than using the best freelance designer in America. Thus, large agencies' continuous efforts of buying out smaller vendors in order to capture the best talent is constantly thwarted. The top talent forever gravitates to the smaller shops, often leaving as soon as practical after an acquisition. That top talent simply *must* be hired to win the work, even if it means hiring an outside vendor. So the cycle begins anew.

HOW TO WORK EFFECTIVELY WITH
OTHER AGENCIES AS CLIENTS

First, and most obvious, be awesome at your core skill, and make sure everyone knows you are awesome. Make it clear to your clients that what you do for them is not easily replicated.

Next, diversify your client base. This is important regardless of whether you're working for agencies or not, but is especially so with agencies. They will leave you one day. Make sure your firm can withstand this.

WORKING WITH AGENCIES AND GETTING ACQUIRED

If you're building your shop to get acquired, first and foremost, make sure you have done a lot of work with the acquiring agency. If you're going to sell, better the devil you know.

Secondly, ensure that not all of your work comes from agencies that the potential acquirer may perceive as competitors. They don't want to buy you and see all of the work disappear. A small percentage from other agencies is fine—but ideally, you'd have some direct clients of your own. If a significantly large chunk of your work—say, over 50 percent—comes from an agency held by a competing holding company, this may factor into the equation. If they're interested in you for the quality of your work, they may want you anyway, but their overreliance on their competitors is a risk.

THE JOURNEY FROM AGENCY VENDOR TO AGENCY COMPETITOR

Over time, we built up our client service department so that our team could stand on its own without having to take work from a big agency. We did this by hiring one talented, experienced client service executive, Shelby MacLeod, and helping her win her first client. From there we grew client service.

This whole process took about seven years, from the beginning of our company to where agency-related work was less than 20 percent of our work. We still took agency work from time to time—sometimes the project is just too potentially interesting. Sometimes it's good for a quick hit of cash. Sometimes we wanted to work with an old friend. So we never completely stopped, even after we had been acquired.

The big challenge here is not to let your agency clients start to think of you as a competitor. We built our direct client relations from scratch, never trying to poach work from the agencies we worked for. I'm not sure they cared, since even at our largest size, we were never more than a fraction of the size of our agency clients. Getting your own work and not taking work from your agency clients might seem difficult, but for us, in reality it was easier than we expected. Many brands don't care what "type" of shop you are. They simply look at lists of "best digital shops" or "best designers" or "best branding companies" and just call you up, not really caring or knowing that you work primarily with agencies. The distinction between an "agency" whose work is from clients and a "production shop" whose work comes from agencies is an obsolete and a false divide. Eventually the inquiries coming directly from brands will start piling up, and you'll start answering them when the time is right.

10

PRO BONO WORK

There will come a time when every shop such as yours is given the opportunity to do some pro bono work. This is work, typically (but not always) for a nonprofit organization, that you do at a reduced rate or without charge.

At The Barbarian Group, we did some hugely rewarding pro bono work. The most successful was with our partnership with Droga5 and UNICEF, The Tap Project, which went on to win several major awards. We also did rewarding work for The New Museum, Helping Hands: Monkey Helpers of Boston, the Berkshire Film Festival, the City of New York, and several other organizations.

These are legitimate charity organizations that need discounted work and would otherwise have trouble paying for it. Additionally, this work will almost certainly likely see the light of day. This means it can have a positive effect on your reputation.

There are, however, some risks.

WHEN DOES PRO BONO MAKE SENSE?

There are times when pro bono work makes more sense for you. First and foremost, you'll need to be able afford to do the work. This tends to mean that it is easy to do pro bono work when you are very small, and when you are becoming rather large. In the middle of your shop's arc, when you're in high growth mode, it is a little more difficult to fit in pro bono work, as margins are razor thin and most of your excess energy and capital are being plowed back into your business.

PRO BONO WORK IS GOOD KARMA

Karma is, of course, a huge reason to pursue pro bono work. It feels good to do good. This may be especially important to you, and you may want to set aside a fixed percentage of the time the company spends on pro bono work. If you believe strongly in a cause and want to help, it can be hugely rewarding to bring to bear the resources of your company for a cause you feel passionate about.

PRO BONO HELPS DEFINE THE CULTURE OF YOUR SHOP TO EMPLOYEES

For all of the reasons mentioned above, pro bono work can be hugely reward-ing for employees, and a significant booster to a company's morale. When chosen well and when the work is going well, it can be a powerful rallying cry within your organization. It may even become something that your company is known for, thereby helping with recruiting and retention. It can also be a way for individual employees to spread their wings, taking on increased responsibility or developing their craft. The attendant galas and balls with which pro bono workers are often rewarded can also bring significant joy to the employees.

RECOGNITION, CREDIT, AND FULFILLMENT, ALL AT ONCE

The vast majority of pro bono work is done with the aim of bringing your firm both recognition and credit. Pro bono clients are a great way to quickly develop great work and get the word out about it. Therefore ensuring you get the credit and recognition for the work is key to accepting the work. Be frank about this concern upfront—most charities are totally okay with the concept of giving credit to the people who helped them. You can also ensure the right people see the work by sending it out yourself, which has the added benefit of promoting the cause at hand.

CREATIVE FREEDOM CAN BE A BENEFIT OF PRO BONO WORK

Creative freedom is another powerful reason to consider pro bono work. With-out the usual myriad concerns of a paying client, it's often possible to push cre-ative boundaries with pro bono work. To do something you've been longing to do that's been difficult to sell a client. To show the world how something could work, so that you have an example to point to in the future for paying clients that need a little extra reassurance. To make a really great portfolio piece. To win a few awards. There is, of course, a bit of a backlash in sentiment when a pro bono piece wins an award. Many practitioners of a craft understand that successfully navigating the constraints of a paying client with a business case is a more difficult challenge. This is why we often see pro bono work in separate categories at awards shows. There's still ample respect for the award, and ample reward in doing something creatively satisfying. And in any case, it's not as if most nonprofits don't have constraints or business requirements (you'll notice an overweening obsession from most pro bono clients with giving ample consideration to getting to the donation page on their website, for example).

At TBG we took this to the extreme when we worked with Helping Hands: Monkey Helpers, a Boston-based organization that helps adults with spinal cord and other injuries live more rewarding lives with the assistance of a monkey. Not only was the work rewarding but we got to see a monkey throw the first pitch at Fenway Park, and appear with David Sedaris and the Boston Symphony Orchestra. Fun!

WORKING WITH NEW PEOPLE

The networking opportunities of pro bono clients can be powerful. Many nonprofits have very high-powered boards, and attending the galas and board meetings of these nonprofits can reap many great introductions. We've also had great success asking for our logo to be listed among the partner logos in the gala programs and in the on-screen visuals at a gala. If this is why you're pursuing a specific nonprofit client, be sure to talk about this upfront. Working on a project does not necessarily ensure face time at the board meeting or the gala. Also, be sure to leverage this opportunity, bringing your hustler to the appropriate events, along with the people who did the work, though, here, too, a word of caution. One of the rewards, as an employee, of doing pro bono work is getting to go to the gala. Don't sell the team short that worked hard on the project so that your hustler can reap all the rewards. Find a balance.

WHAT CAN GO WRONG?

Pro bono work is not without its drawbacks, however. Be aware of these. One nonprofit is different from another. It's kind of amazing. When you think of the nonprofit world, you may think of diligent, passionate people working hard to change the world. Or perhaps you think of stifling bureaucracy, massive waste, and sclerotic organizations filled with wasteful, moribund amateurs, far removed from the actual work of helping people. Turns out, in my experience, both of these are true.

PRO BONO WORK IS NOT ALWAYS PLEASANT

Some of my worst clients ever were nonprofit clients. One client was so used to major marketing firms dying to do work for him for no money that he had come to expect it. He treated vendors with disdain. He spoke like a gangster on the phone. He used the phrase "ruin you." Wow. He was, for lack of a better term, a complete bastard. What's worse is that none of his rudeness, and none of his aggressiveness, was marshaled in support of the work that the nonprofit was doing. When nonprofits go bad, it's hard to understand why you're there at all. Fact is, there's probably no good reason. It's probably best to just get out. Explain to them politely why the relationship isn't working, and get out. Even now, years later, when the topic of the charity that this person works for comes up in conversation, or the recipients of that charity, I have to stop myself from ignoring them out of spite. Every plea for a good cause that falls upon my ears is a reminder of the humiliation that I received at the hands of this client. It's funny when you find yourself resenting a good cause against your will. Best to cut the cord quickly on this sort of relationship, find your inner good, and work hard to let it go.

DISORGANIZATION WITHIN THE ORGANIZATION

Perhaps the greatest risk with working with nonprofits is their propensity for disorganization on all matters marketing-, design-, and branding related. The large ones have quite robust budgets and sophisticated marketing departments when it comes to traditional techniques. Yet even they have challenges with emerging technologies. The smaller ones are even more challenging. You can't really blame them, after all. Most are run on shoestring budgets, and a good charity spends most of its resources helping those in need, not on design. The trick here is to think of them as regular clients, who, you may have noticed by now, can often tend toward disorganization. Use the same tricks and techniques. Resist the urge to skimp with a lightweight team. Do it right. Set deadlines. Stick to the process. Ensure client service at your organization is engaged. Cutting corners on these sorts of clients will bring heartache and misery. Be especially careful if you're trying to "fit in" a pro bono project between other, paying work. These situations call for the even-more-disciplined application of process.

CULTURE AND EMPLOYEES

Beware potentially divisive pro bono work, such as politics and political causes. While there may appear to be some political cohesion in our company, this sort of work is exactly the kind that exposes some rifts that perhaps best lay dormant.

One possible approach is to make the pro bono work volunteer only, for those who are passionate about it working, say, after hours or on weekends, for the cause. This can work, but is also accompanied by risk. It can foster resentment, jealousy, feelings of favoritism. It can make employees feel that the work is required, despite outward appearances, to get into the "in club." Tread with caution.

WHEN TO TAKE PRO BONO WORK

Doing pro bono work early in your career is good as it allows you to build up experience. Doing it later is valuable, as it can keep employees engaged (provided it is a pleasant experience, with pleasant and organized clients—see below). It can also be useful in doing some groundbreaking work, exhibiting your shop's creative prowess, and reinforcing the maxim that *being known for a good idea is more valuable than being paid for good idea.*

I find that there is a natural, U-shaped arc to how much pro bono work you can do over time: lots in the beginning, not so much in the middle period, say, up to 100 employees, and lots of work once again after that, as you have more substantial resources.

Some companies find the power of pro bono work to be compelling for recruiting and retention. Alternatively, you may want to focus now on growing your company as quickly as possible so that in the future you can find the time and resources to give back. Every company will need to find its own balance.

Be sure to include your partners in these decisions, however. It's quite acceptable—even ideal—for the partners to talk, early on, about their desires and hopes in this field and develop a consensus understanding. It may even be worthwhile to write a short pro bono point of view document at the outset of your company.

THE PARTS YOU NEED MONEY FOR

Pro bono implies free, but the reality is that it's not always possible to do the work for 100 percent free. There may be fixed costs that cannot be avoided, such as third-party hosting providers, or credit card processing fees. Work to be a good partner to see if you cannot find third-party providers that cater to, or at least support, nonprofit clients. There are many of them out there. Nonetheless, in the end, some things will need to be paid for. Explain this clearly to the clients up front. It may not always be obvious to them what you can and cannot do, what a hosting company is, or why some specific Application Program Interface (API) needs to be paid for. Write out an estimate, in advance, like you would any other project, and walk them through it.

ESTIMATES AND INVOICING

In the estimate, include the price for how much your work would cost normally, and line item it to zero with a discount. Finally, at the end of the project, submit invoices, like you would to any other client. Show how many hours you worked, and how much this would have cost. Show the discount to zero. Make it clear how much work you put into it. This is useful for a few reasons: first, it lets the client know the value of your services, which it may not fully comprehend. It may think it's getting $10,000 of free work, when it's actually getting $100,000. This may inspire them to give you a better promotion package, better signage at an event, or more tickets to the gala. It may also simply help with keeping the nonprofit appreciative and making each party understand how much is being given. One final perk, should the time come: it will be useful for the accountants of any potential acquiring company to see where that time went, how much it cost, and so forth, so it can be calculated into what your true potential margins are, and not written off as overhead.

I'll close by saying that some of our pro bono clients have been some of the most rewarding work we've ever done. Every time I visit the New Museum, for example, or go to its website, I am tickled pink to have helped such a great New York institution make its giant leap into its award-winning new home on the Bowery. And I am especially rewarded by the work we did for the Women's Sports Foundation, a nonprofit started by Billie Jean King that is dedicated to advancing the lives of girls and women through sports and physical activity. These kinds of projects are some of the most rewarding work you can do.

PART III

NEW BUSINESS

11

THE BASICS

This is the immutable truth: the work you have already done is 90 percent of your new business effort. Every marketer looking to hire a company like yours should want good work, and ignoring the past work of a company would be, to put it mildly, idiotic. This should go without saying.

There will be times that you, or another shop, will be chosen on the basis of something other than the work. But it will rarely happen that you'll be hired despite your not having any good work to show. All of your new business efforts will be exponentially more difficult—if not downright impossible—if your work is mediocre.

It's important to remember that everything in this section is secondary. If the devil came down today and forced you to choose between perfectly following every bit of advice in this section or just relying on a previous body of good work, choose the latter. Every time.

There are *many* different people involved in a client's choosing to hire an outside shop these days, and if your project is creatively genius, but technically crappy, the client IT director—who very well may be on the procurement committee—may dismiss you as "hacks" and vote not to hire you. Conversely, if your code is rock solid and you speak her language, she may become your biggest advocate. The good work is not always work that you, or a layperson, can easily see. When I say that all your work must be good, I also mean every individual project. Some agencies do half-assed jobs on some work, and then focus on certain other work to showcase. Avoid this. I've found that as the years go by, you'll find yourself pitching in different sectors. For example, you may be pitching a bank one day. And three years ago, you did a quickie project in the financial services category. Your chances of winning this new bank account are radically improved if you can show with pride the past work you've done in the financial sector. We never know when that old project is going to come in handy.

In the digital age, where there is a ton of production work to be had, and no shortage of crappy work and underbidding, it is probably possible to build a services company on mediocre work. While you will need to do everything in your power to build an efficient business that can compete with these people, you'll only ever be able to *truly* compete if your work is excellent.

Besides. Do you want to work at a company like that?

YOUR NEW BIZ TEAM

Tactically speaking, any good new business department has three distinct roles. These are the hustler, the pitcher, and the proposal jockey. Each of these roles is distinct, though occasionally a truly talented person can handle more than one of them. In the early days, you may need to double up on one or two of them, but in time you'll want to give these roles to different individuals. Each is a totally different set of skills and traits. Each takes years to perfect, and each takes many hours to perform. While the list of the hustler, the pitcher, and the proposal jockey is not ranked in order of importance, it is pretty much ranked in order of hire. For without a hustler, you have no work at all. Without a pitcher who inspires the client and gets it excited, it's harder to win work. And without a proposal jockey, it is very difficult to win the larger projects and to minimize any potential veto votes on the decision committee for larger pitches.

Remember: this team needs to operate in tandem with some effective PR, at a shop whose brand aligns with its vision and stands for something. A new business department isn't a substitute for great work, passion, and vision.

DON'T BE AFRAID TO SAY NO

A warning: don't be afraid to turn down new business. If you have a bad feeling about it, listen to that feeling. Remember that a great client relationship should be a partnership. There will be times when pursuing a piece of work will be profoundly tempting, but not the right thing to do. It'll be hard to turn it down. It can be excruciatingly difficult to figure out whether you're being too picky, paranoid, or careful. If you find yourself turning down *too* much work, maybe the problem, as they say, is with you. But the selective turning down of clients and projects that set off warning bells is a good thing. You are not compelled to pursue every job that comes your way. Indeed, you shouldn't.

ZEN AND THE ART OF NEW BUSINESS

New business will be a massive part of your attention and energy for the next few years. There will be times when it feels like half of your company is working on new business. And indeed, that may well be the case. It can also be a massively frustrating endeavor.

When the layperson thinks of advertising new business, they inevitably think of The Pitch. Let me stop you right here. In reality, this is a minuscule part of winning work—and a comparatively rare one. There is much, much more to it.

It's true that part of your new business life will be spent pitching. And it's absolutely true that mesmerizing presentation skills and a perfectly delivered emotional plea can make or break a pitch. But there is more—much more—to the equation.

Lao Tzu, in *The Art of War*, says, "The supreme art of war is to subdue the enemy without fighting." The same is true in advertising new business. Or how about John Hegarty: "Great agencies have started winning the pitch before they've pitched."[1]

ORGANIC, LANDED, AND PAID

In reality, there are *three* types of new business within your firm, all going on at once.

There's organic growth—work that you obtained from a client you already have, without a competitive pitch.

There's new work that just landed with you—work that you won from a new client without a competitive pitch.

And there's pitched work—work that you won in a competitive pitch.

Each type of work carries a different cost. Organic Growth is obviously the cheapest, and indeed, it might cost you negative dollars if you won the work in the course of profitable business. Landed work is the next least expensive. Its price can vary greatly—some companies may know for a fact that they prefer to work for you, but still make you go through a pitch to win it. Others will just hand you the work, especially if the client is an individual who's worked with you before when one of you were at another company.

Pitch work, by contrast, is extraordinarily expensive, and it is getting worse. The former chairman of one of the world's largest agency networks recently told me that they would easily spend seven figures on a major global pitch. On a smaller scale, more relevant to our interests, it's easy to spend

$50,000 winning a million-dollar piece of work. Given the razor-thin margins in the increasingly competitive world of digital marketing, and the fact that the won piece of work has to pay for the pitch spends on all the *lost* pieces of work, it is entirely possible that, in the short run, winning a piece of pitched work will cause you to *lose* money.

It's true that winning some work in a competitive pitch can carry lead to repeat, or recurring work, where the future cost of acquiring work is much lower. The won pitch may eventually yield a large amount of *organic* work in other words.

Unfortunately, winning a pitch doesn't necessarily mean more work will follow. Indeed it's becoming increasingly infrequent.

Therefore the application of Lao Tzu's words should be clear: *strive for the majority of the work that comes into your firm to be organically won or landed without a pitch.*

RATIONAL VERSUS EMOTIONAL

If the organic-pitch axis is one way to view new business, let us consider a second axis: that of emotional versus rational.

An emotional sale is one in which the buyer does not listen to—or yield to—logic. They *want* to hire you. They're basing their decision on intangibles, such a piece of your past work or the fact that they just *like* you. Often buyers attempt to couch the emotional in the rational—your past work is good, so they can rationally expect that your work for them will be good, or they've worked with you in the past with good results, so they can expect to do so in the future. It is, of course, possible that you actually will cost less, but it's not a 100 percent rational decision in the same way as "this company has lower rates."

And more to the point, this work is won without extra costs incurred by your shop. For you've already done your past work—your portfolio already exists—and you are already you.

ALLOCATING YOUR NEW BUSINESS EFFORTS

Management experts W. Chan Kim and Renée Mauborgne talk about a "blue ocean strategy" in their book of the same name. The general gist is that great companies position themselves where there is business to be done, where there are few competitors. This is in contrast to a "red ocean," where many other companies—predators—are competing heavily for business—the fish. This is worth thinking about in terms of new business, and some agencies make great use of it. Big Spaceship, for example, got its start by doing a lot of work for the film industry. Many agencies, The Barbarian Group included, eschewed film work for its low revenue and margins. But Big Spaceship found a way to make it work, where few others dared to tread, and built a foundation for its larger business from this. This is worth exploring. Is there an industry segment in which you can grow your business relatively uncontested?

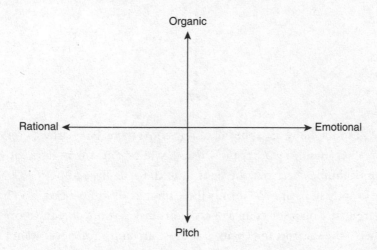

If we were to look at the cost of incurring work in each of these quadrants, it might look something like this:

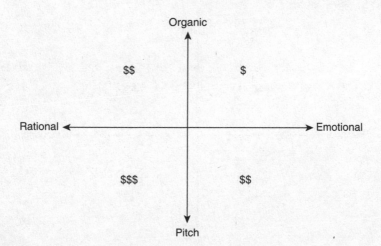

This would indicate to us that the top right quadrant is our sweet spot, the best place to expend new business effort:

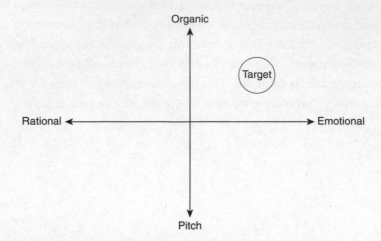

We cannot, however, apply all of our effort there. For starters, every client only has so much work from which to win organic work—and early on, the opportunities here may be light indeed. Secondly, as BBH CEO Nigel Bogle so aptly sums up, "We're only three phone calls from disaster."[2] That is, an overreliance on just a couple of accounts makes your company more susceptible to the vagaries and changes at those accounts. You never want to get to the point where you will go out of business by losing a single account.

We must, then, apply the largest measure of our work to the primary target quadrant, but not neglect the others. A sound, well-rounded business strategy might look something like this:

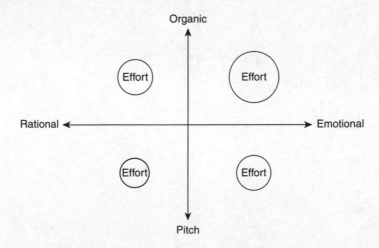

NOT ALL PITCHES ARE THE SAME

Ah! You might protest. *But how am I ever to win a pitch in the rational, pitch quadrant spending so little money when my competitors are spending so much on them?* And right you are to ask. For here you get to the heart of the matter: not all pitches are the same. It is not so much a matter of how much you spend per pitch—though that is relevant—as *which pitches you choose to pursue.*

AKQA head Tom Bedecarre puts this in mathematical terms. "Agencies must balance the costs of time and resources put into a given pitch against the potential benefits of winning the business. If the odds of winning are 1 out of 2, your expected value of the pitch is 50% of the assignment. If the odds are 1 out of 6, then the expected value drops to 16.7% of the assignment."[3] The number of agencies in the pitch is a huge factor in your chances to win. There are other factors as well. The odds matter, and the odds are not universally consistent.

Some pitches work more in your shop's favor on rational measurements than others. Perhaps you have an office in their home city, whereas others do not. Perhaps you have extensive experience in the industry. Perhaps you can charge less. Look at the rational factors in deciding which pitches to pursue that will be won on purely rational terms, in a pitch process. Look for pitches where your firm has a natural advantage.

12

THE EMOTIONAL

Any good advertiser knows that the emotional side of the brain is nirvana when attempting to influence the purchase decision. The emotional side is where we can appeal to factors that cannot be quantitatively measured. The advantage here is that the potential upside result of any argument could far outweigh its expense. So too is this the case in selling your agency. I can say with firsthand knowledge that appealing to the emotional side of the purchase can be tremendously powerful and profitable when trying to sell your company. At The Barbarian Group, we literally had clients who dreamed of working with us and would go out of their way to find projects to do with us. Winning these jobs cost us nothing.

But how does one appeal to the emotional side? Four factors are at play here: the work you do, the PR that your company undertakes, the brand that your company imparts to the world, and the amount of networking that your executives undertake to the advertising industry.

THE WORK THAT YOU DO

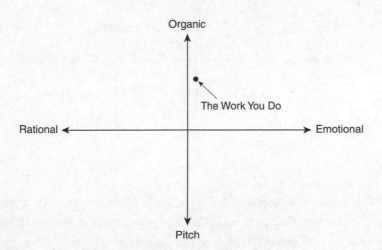

There is an argument that "the work you do" is not an emotional component, but rather a logical one. Indeed, it is in the company's interest—it is in your interest—to further this perception. The work you do costs you nothing—the expense was already incurred in the past, and presumably even then you got paid for it. It *acts* like an emotional appeal. It is appealing to some part of the brain that wants good work too. But it is disguised as rational. Your agency's having done great work in the past allows potential clients to rationalize a decision they want to make anyway. And did I mention it costs you nothing?

Because it is in the company's interest to pretend the emotional is the rational, we encourage this through the quantification of creative quality, despite this actually being secretly repugnant to us. This is most clearly manifested in awards shows. We talk about how many we've won, how many Lions and Clios we've got stacked on our shelves, as if this is a rational indicator of quality of work. Never mind that only the work that is entered wins. Never mind that many smaller shops can't afford the (hundreds of) thousands of dollars of entry fees. Once we have a bunch of awards, we encourage the misperception that these awards are a quantitative, logical indicator of quality. Because it is in our interest to do so.

PUBLIC RELATIONS

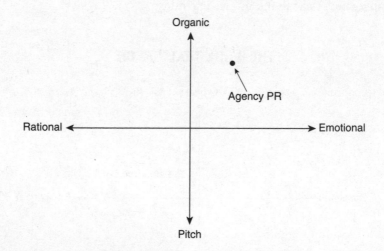

PR cannot be underestimated as a tool. When we were first getting started, my partner Benjamin made the canny decision that our first full-time hire would be a PR executive. Most of our designers and developers were still freelance and contract, and to me it seemed to be an unwise, or at least questionable, decision. But Benjamin held firm. He knew, far before I did, that PR would be a tremendously powerful tool in positioning the shop to get the work we wanted, and to get that work for less money than we would in a competitive pitch.

He proved to be massively correct. Our PR executive, Eva McCloskey, performed miracles, getting feature stories about The Barbarian Group in every major advertising and design publication, even at a very early stage when we only had a couple of great projects to show for it. This continued all through our career, and had a tremendous impact on our bottom line. Eva also worked to get us high-profile placement by speaking at conferences and writing columns for such advertising and technology publications and major blogs. Many firms "outsource" PR, handing over the PR duties of their firm to an outside specialist firm. I am often asked by small shops what firm they should hire for their PR. I tell them every time that it's best to hire in-house when you can. It's also good to hire someone who has experience with the practices of PR. Eva had had extensive experience working for the John Hancock Corporation. She did not have advertising experience or knowledge—that was less important. The experience she had was the ability to target the best and most appropriate publications and journalists, figure out what stories they liked to write about, and the tactical knowledge of how to pitch them ideas, speak their language, attend their gatherings, and generally how to make things easier for them in choosing to write a story about us. There is a story about Donny Deutsch starting Deutsch advertising. He took out a full-page ad in the *New York Times*, announcing his new agency. It is said that the ad was ineffective. He then took his resources and moved them into the more traditional approach of hiring a PR firm—in his case the high-powered Rubenstein Associates—to raise the profile of the firm. Said *Brandweek* in 2006, "And it worked."[1]

PR is fuzzy—results will not always be obvious. It is also, however, relatively cheap, and I have seen excellent results many, many times in our world. Different types of firms will have different luck pitching to publications—a design firm with gorgeous comps and screenshots of work is catnip to a publication looking for something interesting to publish. The story of a brave coding adventure, perhaps less so.

Also be aware of ensuring that your PR is targeted correctly: you want the stories to run in publications your clients read, not you. Work with your PR exec to ensure the strategy is sound.

The age-old question of whether services firms should advertise is becoming moot. The very nature of advertising is changing. It's not just about measured media and purchased ad space anymore. We all know this. It's about social; it's about a digital presence. It's about being where people are when they are thinking about hiring you. It is about your brand. Agency advertising is now agency PR.

YOUR COMPANY BRAND

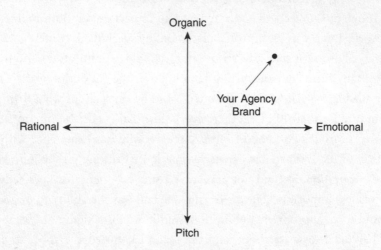

And here we come to a very important point, essentially Advertising 101, applied to services firms: your brand is not just your advertising. It's your work, it's your vision, and it's your soul. BBH's John Hegarty said, "The best definition of a brand I ever heard is this. A brand is the most valuable piece of real estate in the world: a corner of someone's mind."[2] This is what a brand can achieve—and this is what your brand must achieve.

For a company's *brand* is different from whether or not it advertises. It's what it makes potential customers feel. While advertising your shop may not be vital, what is vital is applying excellent brand marketing to your shop.

Your brand's value lies in the perception of others.

Hegarty again: "Behave like a great brand. It's amazing how so many agencies never behave like brands despite the fact they're constantly advising their clients on brand behavior. Great brands have a point of view—they stand for something.[3]"

As Strawberry Frog founder Scott Goodson says, "Agencies—both new and old—don't put a lot of thought into differentiating themselves in the market place. Clients have a hard time knowing the difference between agencies, even the old ones which have been around forever. So if you're going to set sail for the glorious land of opportunity you need to stand out and have a different point of view.[4]"

Your shop needs to be your brand. Your brand needs to tie into your vision. You need to "have a different point of view." You need to "stand for something." And you need to shout it from the rooftops through your PR.

This brand, of course, comes from the vision of your company. If you have not heeded my advice about figuring out, from the beginning, what your shop stands for, all of this is moot. This incredibly powerful—and free—tactic for developing new business will be lost to you.

You may find yourself reverse engineering this—bolting a sales positioning-based brand message onto an firm that has no inner vision or soul. It may work, briefly. But it is unsustainable. Fix the problem at its core, regardless of how much time it is going to take.

NETWORKING AND HUSTLING

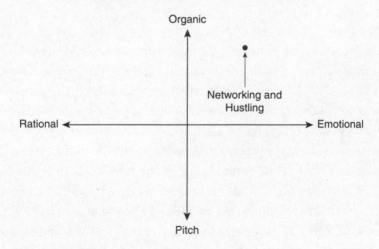

It's vital that your agency possess someone with the preternatural ability to go out practically every night, and most every day, and convince people to give your agency a shot. This is almost a full-time job. The importance of networking cannot be overstated. Looking at our organic pitch axis above, it's one of the key drivers of a solid new business pipeline of organic work. Your hustler needs to be inspiring and fun, instilling a sense of desire in others to work with your agency.

This means the hustler will be going to every advertising mixer, conference, and party under the sun. It means they will accrue a LinkedIn network the size of a small state. It means they will spend their days chatting on the phone. They'll be heading off to agencies and brands around the country doing dog and pony shows. They'll talk about the amazing work your agency has done and can do for you, the client, if you hire them for your next gig.

The hustler should have a title commensurate with his external role. This will seem unfair to others, but will be necessary. When that potential lead calls, jazzed to be working with your firm and your hustler, they need to feel like the hustler will still be involved. Having a title like "new business associate" will make that more difficult.

This all sounds pretty logical. Why, then, do we place networking under the rubric of "emotional?" Because your hustling and networking do not yield a rational response. Sure, some of the things your hustler will tell people will *sound* rational. "We can do a better job." "We could have done that faster." "We could have done that for less." But really what they are doing is appealing to the emotions of the potential client by fostering regret of hiring someone else in the past, and a desire to hire you in the future. Intangibles will also come into play in a big, big way.

Ideally your hustler should be *cool*.

Coolness is a strange thing in the marketing and advertising world. Sure, everyone *looks* kind of cool, but there exists in the advertising world a deep latent vein of self-loathing and thwarted ambitions. Even the people who aspire to do nothing more with their lives than to create great advertising are dimly aware of it. This is not to say that everyone in advertising hates their jobs or their lives—many people are super, super into it—but all are subconsciously aware of advertising's traditional second-fiddle-ness. At an Art Director's Club party one night in 2007 or so, I met a man who seemed cooler than everyone there. It turned out he was. He had recently arrived in New York, and he was English. He was called in to be an Executive Creative Director by the cool new CEO of a storied old agency that was in turnaround. He wasn't an ad man. He had directed music videos, done theater, and was a former partner at one of the coolest traditional graphic design shops out there. His bearlike physique, unkempt beard, and chain-smoking-after-it-was-cool told me that obviously he did not give one fuck about anything. I immediately wanted to find some way to work with him. Our agency, at that moment, was way more cool than the storied old agency in turnaround, but I suddenly found myself plotting various ways to do work with them. *That* is the kind of cool you want your hustler to have.

You do not, and should not, be taking an approach of hiring a gorgeous hustler who relies on their looks. But rather you want someone of either gender who is energetic, charming, witty, funny, and has a marked tolerance for massive consumption of alcohol. You want someone who can hang with people who are living to excess, but not take part, for they are working, but still not make anyone feel like they are being judged.

The hustler isn't a *salesman*. There aren't really commissions for this job. It is, in many ways, pure personality. But it's not a role for just a pretty face. They need to be able to shift gears from talking shit about a pretty sunset on the beach at Cannes at 4 a.m. to talking about the future of advertising, after eight beers, without missing a beat or sounding like a pompous ass.

Everyone in the office may well grow to resent this person's lifestyle, so the hustler should possess some measure of discretion. And above all, results are necessary.

A good hustler is a chameleon. The Barbarians once misjudged someone we were networking with, thinking he was a person of a certain hedonistic bent, by dint of his industry, dress, and mannerisms. Turns out we were totally wrong, and he was in fact a tee-totaling, nonswearing, devout Christian. A good hustler does not make anyone feel left out or uncomfortable.

If this works, you will be developing a steady pipeline of organic work that, most importantly, you *often will not have to pitch for.* Sure, there will be times your hustler's charm and networking yield an invite to a pitch you otherwise would not have gotten. In that case, refer to our axioms above about pitch spends and which to pursue. Sometimes, even here, the hustler can play a part. "No, man, you know, we just don't really do that sort of thing, it's not really our gig. If you want to hire someone like [crappy company X] or [crappy company Y], you should totally do that. But we're going for something else." The true gems are the work that just lands in your lap, without any competition. And the hustler is your number one weapon in that arms race.

13

THE PITCH

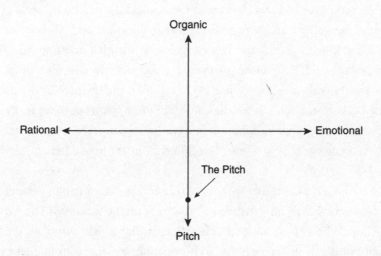

No part of advertising has been as romanticized as the pitch. From Don Draper's meandering, bordering-on-incomprehensible emotional journeys during pitches on *Mad Men*, to the horrible reality show *The Pitch*, to every book ever written on advertising, the pitch seems to exude an aura of romance, gladiatorial battle, and excitement. Witness John Hegarty's florid prose when talking about the pitch: "We love pitching—it brings out our competitive spirit like nothing else. We snort the energy of battle....When a 'big pitch' is on you can feel the adrenaline running through an agency. There are endless ideas, positionings, strategies and flow charts pasted on to walls, late-night meetings and discarded boxes of half-eaten pizza scattered around the building. There are cancelled social lives and late-night taxis home and then a quick shower and a clean shirt before a rapid return to the frontline. We thrive on this kind of energy. Failure is not an option."[1]

What is it about the pitch? I suspect it's the subconscious feeling of being drawn to life's moments of truth. Yes, it's only advertising, and, yes, it's only a job, but the pitch is one of those moments where it's all coming together, it's all happening *right now*. You have to perform perfectly, everything must gel, and even then, there's a good chance that it will all go to hell.

Now, in many ways, this is irrational. We spend much of our life plotting and planning to avoid exactly these moments. Most people do not consider it, for example, a viable financial planning path to wait for the lottery. They know that the odds are an unkind mistress, and the best way to increase our odds of success is through methodical hard work and patience.

There have been times that I've been in a pitch, and I've made some great, sweeping, emotional claim, and I've looked down into the eyes of my potential new client and seen nothing but inspiration and admiration and knew I had killed it, and *knew* we were going to win that account. And yeah, it felt pretty good. I can close my eyes and picture one now. But you know what? I will say this: that pitch had no bearing on the finances or reputation of The Barbarian Group. And you know what else? None of them really did, not even the ones that had that invigorating moment. These moments—as much of a rush as they are—are decoupled from the actual benefit for your firm.

In looking back, I can only think of one competitive pitch in which I had even remotely that feeling, that had any bearing on the success of The Barbarian Group. When I look back on the work that shaped our company, the vast majority of it was either won due to networking efforts (with 80 percent of that credit going to my partner, Benjamin), and/or boring, staid, stolid proposals that were utterly devoid of drama.

The pitch is overrated. The emotional moments are nice, they're interesting, and they make you feel something. But by and large, statistically, they don't mean diddly.

Fast Company dedicated an entire article to the flaws of the pitch process:

"Long lead times, long pitch lists, layers of consensus needed to select a partner, layers of meaningless paperwork for RFPs, requests for spec work, lack of access to decision makers, cost pressure from procurement for the agency, search consultants who may or may not be motivated or equipped to arrange the best marriage, giving away IP...when it's bad, it's pretty terrible. Even the wording of recent guidelines from the normally restrained 4A's (the American Association of Advertising Agencies) and ANA (the Association of National Advertisers), referring to 'excessive, unfocused RFP demands and cattle calls,' reveals the extent of the problem when it comes to the process of securing new business."[2]

Recall our overall new business approach: most of your effort should be placed into organic new business, won on emotional terms.

ABOVE ALL, BE CALCULATING

There will be times a pitch feels within your grasp—because of the nature of the work, because of the lackluster pitch participants, because of some special inside connection.

This leads us to the two more rules regarding pitches.

First: *pursue the pitches you have a better than average chance of winning.* Have an advantage. Have a reason why you believe you can best the competition.

Second: *budget your pitch rigorously and don't exceed that budget.* Do the math in a holistic way: we can afford to spend this much on pitches this year, we need to win this much work, our pitch sizes are X amount, and we get about Y pitches a year. This means we should pursue Z number of pitches and apply this much money to the budget of each one of them. You can be more complex and have two or three different pitch sizes with separate economics—we had a six-figure pitch approach and a seven-figure pitch approach, for example. But the principle is the same. Establish budgets and stick to them.

In the early years The Barbarian Group radically applied the tenets of the new business philosophy I'm espousing at a low-dollar, high-volume level. We did literally dozens of pitches a month. When we decided to pitch, our calculations told us that we shouldn't spend more than, say, $5k on the pitch, and therefore we wouldn't spend a dollar more, even if we knew that our pitch competitors would be spending thousands—or hundreds of thousands—more.

It worked.

Some would say we half-assed them all. Did we apply ourselves to the utmost on these pitches? Not even close. At that time, we were operating from a position of incredible demand for our company's services. In hindsight, we were essentially going into every pitch as the front-runner. We could *afford* to half-ass them, and our win ratio would still be solid. Would we have been better served focusing on fewer pitches and putting more effort into them? I believe our pitch success rate on *attempted* pitches would have gone up. But I don't believe our total number of pitches won would have gone up. In fact, owing to our specific situation of having many easy-to-win opportunities thrown at us, I think it would have gone down. And we needed to win as many as possible.

This, of course, did not last forever, and it may not happen to you. But the basic concept remains the same: only pitch the ones you think you have a chance of winning, and only put the amount of resources into pitching that you can afford. Be disciplined.

Over time, the situation and our calculations changed. We focused on fewer pitches, the ones we knew were most winnable, most profitable, and the best for our shop. And we put more effort into fewer pitches. This is because we got more large pitches. Whereas before, we needed to win, say, two six-figure pitches every month, things eventually evolved to where we needed to win one seven-figure pitch every three to four months. And, unlike previously, we were now getting invited to enough seven-figure pitches that this seemed possible. We were also competing against a new cohort of competitors, and our chances of winning each individual pitch had changed. Yet we were still rigorous in our discipline in not letting costs get out of hand.

The pitches you pursue are the ones that you think you can win.

THE MECHANICS OF PITCHING

Winning a pitch is more than a good speech. You must win a pitch on emotional *and* rational terms. You must inspire, but you must also have your shit together. You need to explore the soaring heights of rarified emotional planes, and you must make sure that your QA engineer's price is within a specified industry-standard range and that your C# technical implementation case study is up to snuff. It's simultaneously operatic and mind-numblingly tedious.

THE REQUEST FOR PROPOSAL (RFP)

Most pitches start out with an RFP, or an inquiry. Someone will call you, or your hustler has done his job, and you'll get an email document laying out the pitch. It'll define the parameters of the engagement, how the whole pitch is going to go down, and the general details. Some RFPs are masterworks of thoroughness and intelligence. Others are a painful warning sign of how bad things might be with this client. Treat the RFP as a Ouija board that offers you insight into what working with this client will be like. Some RFPs are filled with manifest contradictions that indicate the whole company may not be aligned in its thinking. Others very pointedly omit salient details, and that may say something about the company as well. Some of them are detailed documents outlining every step, verbose and intricate, leaving nothing to chance. Some are written almost as manifestos.

The most important parts you care about are the *brief* and the *requirements*. Essentially, you are looking for the goal of the pitch, the marketing aim. Next, you are looking for the stated requirements of the pitch process. Some pitches will be about money. Some will be about past experience. Some may require you to fill out lengthy past case studies, resource allocations, individual hourly rates, and list past relevant technical expertise. Some will explicitly say the pitch is going to be on a certain day in a certain place. Some will kindly tell you all the relevant parties who will decide the winner of the pitch—this is always nice. Some will explicitly tell you what the decision criteria are. This is always nice too. Some won't tell you anything, and are just asking for an idea.

Get everything you can out of the RFP and assign the team to various parts of it as resources permit. Some should pursue the brief. Some may need to work on pricing. Some will work on the requirements materials. If you're small, this whole team may be you.

THE FIRST TALK

With most every pitch, there is an initial conversation between the potential client and your team. If there isn't, you should certainly ask for it on all but the most inconsequential pitches. It might be a one-on-one meeting with the potential client and your company. This is best, and it's best done in person. Sometimes it's a group conference call with all participating firms. These can be annoying as hell, but also fruitful for intelligence. In some formalized, larger pitches, there are formal "chemistry meetings." These often feel like invasive medical checkups.

If it's a one-on-one meeting, push for in-person. Your goal here is to get the client comfortable and talking. The successful first talk is informal, chatty, and conversational. Pitches can be won or lost on the first meeting. Both are rare, and the odds are you'll be able to see it coming if it goes to that extreme, so stay aware. Ask lots of questions. Keep the client talking about its problems. Ask, ask, ask. "While business relationships are no doubt a different beast than personal relationships—more formal, thankfully less intimate—the human behavior behind forming these bonds is the same. As in love, chemistry—or fit—is the most important element to a fruitful partnership, and the rigid, often arms-length way in which new partners are engaged does little to help foster the necessary connection to make professional fireworks," says *Fast Company*.[3]

Don't offer too many potential solutions on the spot, but do ask about certain areas of exploration and whether that "sounds potentially helpful." Every idea you offer is a potential avenue of exploration that can be cut off with a premature no, and an area of potential embarrassment showing you don't understand their business yet. Says Hegarty, "Ask your client what the business problem is that you are trying to solve with your advertising? That's probably the most important thing you should have in mind when you talk to a client and, if you genuinely believe in it, you'll have them eating out of your hand…"[4]

But above all: Never act like you really need the work. Sounds like an interesting problem. It seems like a fun problem. Reminds me a bit of what we did with client X.

If it is a group call, I find the best thing to do is to stay quiet. Don't tip your hand to your competitors. They will ask most of the questions. Most companies on a group RFP call think they have a chance at differentiating themselves from other shops by asking lots of questions. This is a mistake in a group setting, and comes off as posturing. Better to lie back and just take notes. There is also the risk of asking questions unsuited to the client on the phone. I've heard many firms annoy and confuse in pitch calls by drilling down into super detailed technical questions when no IT person is on the call, for example. If, for some reason, no one asks about a vital piece of information you need to know, or you want to screw with your competition to throw them off, you can ask a single genius question. Maybe re-elevate the conversation after it gets too technical or bogged down in budgets. Maybe ask something sort of left field, like, "if you had to equate yourself to Donald Duck or Howard the Duck, which would it be?" Don't announce who you are. Leave everyone wondering. Throw them off. Plus, if, at a later date, your seemingly left-field question clicks in your pitch with a larger genius strategy, the client will experience a profound ah ha moment. This is good. Unless you screw it up. In which case, act forever more as if you had never asked the question. The client will never know for sure.

There are things that the client may not want to tell the pitching shops, but it is totally acceptable to ask. Specifically, it's acceptable to ask the budget, the decision criteria, the stakeholders at the company, the timeline, and who else is pitching. Clients will often be dodgy on all of these (often to their own detriment), but it's absolutely acceptable to ask about them. If they say they can't tell you, your immediate follow-up should be "what *can* you tell me?" Talking about money can be tough, but you should absolutely try. "For whatever reason, talking about money is a delicate conversation that most people dance around. But in the pitch process, it's crucial to talk about...right away," says *Fast Company*.[5]

I cannot stress this enough. The most heartbreaking pitch is not the one you lost. It's the one you won only to realize it has no budget.

There may occasionally be follow-up materials from the first meeting or pitch call. Incorporate these into your pitch prep as you get them, but don't wait for them.

PITCH PREP

Now it's time to get to work. This should be obvious by now, but let's be clear: 90 percent of the pitch work is done before entering the room. If you're lucky, and run a tight new business operation, up to 50 percent of the pitch may be done before you ever receive the RFP. You may have a great reputation and brand through quality vision and PR. You may have a lovely body of relevant work to show, and you may have already developed the relevant case studies. You might have most of the detailed questions from the RFP already answered, because you have a robust new business department that follows the Boy Scouts' mantra of "be prepared." We'll talk about the details of this, but it's important to state here: the shop that has to pitch from scratch is at a serious disadvantage.

Either way, though, you need to get started on *this* pitch. First, you need a team.

THE PITCH TEAM

The size of the pitch, of course, dictates, to some extant the size of the team, as does the size of your company. Make sure this stays true: smaller pitches get smaller teams. There is power in a single individual's delivering something coherent and ambitious. When you're small, this may be your only option. In other cases, the team will grow. In either case, *keep the pitch team as small as possible*. Never stop keeping an eye on this. People are by far the biggest expense on a pitch, and it is important to keep the team lean.

I've never been a big fan of multiple creative teams. It's occasionally required, but I find there needs to be a good, explicit reason for it, and the default should be to one team, even if you need multiple ideas. Pure cost is a good enough motivator. One team is expensive enough. Two, more so.

INTELLIGENCE AND RESEARCH

Companies such as yours tend to spend a lot of time on *research*, or the delving into the stated problem at hand: learning as much about the client's brief, its customers, the challenges, opportunities, and so on. Many conduct man-in-the-street interviews, focus groups, and more. On some pitches, this is necessary. On others—say, for a website redesign—it may be less so. I can say definitively that having a few insight-based stats in your pitch can be powerful. I have won pitches owing to the fact I had gone out and gotten one interesting new statistic.

But you know this. You are a competent practitioner of your craft, and whatever craft you are toiling in, it already has a perspective to research, and you have your methods and opinions about it. Apply them—diligently and wholeheartedly, within the confines of your stated budget.

On of the flip side of this coin—intelligence—I find that many shops don't do enough digging. Look into the past experience of the pitch stakeholders on the client side. Learn the business press's point of view about the company. Is its stock depressed? Is the CEO on the ropes? Is it the darling of financial analysts? Have there been recent management changes? What's its track record of putting new products in the market? Are there significant expectations around this product? How long has your client been there? Does it have the political clout to effect disruptive change? All of these answers will have an impact on the kind of work you can sell and that the client can buy. A company at the height of a stock run with a well-respected CEO can take more risks than a company that has a ton of shorts on it in the market. These things matter, and they are weighing heavily on your potential client's mind. To address them—even tacitly, if discretion dictates—is to show the client you understand them.

This is also true for your pitch competitors. Many pitches won't tell you who you're pitching against. Often, it's not hard to find this out regardless. Invariably someone screws up an email thread. Scroll down on every email and look for addresses. Ask around the town. You can usually find out. If you've not heard of the shop before, do your research on them. Check their site. Check LinkedIn for new connections between other shops and the pitching company. Check Glassdoor. Learn, learn, learn. Over time, you'll know more and more about competing firms. Many clients will, after the fact, quietly give you the pitch decks of the competitors you beat. This is morally ambiguous, so don't ask for them. But if the client gives them to you, it's silly to not make use of them. Keep them all. Store anything you learn about potential competitors in a centralized location, and consult it on relevant pitches. Know thy enemy.

THE IDEA

The idea, of course, is terribly important. It is, however, probably not *quite* as important as everyone seems to think. I've won pitches on lousy ideas and lost on great ones. And there are certainly a number of times I've just thrown up my hands and thought, "Who the hell knows?" It's an eternal mystery why some pitches are won and some are lost, even when the client gives you a reason. You'll find yourself thinking about this constantly.

However, all that thinking is academic. Yes, you can win on a mediocre idea, but your goal, always, should be to find the best idea, *the best idea*, and pitch that.

Once you have the best idea, *just pitch the best idea*. I'm not a fan of pitching multiple ideas any more than I am of multiple teams. There are times in the course of a client engagement where pitching three or four ideas for a campaign is right and proper. The pitch is rarely one of them. The temptation to hedge your bets with multiple ideas can be immense, and some shops have good luck with pitching a solid idea, and then having another idea in their back pocket that is secretly bolder and more brave. These are the tactics of experts. We have to learn to fly in formation before we can do complex maneuvers. Over time, you'll develop your own tactics.

BEYOND THE BRIEF

Some people believe that straying from the brief in a pitch is risky, and that a concrete- sequentially minded client will get irked that you haven't "listened" to them. This is indeed a risk. Yet at the same time, briefs can be somewhat constricting, and clients are paying you for your insights, and if you believe the brief is misguided, it's your duty to say so.

Nothing is more irksome than someone who is clearly uninformed challenging the brief. If you're going to challenge the brief, know your shit. Additionally, if you're going to deviate from the brief, acknowledge this and explain why. Have a concrete, strategic reason for doing so.

But above all, your idea must elevate the brief to a higher plane, not change it. Says *Art of the Pitch* author Peter Coughter, "if you do what the client, or new business prospect expects you to do—they will be disappointed. You need to go above and beyond and bring them something that surprises and delights them."[6] The key words there are "above and beyond." You are not throwing out the brief. You're exceeding it. You're taking it further.

Hegarty concurs. Shorten the odds, he says: "Change the rules. One of the surest ways of shortening the odds is to uncover some insight into the brand or the market that changes the rules."[7] A key characteristic of an idea that works well in a pitch is that it must be remembered in a sea of three to ten (or more!) other ideas from other shops. It has to stand out.

PRESENTING

A pitch is a team. Many people will probably talk. It's a symphony. An orchestration. There will be different topics, different areas, and the whole pitch team may well take part. And each of these people is equally important. There is no "lead pitcher" who has to do all the hard stuff, while others can get up and mumble their way through some surveys and graphs. Each person is the pitcher. Each person must inspire, and each person must deliver.

No better work has been written on this topic than Coughter's *The Art of the Pitch*, and I urge you to read it. Coughter sums up the basics of a great pitch in 11 easy chapters. If you're going to pitch, you need to read this. But here are the basics.

First, learn to speak in public. Practice, practice, practice. Learn to take pauses. Learn to tell stories. Learn to connect with your audience. Learn to keep them engaged. Learn to ask questions. So many people don't learn the basics of public speaking, and their only rehearsals are the actual pitches. Don't make this mistake. Join a band. Join toastmasters. Hit the lecture circuit. *Anything.* Get experience in public speaking. Learn to pause without saying *ummmm.* Learn to laugh.

Elevate the pitch above advertising. "Don't make your pitch just about the advertising. The greatest failing in any pitch is to keep it in the world of advertising. Fall into that trap and, ironically, you lengthen your odds rather than shortening them."[8]

Sell them on the idea before the execution. "The secret to selling great work is to sell the idea of the work before you sell the work."[9]

Be confident and authentic. Be yourself. "They're deciding all that and more, based upon your attitude. If we sound and seem confident, they will tend to believe us and share that sense of confidence. If we are enthusiastic, they will tend to be excited about what we're saying. In short, the audience will tend to mirror the emotion that we establish via our attitude."[10]

Don't make it about you. Above all, connect.

THE SLIDES

Pitch slides are different from other slide decks in the business world. These days, I spend a lot of time in the venture capital world, and slide decks have a completely different paradigm. This is also true of MBA students and bankers, both of whom have certain practices, habits, and conventions of their slide decks that do not jibe with the needs of a pitch deck. Decks in these industries are *wordy*. And ugly.

A pitch deck is something different. These are *presentation* slides. These are visual aids. They are not the presentation itself. *You* are the presentation.

We cannot let PowerPoint (or its stylish cousin, Keynote) rule us. We must be the master. Limit your slides to comps of the work you are proposing, gorgeous photography, unannotated, simple charts that reinforce what you are saying, and maybe one or two large, large words that drive home the main point you are making. Think of the slideshows that run automatically on your new Mac when the screensaver kicks in: bold, beautiful imagery.

There is a distinction between the slides you show during your pitch, and the materials you leave behind. You need to make both. They are separate documents.

You are working the night before. And you find you need to make changes. It's a pain in the ass, no doubt about it.

But it is worth striving for. It will make a difference.

The pitch deck is not the leave behind.

THE ROOM

You are better off on a pitch if the client can come to you, and you can prep the presentation space. When I worked at Arnold, we had a man, Tony the Room, we called him, whose job was nothing other than to prepare the room for the pitch. I find that this is a circumstance of overall budget. A good figure is spending 1 percent of the pitch budget on the room preparation. In the early years at TBG, owing to low budgets, we didn't worry about this at all. We much later got to the point where we occasionally (when circumstances and budgets warranted it) rented gorgeous spaces to do the pitch. Former ad exec and novelist James Othmer, in his survey of modern advertising, *AdLand: Searching for Meaning on a Branded Planet*, recalls rolling out the red carpet for a major pitch and renting an off-off-Broadway theater for a pitch. "Over the years the theater had been the home to world-premiere performances of works written by the likes of Arthur Miller, Sam Shepard, Edward Albee, and August Wilson."[11] This type of theater (literally, in this case) can work, but is not necessarily required in the early days. At all levels, do pay attention to messes, and think through things like logistics, audio, visual, proximity to restrooms, snacks, and whatnot.

These days, it's often the case that you have to pitch at the client's headquarters in some dingy room. Sometimes the client will rent a space in town, and expect you to come to it. If this is the case, try and get a little prep time. Spruce the place up. Storyboards—decorating the room with comps and inspirational imagery—were a popular prop early in my career. Home field advantage is powerful. If the competing firms are spread out throughout the country, a pitch that's in your town will give you an advantage. There is power in sleeping in your own bed. And there's power pitching in your own office. AKQA's Tom Bedecarre stresses the importance of the client's coming to you. "If you are hiring an agency, then you are hiring the people, culture and work environment of that agency. It makes no sense to have pitch meetings at client offices or neutral locations because it shortchanges the opportunity to learn more about the people, culture and work environment of the agency you are about to hire."[12]

PITCHING ORDER

People often obsess about when in the pitch order they are pitching. Is first best? Is last? Conventional wisdom has said that pitching last is best, as your ideas are fresh in the client's mind. I've found no evidence of this, and indeed, I can't help but wonder if an idea is fresh in the client's mind because it was last, that they wouldn't subconsciously discount it because it was the last idea they heard. This belief was given quantitative credence at famed ad agency BBH, when partner John Bartle decided to do a statistical analysis of all its historic pitches and where in the order the company pitched. The result?

"There was absolutely no relationship between where we pitched and success and failure."[13]

I like to go early. One reason: there is a subset of pitches, profoundly hellish, where every party has to show up in order. You're always running into the other pitching shops. If your intelligence efforts failed, you may not even know whom you're pitching against, and if you respect or fear them, learning this can be profoundly dispiriting. Better to see them on the way out of the room than on the way in. I operate better in the afternoon, but I find more clients are alert in the morning, and are getting bored later in the day. Better to get them bright eyed and bushy tailed.

THE PITCH DOCUMENTS

It is expected that you will leave behind a set of documents related to the pitch that drills down into more detail. These will offer up the things you don't necessarily talk about in the meeting, like technical specifics, cost, timeline, and so forth. You might touch upon these topics in your pitch—and you should, if any of them need to be specifically called out—but for the most part, the material will just be left behind.

This is a key point: the "leave behind" documents on a large pitch should not *just* be the presentation you gave. They should be more detailed. They can include the presentation, though a great presentation might make no sense without the presenter. So a reworked version for the leave-behind documents is often in order.

Remember, too, that not every stakeholder might be at the pitch. You need a set of pitch documents that not only dots the I's and crosses the T's on the details but also does something to recapture the magic and emotion of the pitch. I often find it is useful to include two documents: one that is a *only slightly* more wordy, portable version of the pitch presentation, and one that is akin to a proposal, offering all the details of the engagement.

It's important to discover whether these documents are *expected*. It may say so explicitly in the RFP, but it may not. It's often unspoken that these documents are expected, and going in with only a pitch presentation deck may put the client off, who may view your company's thinking as slight. If you're thinking of skimping, best to call the client directly and ask about proposal formats.

The most popular way of reducing the workload is using the speaker notes section for the bulk of the text of the slightly wordier leave behind, so it does not show up during the pitch. You can then add a couple pages of details if need be. Get to know the notes functionality in PowerPoint and Keynote. Make it your friend.

THE VETO VOTES

Be aware of the veto votes. Most larger pitches are done by committee. There is often someone from marketing, someone from IT, someone from the web team maybe, and probably someone from procurement. Sometimes there are multiple brand managers working on different brands. Perhaps a lesser brand generally feels snubbed because all the attention goes to the larger brands, and will cast a vote against an shop that doesn't pay attention to their little trooper of a brand. Be aware of these dynamics. Have a little something for everyone. Address all of the votes. Too many shops seek to identify the power player, the lead marketer, and direct the entire pitch to her, ignoring, at their peril, the surly IT exec in the back who may have to approve any new vendor. Getting these people on your side can be a powerful weapon in a close pitch, and antagonizing them can be the death knell.

REHEARSE

I saved this for last because I wanted you to remember it. Rehearse. Rehearse. Rehearse. Individually. As a team. No one is immune. No one is exempt. Not you, not the boss, not the wunderkind. *No one listens to this advice.* It is maddening. It is, of course, a pain in the ass. People are busy. The script is always changing. But do it anyway. Do it with a rough script. Do it when someone's missing. Just keep doing it.

Because it works. If you do it, you will double your chances of winning. If you don't, you will double your chances of losing. It took me years to accept this. I thought we were good enough without rehearsing. I was wrong. I shudder to think where our awesome company would be now had we learned this years early. I bitterly regret being so stubborn on this point, and urge you to not make the same mistake.

SOLICIT FEEDBACK FROM THE LOSSES

It's a sad truth that you will not win every pitch. When you lose, ask for the harsh, honest feedback about what was the deciding factor. Sometimes it's just the breaks. Sometimes you'll hear the idea that won and you'll think "oh, yeah. That is awesome. That deserves to win." But other times it's something you could fix. It might be your pricing. Your case studies. A call to a past client. An errant comment at the pitch or at a conference or on a panel. Find out what went wrong, so you can fix it.

ON PITCH WORK

One of the most frustrating aspects of a service business is the requirement that you often give away your work for free in a pitch to win the work. It can be very easy to latch onto this, and focus on how much it's costing you. This can be significant. Without careful consideration, you could put your company out of business with free work. As we've said, the best work is the work that is free to land. But this is not always possible. Some work takes work to win. Finding the right balance between never giving any work away for free—often at the cost of not winning jobs you really, really want to win—and giving so much work away that you can't maintain a healthy profit margin is devilishly complex.

There is, without a doubt, a business environment these days that is monstrously balanced against the vendor in favor of the client. Marketing and agency-related services are in a massively competitive period right now. Many, many jobs that you seek out will have several other firms competing for them. You may be the best qualified company, you may be the cheapest agency and the most talented, and it can be incredibly maddening when a competitor wins a job because it did the whole job for free, or did half the job for free as part of its pitch. It can feel profoundly immoral to have someone expect you to provide for free the very service that puts food on your family's table. And yet, at times, not only is it necessary but it can also be ideal for you.

There are, from time to time, industry efforts to tilt the balance toward the vendors in this power dynamic. People will try and organize guilds, or trade organizations, or institute some industry best practices. Most of these are well intentioned but ineffective. (As another aside, beware of pricing guilds. You will, from time to time, get pitched on the idea from some other colleague that you should all band together against the evil clients, agree upon some pricing, and stick to it. It is very tempting, but it is the dark side. More than that, these sorts of engagements run the risk of running afoul of antitrust regulations if they become successful enough. And if they are not successful, then what's the point?)

You can engage in these industry endeavors if you want, but think of them as a hobby. It's got nothing to do with the day-to-day dilemma of the miserable state of free work and pitch work today. It's probably more productive to keep your head down and work.

CHOOSING WHEN FREE WORK IS WORTH IT

Free work can be broken down into three categories: risk mitigation and expectation alignment, gaining competitive advantage, and economic predation. While all three situations call for some modicum of free work, each is in actuality quite a different situation. Let's look at each one of them.

RISK MITIGATION AND EXPECTATION ALIGNMENT

There's a scale of complexity that needs to be considered here. The less complex the job, the less pitch work should be done. For a simple banner or a single page of design, I don't see any reason why there should be pitch work at all. The potential client can look at your portfolio and judge for itself whether you are competent to handle the job. A full website, by contrast, is somewhat more complex. It's not completely crazy to see a couple thoughts toward your initial thinking, be it an initial comp for a single page or an "inspiration board" à la Pinterest, of the inspirations for the design. Finally, a major, full 360-degree campaign consisting of a website, an iOS app, perhaps a game, some display advertising, and a year of social media management is a major commitment, probably costing well into the seven figures. It helps not only the client but also you, to show somewhat more of your initial thinking. The "pitch work" in these instances is all but avoidable, and should be thought of as a road map, or plan, for the whole project.

How much needs to be shown to give the client a good idea of the project, without doing extra work, without its entering into the realm of free work? Let's think about client risk for a moment. There is a low risk in a client's spending $1,000 on a banner ad from a designer and not having it work out. There is significantly more risk in a client's hiring a dev firm for $100,000 to build a website, without having an idea of what the vendor is considering building. Finally, there is exponentially more work when it comes to a $5 million integrated campaign.

Some modicum of "work" must be done to ensure the client and the vendor are on the same page, to align expectation and risk. This work is your friend. It is insurance against taking on a project that will go horribly awry, make everyone unhappy, and cost you lots of money.

A good rule is 10 percent of the job. Expending 10 percent of the total effort of the job on initial work that aids in winning the job is not out of the realm of sanity.

GAINING COMPETITIVE ADVANTAGE

You really want to win. You have a great idea that is so revolutionary that it needs to be more fleshed out to explain it to the client. You're proposing a path different than what the client asked for, for the good of the client's needs. You have free time. Your bid is going to be more expensive than your other clients'. Your team is incredibly stoked to get this project and really, really wants it. And you need the money. There are a whole host of reasons why you may, from time to time, go all out on a pitch. *These are totally valid.* The key here is to use them selectively and know why you are doing it.

On any given pitch, your competitors will feel a variety of emotions on receiving the RFP. They may also desperately want it, yes, but there may be times when they are slammed with work, or a key resource is on vacation, or they are just not feeling that jazzed about this individual project. If you can go the extra mile in your pitch, while your competitor doesn't, it can radically improve your chances of winning this job.

It may be tempting to think that if this is the case, then perhaps you should do this every time. However, I have never, ever seen a company join the hallowed ranks of "the best" who can sustain this approach. We are all facing the same economics. Within certain boundaries, we all pay the same salaries and rent. It's true that significant performance benefits can be exacted through the same economic parameters, through the disciplined creation of a passionate culture. And it's true that this can provide your shop with an extraordinary competitive advantage. The challenge here is that *the very act of going the extra mile on every pitch can profoundly negatively impact the culture of an organization.* Throughout my career, I have been in innumerable pitches where some competitor routinely ruins it for everyone by going the extra mile on the pitch. There have been times when I've seen that the competitor that is doing so has been the same competitor, routinely, for several pitches in a row. Not one of those competitors is a company of note today. The shops we pitched against that would beat us—AKQA, RGA, Big Spaceship, and so on—were the ones that selectively applied the great pitch when they thought it would yield a significant advantage. The rest of their pitches contained a minimum of free work.

There's a rough mathematical equation here: *apply extra effort on a pitch when the chance of reaping potential benefits of the extra work is exponentially greater than the energy expended.*

A final note of caution. Let's talk about the "trophy pitch." These are the pitches that everyone really wants to win—the prestige client and the account that everyone is talking about. The cream of the crop of the most desired clients in America at any given time. Nike, Apple, Virgin. Whatever it may be. These are the pitches where your competitors are all going to *also* be going the extra mile. The rule above still applies here. Because all of your clients are going the extra mile, the cost of your going the extra mile is unlikely to reap exponentially rewarding benefits. It is my strong advice to stick to the rule in these situations, and do your normal amount of preparation for these pitches. This can, occasionally, have the paradoxically inverse effect, showing the client that you don't really need the work, and that you are willing to stick to your guns. Play it cool, be smart, ask questions, and be laid back. You won't win all of them, but over the long term this is the only way to make these pitches work to your advantage. You'll win your share, and do so at far, far less cost.

ECONOMIC PREDATION

There is, however, a more pernicious form of free work that will be foisted upon you: that borne of economic predation.

Explicitly speaking, beware the client who dangles the prospect of more work in the future for free work now. There's a difference between your choosing to go the extra mile and do extra work for a pitch, and a client's asking for it. The client who is asking for free work is a major red flag. What I'm talking about here are the people who want free work outright.

Beware the silver-tongued devils who name-drop, with a strange compulsion to repeatedly list their past resume, unbidden. The promises of future fortunes will be vast. They will dangle the possibility, nay, the certainty, of more work, great work, lots of work, *the best* work.

It. Will. Not. Happen.

I have noticed a sort of "promise escalation" with these people. Back in the early '90s, such a person would simply promise more work, ask for a "test" job. Now, however, they promise the moon. They promise parties with celebrities or meetings with powerful people. They promise the best clients. Whereas they used to just promise that the next job would be paid, now they are promising you lunch with Justin Timberlake, and the Nike account.

They've also learned that they need to introduce a smidge of fuzziness, on the "no payment up front" game. They may pay a nominal amount for the first job.

They may even get you into that Justin Timberlake concert. The truly talented hustler may even get you in to meet him for a few seconds. That's usually the moment of truth. You can tell in two seconds whether Justin cares or not. Don't be blinded by the light. These people shake the hands of anyone whom their handlers put in front of them. And the handlers use this as a currency not just for the celebrity's aims but also for their own. This is understood, and is the reason why the handlers make no money. Access is their salary. If the celebrity doesn't exhibit the least bit of understanding of the supposed project or reason why you're there, this is sign of the huckster's long con.

I will invoke another 10 percent rule here. Take the total amount of time the potential project—the first supposedly high-paying project that Grima Wormtongue is dangling in front of you—and divide by 10. In the time frame of the first 10 percent of the project, things should be worked out and normalized, and free work/cheap work should be off the table for good.

This extends to whole industries. And here I will be explicit: the fashion industry. The movie industry. The music industry. Now, I can find it in my heart to forgive the music industry these days, owing to its gutting by the Internet, but the same cannot be said for the film and the fashion industries.

I find that people in these industries are far, far more likely to ask for free work "to get a budget" or "to try and sway people this matters." To them I usually say some variant of "Look. By this point I think we have figured out that marketing [or whatever segment within which you toil] works. If you need to do some marketing to prove marketing works, you are working with idiots. Consider a new job." But they often don't. Because they want to work in fashion. Or music. They are slaves to the cool. Be one at your own peril.

Your employees will be excited to work on these projects. It will be sad to shut down their excitement. But often, you will need to.

The dilemma here is that there will be some work that you will want to take that pays little or nothing, but that is *awesome*. That's your prerogative. If you want to do Shakira's website for no money and the chance to meet her, go for it. I did this, and it was awesome. She is very nice. But don't kid yourself: you're taking the job because you want to. And remember: most importantly: *it's okay to take low-paying work if you want to do it, but if clients are asking you to do it for free with the promise of more work, run.* The good clients will be frank about it: "What can I say? Bob Dylan only wants to spend $50,000 on his website. Take it or leave it. If it's too little for you, I understand. No hard feelings. But it'll be fun. It's Bob Dylan." These exact words were said to me once. *I appreciated the honesty.*

SOME PRACTICAL ADVICE ON CERTAIN TYPES OF PITCHES

Let's take a moment to offer some practical advice on certain aspects of pitches.

REUSING THE PITCH WORK IN THE REAL JOB

When a lot of work is done on a pitch, especially comps for a website, there is a tendency to want to reuse this work on the actual project after the pitch is won. This may also apply to provisional brand positioning, logos, and taglines. It may seem practical and efficient. The client may also have become attached to, and really begun to love, a piece of work that you showed. I strongly caution against this in all regards.

Practically speaking, pitch comps are not production comps. We often overlook many details necessary on real websites that aren't necessary to see on the pitch comps: copyright notices, social media buttons, privacy policies, email list registrations, and the like. We also may not have bothered to procure the licensing for the imagery. When the time comes to produce, you'll need those licenses, or you'll have to find new assets. Take the pitch comps, give them to a UX designer and/or a designer, and have them redo them for production. Thank me later.

The same applies with branding-related deliverables. Yes, that tagline may seem the best. That logo may seem brilliant. And you know what? In the end, they may be the winner. *But take the time to be sure.* Test the branding. Explore alternatives. Refine. Refine. Refine. It will, almost always, make for better work. You will find out in the end that it is less than 5 percent of the time that the best idea in the pitch is still the best idea in the end of this process.

PITCHING WITH AGENCIES

Let's talk about pitching alongside an agency. Not pitching *to* an agency to be your client, but going in, side by side, with another agency, and trying to win a pitch together. Jointly.

This falls into two camps: helping an agency win a pitch as a project in and of itself, or helping an agency win a pitch with the hope of getting some of the work when the agency wins the pitch.

With the former, I like to price this one of two ways: a straight project cost or a percentage of the pitch budget.

The straight project cost is simple: pay us x amount to do some pitch work for you. Clean, simple, great. No hassles, no commitments. It's quite nice. The downside, of course, is that the agency has to pay you either way. Large agencies spend tons of money on large pitches, several hundred thousand dollars. It's not unreasonable that they spend some of this on you.

The flip side to this, of course, is that they are spending hundreds of thousands of dollars, so how can they pay any more for you? Furthermore there's a difference between spending the money on the salaries of your employees versus spending the money on an external vendor

The answer here, then, is the percentage. "Okay, if you win, you give us 1–2 percent of the total budget. Sign here."

I love these agreements in principal, but I find that many agencies dodge. Once they do the math, they realize this is really, really expensive. Agencies are also reluctant to sign away a percentage of the winnings *they just won*. I don't blame them, for several reasons. It's expensive. Agency margins are razor thin as it is. The agency may not know exactly what its getting. It's an accounting headache.

You can get around this by ballparking: if you win, you'll give us $200k. That's okay. Make sure this number is higher than the number you'd get for just being paid outright for the pitch, so that you have a potential upside. Win some, lose some, and hopefully it all comes out ahead.

Of course, if they're going to be paying you anyway, they may as well get some work out of you. This brings us to the promise of your getting the work if they win. *If* they win. This, too, sounds great in concept. In reality, it's basically a derivative of the economic predation we caution against above. Because now you're doing the pitch for free, and then MAYBE you're going to get some work for which you are only going to be paid market rate. Best-case scenario, you still did free work.

And even if you win, the agency may well renege. There's also the risk that the client will negate the whole deal as a condition of the win. "We like you, but you have to use Vendor Z." It happens. And how likely is it that the agency will fall on its sword for you?

Pitching with an agency can be frustrating because in reality you have limited impact on the pitch process. At best you'll be the "Internet person" in the room (or the "PR" person, or the "design" person, or the "social" person—whatever it is you do). You might get five minutes to talk. That's the best-case scenario. More likely, you'll deliver your materials, and they will go present them. And the odds are they won't present them as well as you will. Because the materials don't belong to them, and the subject area is by definition not their forte. It's an undeniable reality that on most large brand pitches, any one component aside from the overall strategy is only a small fraction of the whole pitch. Often, your component won't even get mentioned. It's relegated to maybe one or two comps or bullet points, that are flipped by with two to three seconds each. I am not exaggerating.

Conversely, your firm may specialize in exactly the component the agency is pitching. Perhaps brand strategy or packaging design. Here, there may be a stronger argument for hitching your wagon to the agency, and everyone's winning together. In this case, I would question what the agency is doing there.

In our case, even when agencies agreed to the "win with us and we'll give you the work" approach, almost every time we entered into this agreement, in the end the agency reneged. Remember that old maxim that "success has many fathers, while failure is an orphan." The minute the account is won, all decks are cleared, the reset button is pushed, and everyone freaks out and gets to work.

I do have to say, though, that I actually love pitching with other agencies. It's fun, and I like the quick turnaround nature of it. For that reason, despite the inherent risks, it was important for us to find a way to make this work.

In the end, getting paid cold, hard cash turned out to be best for us. When that didn't work, we'd insist on a reward for winning, not tied to additional work. They could then hire us for additional work against that reward if they so desired. It seemed to me, at first, that agencies wouldn't be willing to pay for pitch work. If you hold fast, this will eventually turn out to be untrue. Stay firm.

PAID PITCHES FOR CLIENTS

A paid pitch is when the client brand—not an intermediate agency—offers you some nominal amount of money to pitch it to win the larger job. These fees range from a token $1 to something more substantial. In our scope of pitches, we would often see something in the $10,000—$50,000 range for a low multi-million-dollar pitch. In the large, global, nine-figure campaign pitches, these can go higher.

This amount is nominal and arbitrary, and not tied to how much you—or your competitors—will actually spend on the pitch. *Adweek* concurs: "That's a fraction of what a pitch can cost, which generally runs well into six figures."[14]

Legal departments have sowed some fear into brands, and there have been some lawsuits in the past, where ideas were presented to clients, and the ideas were then supposedly used in larger campaigns without compensation to the agency. In the old days, this was understood to be a risk, and the clients were understood to abide by a code of ethics. Says our old Barbarian Group lawyer, Rick Kurnit, in *AdWeek*, "These type of client demands grew out of the old agency-client model, where agencies spent lots of money to pitch business with the understanding that if they won, they would recoup the investment via a 15 percent commission over a long relationship....Today's fee-based arrangements, coupled with shorter client-agency marriages, underscores the need for a new approach."[15]

While there are ample stories in the press about agencies getting up in arms for clients wanting to own the ideas in a pitch, there don't appear to be many stories where the brand sues the agency for reusing an idea. They are predominantly interested in making sure you don't take their proprietary material and use it to gain an advantage for a competitor in the future. So, don't do that, and you should be all good. And, of course, an idea requires context. Using puppets for a competitor's brand, after you pitched this to a client, is one thing. Puppets, someday, in another campaign in a completely different industry and with a completely different plot, is another thing.

I will also say that compared to getting jack for an idea, getting $25,000 isn't so bad. I mean, hell, when you're in the right creative headspace, and you've trained yourself, you can generate ideas by the dozen. Not a bad return on any one of them.

CONCLUSION

Because of the romance and adventure of pitching, there are innumerable books on the topic, by very talented practitioners. I have quoted liberally from a few of them. This should give you the basics.

Remember, though, *that the best way to win a pitch is to not have to pitch.* Remember, too, that pitching should be done sparingly. It is but one tool in your arsenal.

And remember that even the best pitch must be accompanied by the detailed substance of the nitty-gritty. It is profoundly depressing to be told your ideas were the best, but they did not choose you because they were worried about your ability to execute. Your ducks must be in a row.

14

THE RATIONAL

This is where we focus on the nuts and bolts of sales for a services company, and develop a library of tools and tactics that allow us to routinely win new business.

CLIENT DIVERSIFICATION

Why have a new business department at all if you are already winning work through organic and emotional? One reason: It's vital to diversify your client base. What this means is that no single client should make up more than one-third or so of your total revenue. The financial impact of losing a client larger than that can be devastating. Even losing a third of your revenue suddenly will have a profound impact on your company, almost certainly leading to some level of layoffs. This is related to new business in the sense that *we cannot solely focus on organic work from one or two clients*, and no matter how great things are going with that client, we are going to have to do some modicum of new business no matter what.

It can be very tempting to ignore this problem, and in certain situations it can be a lot of work to break out of it. This is especially the case if your company was born through the work of a single client. You started your company with this client, and it's been around forever. It's impossible to imagine that you'll ever need another client. I have never known one of these situations to work well over the long run. Unless you want to completely rebuild your company from scratch when this client inevitably leaves, it's absolutely best to be insulated against the fallout by having other clients.

The logical component of new business can help immensely in client diversification. Besides, having multiple clients is fun, and it's half the reason you're doing this, other than just working for someone else on a single account, right?

EVENTUALLY YOU'RE GOING TO GROW UP

When you're younger, you may well be a hot shop. But as any follower of style or fashion knows, what was once cool is inevitably boring. It's one thing to be invited to a pitch because you are a cool shop and they have heard good things about you, and you go into the pitch with a strong advantage. This is great. When it happens. But we cannot always rely on it. At TBG, we had great luck with this for many years, but eventually it was inevitable that we mature as a company and develop a more robust, rigorous, methodical new business practice.

In addition to Benjamin, who worked predominantly as our hustler, and to myself, who specialized in winning organic work, we began to staff out a new business department with a staff member focused solely on the world of winning new business through the logical and methodical processes of sales. Had we spent all our time relying only on organic, word-of-mouth and our innate coolness in pitches, we would have eventually gone out of business.

Let's turn to the tactics and tools of the rational new business department.

PROPOSALS

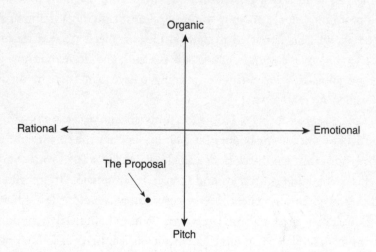

Let's start with the most important tool in the rational winning of new business: the proposal. We've talked about receiving the RFP and the component pitch presentation. We will also need to deliver the proposal itself. Additionally, many proposal opportunities come in that do not require a formal pitch.

What is a proposal? It's a written document that outlines your company's qualifications for a specific job, as well as how you plan on accomplishing the project. It's a document written to answer as many questions as possible up front that the client may have.

In many ways, the proposal is the exact opposite of the type of work you are looking to win. It is won on nearly completely rational grounds. The pitch presentation isn't a tool available to you to inspire potential clients. You've got to rely on paper. Proposals fall on the "pitch" side of the pitch-organic scale, thus meaning you have no real inside advantage.

Prior to my career in advertising, I worked in management consulting at Ernst & Young. Specifically, I worked in the marketing department, and a good chunk of my job was to prepare proposals for multi-million-dollar engagements with the largest companies in the world. Now *those people*, they wrote proposals. One hundred-page documents were the rule, rather than the exception. This background has been a blessing and a burden for me in my time in advertising. In the beginning, I confess I massively overestimated the amount of effort that I needed to put into a proposal. I recall one early job, where the client asked me to send over a proposal for a job estimated to cost somewhere in the neighborhood of $300,000. This was a mammoth amount of money for us at the time—our largest job up to that point had been around $50k. I went all out, producing a 50-page proposal that, while a little light by EY standards, was still a gloriously comprehensive document of every conceivable issue at hand. The client politely said thank you and asked if I minded providing her a one-pager with just the timing and costs, since that was all she really needed.

It was an important early lesson, one that made me realize that *the goal is to only write as much as you need to in a proposal, and not a word more.* Ten years in, as The Barbarian Group battles for multimillion-dollar projects, the types of proposals I was writing in those early days are the norm. But back then, they were wasteful overkill.

Thus, *the larger the project, the longer the proposal.*

A couple of pet peeves of mine. First, a client company elicits a proposal from you by submitting an RFP. The thing you are sending back is a *proposal.* You'll hear people say weird, nonsensical things all the time like "response to the RFP." A response to a request for a proposal should be a proposal. When someone asks us for a glass of water, we give them a glass of water, not a response to a request for a glass of water. You'll also find people who call the proposal itself the RFP. I believe these people think RFP stands for "response for proposal" or something. I'm not quite sure. But it is incorrect.

Secondly, I must decry the trend of the last five years or so of answering RFPs with proposals in PowerPoint/Keynote format. This has, sadly, become an acceptable practice in the advertising world, and I do not like it. Now, I understand the reasoning: it is massively easier to produce. It is more quickly digestible by the end client. But as a rule I believe it is shoddy work.

I believe this because *a good proposal is easily digested at any pace*. If a busy executive encounters your proposal, they should be able to skim it, read the executive letter, glance at the timing, price, any comps you may provide, and your past work, and develop a knowledgeable opinion. By the same token, if you have an obsessive, detail-oriented producer who wants to know all aspects of the job, and spend hours pouring over your proposal to learn every single thing about you and the job, why should you not give them that ability? Don't you want a client who cares this much and pays this much attention? Bear in mind that the job may be clinched by winning over either of these two people. I've landed more than one job just because the producer found our proposal the most thorough, and our thinking the most fleshed out.

The PowerPoint/Keynote proposal should be used sparingly, only when explicitly requested by the client, and you know all the other competing shops will also be delivering proposals in this format.

SECTIONS OF THE PROPOSAL

Every proposal has broadly the same sections. Depending on the type of job, some sections may be expanded or removed, but these are the general sections every proposal should have:

- Cover Page, project name, date, client, prepared by, copyright, and confidentiality notice[1]
- Executive Summary—this should be a quick summary of what you want someone to take away from this proposal if they read nothing else. Take care to not make this bland, and not to make it overly formalized. If you believe your comps are going to be the best, say, "Our comps are going to be the best. Go take a look at them." Many

people make the mistake of using this section for such platitudes as "we look forward to working with you" and "let us know if you have questions." Screw that. You should say things like "with our past work for clients X and Y, we know your industry cold, we'll come in strong, and we have some awesome ideas already: we particularly love idea Z." If someone on your team has a personal connection, say so. If you've been working with them before, say so. Hit them hard. *This may be all they remember.*

- About your company—this is a continually debated topic, whether to dive right into the project or start with your company. This can be omitted with regular repeat clients. If it's been a while, or there have been personnel changes, include it. I choose to start with information about my company upfront. Your company's chops, background, and point of view are just as liable to win the project than any specific idea you may have for this project, and starting strong about you increases the chances that you can win on your own merits even if your specific idea about the project is weaker than others'. *It's better if the client is choosing to hire you for you who you are, rather than the specifics of a project.* This section often includes the following subsections:

  - Your beliefs: This is where you make a point to say what you stand for. Put it in here. Show them you're a company that brings a point of view to the table and that you stand for something.
  - Your capabilities: Often, someone came to The Barbarian Group for our design chops or our coding chops, not even knowing what else we were capable of doing. Take this opportunity to list, in a simple bulleted form, all the services you provide.
  - Departmental-specific credentials and information: if this is a design and tech-heavy project, include sections on the design and development departments. If your company does one thing and one thing only, you can generally fold this into the larger "about the company" section, but if, say, you are a great product shop, consulting shop, and design shop, you should briefly outline your skills in each of these areas. This is doubly true if your shop "builds" things and "thinks" about things—that is, if you offer consulting services. Let them know you aren't just hired labor, but you can offer deeper strategic thinking.

- An overview of the project. This is where you turn the conversation to the project at hand. This section should talk about the strategic objectives, research, challenges, and obstacles, strategic approach, creative considerations, and such. If you feel that comps, technical flows, or wireframes are required to win the project, this is where they would go. Note that things may change—that this is just your initial thinking. Be frank about the challenges at hand, but confident you can overcome them.

- Your Team. List out the team members and how much of their time you will be using on the project. Include anyone who might touch the project, including senior leadership. Bios should go in the appendix. If you can avoid it, don't put in the number of hours that each person will be working on the job. A simple bulleted list of names, titles, and roles is best. If the RFP requests it, or if you know from experience that staffing levels are required in the proposal, put them in. But if you can keep them out, do.

- Timing. How long will the project take? If it is a waterfall project, what are the phases? If it is an agile project, what are the sprint lengths and total project duration? Is there a hard and fast launch day, or something driving the timing? Address it here. If timing is flexible, note that. If timing and team are aligned, because, say, different team members are working on the project in different phases, make the two sections sync up and make sense together (unless you can, of course, get away with not showing any of that). If the client is noticeably nervous about the deadline, address it upfront and say something explicit and clear like "we will make your deadline."

- Pricing. In my perfect world, the proposal will simply list a dollar amount and payment terms, like this: This project will cost $145,000, flat rate. Payment terms are 50 percent at the start of the project, 25 percent at approval of the final deliverables, and 25 percent upon delivery. Payment terms are 30 days, negotiable, except for the initial payment, which is due upon start." If you can win on a fixed number, with no supporting justification, that is just great. You want that. In reality, however, most proposals and projects don't let you get away with this, especially as the dollar amounts grow. A more robust payment sheet might include multiple phases, high and low estimates, outside vendors, and more.

- Appendices. After the body of your proposal, you'll have several appendices. These are added as necessary.

  - Response to Specific Questions in the RFP. If their RFP has a section in it that says something like "give us explicit answers to these questions in list form," add this section in. Also add it if they have asked some random questions about your company that are not relevant to the other sections. List each question and then answer it. You can refer to other pages of the proposal in your answers, such as "Yes we do. Please refer to page 23 for our full list of technical programming languages."

  - Case Studies and Relevant Work. This is, in many ways, the most important section of the proposal—the work you have done in the past. When possible, sprinkle some of the work throughout the proposal—we liked to have a few of our greatest hits in the "about us" section. But here is where you show some work that the client may be less familiar with—especially if it is relevant to its project. In a perfect world, you will have relevant case studies rather than just past work examples. That is, not only will you be able to say you worked in its industry and here is a project, but here is a *case study*, with accompanying challenges, approaches, and results. Take care to not use the words "case study" unless they are in case study form. Ditto for the word "relevant." If it is not immediately clear how the work is relevant (say, it's technically relevant, but you wouldn't know from the client or screenshot), write a brief passage explaining why.

  - References. Some proposals require references from past clients. Omit this unless it is specifically asked for. Keep a few clients in good graces and ask their permission before you put them in this section. Most are happy to do it.

  - Bios. This is where you put the work bios of the key team members on the project. Include any work relevant to the project at hand, and list their past places of employment, and so on. At EY we liked to go whole hog and include years of sector experience, but I find that's a bit of overkill in the ad world.

  - Terms and Conditions. Generally speaking, you don't want to hit the client with a bunch of legalese in the proposal. But if it requests a sample statement of work (SOW) and sample terms and conditions, you may need to include them here. There will also be times with repeat clients that the proposal is a quickie, and the desired outcome is their signing the proposal and its becoming the statement of work, in which case, you'll need some legal terms. We'll go over those in a later section.

- Enlarged comps. I find it is useful to include larger, full-page comps here if you did not in the proposal above. Sometimes the comps in line with text are a little small, and it's good to show them a little larger.

WRITING STYLE

The writing style and voice of your proposal are of massive importance. Too many companies ignore this to their detriment. Too many companies leave proposal writing to people who don't know how to write. Even if I am a client who loves to delve into the nitty-gritty of a proposal, that doesn't mean I have a high tolerance for crappy writing. I'm still pleasantly surprised when the writing is casual, conversational, has a slight sense of humor, but is still obviously professional. That is what you should seek in your proposals. A well-written, coherent, conversational proposal belies a company that intimately, deeply understands the topics at hand, and isn't struggling to convey information. If the proposal is written well, the client will feel, instinctively, that you have your act together.

Most proposals are needlessly bland, and by giving the reader a spark of fun and enjoyment in their day, your company can take advantage of this to win a job. This has happened to me many, many times. People routinely told The Barbarian Group they wanted to work with us because they could tell we were fun from our proposals. This is a free advantage. Leverage it.

READABILITY AND CALLOUTS

Because they must be readable to different types of readers at different speeds and attention levels, proposals are different from other long-form documents you may have written in the past, such as short stories or research papers. The reader needs to be able to drop in and drop out at any point. Different parties will be reading different sections. This means that your proposal should be clearly readable—every section should be titled. Every subsection. Important points should be highlighted in callout boxes, or with bold or italic. Serious book editors will sometimes frown on this habit, but here it is necessary. Someone should be able to flip through your proposal, reading nothing but header titles and callouts, and get the general gist. You will find yourself using header 4 more than you ever thought possible. Sometimes you will boldly go to header 5 or header 6.

WORKING WITH MULTIPLE WRITERS

This need for fluid, engaging writing has all sorts of ramifications if you don't consider yourself a writer. It can be hard for some people. You can work around it in the short term, do what you can, but in the long term, be on the lookout for people who know how to write. In the early days, I wrote all our proposals myself, and indeed, I kept this habit going on the most important ones all the way through. But over time, I found other people who were good at writing, especially their own sections. Creatives, UX designers, and technical directors who can write cogently and fluidly are of vital importance.

This then allows us to assign the writing in chunks to various people, so no one person has to write the whole thing.

The company should develop an in-house style guide, so when different people are writing different sections of the proposal, it still flows. Lay out your preferred capitalizations, words you don't use, words you like, acceptable humor level, and include some dos and don'ts. One area I find particularly telling is when someone stops using contractions. The use of "do not" versus "don't" can subconsciously tell the reader you don't have a firm grip on things. We may think this use of contractions belies formality and respect, but just as often it belies indifference or a weak grasp of the topic at hand.

When using multiple writers, also make sure everyone's writing in the same templates, allowing for easy copying and pasting within the proposal. An alternative is to use a collaborative writing application such as Google Docs. This may mean a more limited palette when it comes to page layout, however, so there are trade-offs.

Ideally when you have multiple writers, someone with editing skills will then go through the final proposal and clean it up for cogency and consistency. This was a job I generally kept for myself, combining it with my final partner read-through for approval. If you find someone you trust to source it out to, God bless them.

DOCUMENT MANAGEMENT

The key to efficient, rapid proposal writing is the extensive use of templates and prewritten passages. All major parts of your proposals should be prewritten: about the company and its capabilities, technical capabilities, design capabilities, your beliefs and so on. Bios of all team members should be prewritten, and photos should be shot. There should be a library of case studies in all relevant industries, with all relevant tech. We had case studies for insurance, financial, automotive, and the like, as well as case studies for viral marketing, Flash, database work, games, strategic consulting, and what have you.

I usually wrote the first version myself, even once we had dedicated new businesspeople. This allowed the new business team to get the straight scoop on vision and beliefs straight from the horse's mouth.

We kept all of this prewritten work in the "proposal template," a versioned document that we were constantly updating. This also allowed us to include instructions in the template itself. We made extensive use of notes and annotations to offer additional instructions to the writer of the proposal, reminding them about writing tone and calling out various rules, approaches, policies, and best practices.

The design and layout of your proposals is exceptionally important. If you are not a professional designer yourself, get someone to design the template for you, including examples of subheaders down to level 6, callout boxes, image wraps, and so forth. And for the love of God, make sure people know how to use style sheets. Take care to title appropriately the final digital file you send. Do not send "Nike_Proposal_v25.pdf." Instead, send "Yourname_ProjectName_Proposal.pdf." They know they are Client X. You want to make sure they know it's coming from YOU. Also make sure to scrub the metadata. Many applications include metadata for author, version, and such. Clean this. Make sure all changes are accepted and they can't turn on "track changes." Send a PDF rather than a native document type.

DELIVERY

Some people like to send "care packages" along with their proposals: swag, gifts, and the like. I never did this. I never felt the need. I view this more as a tactic for the sales team than the proposal team.

Ensure the timely delivery of your proposal. If you're mailing physical copies (some companies require this), use a tracking number, signature required.
If you are emailing them, be aware many companies have spam detection. Try
and send a link rather than an attachment. And send a follow-up email, link,
and attachment free, notifying them it's been sent.

OTHER RATIONAL NEW BUSINESS TACTICS

Let's now turn to some other rational new business tools and tactics.

DETAILED RFP ANSWERS

In addition to the components of the proposal that you will have prewritten,
more and more we are seeing a battery of questions asked of the vendor in
a detailed spreadsheet form. It's often explicitly stated that this is a separate
document from the proposal. What's going on here is that the proposal is for
the marketing purchaser of your work, and the detailed document is for the
procurement department. Thus, the types of questions they are answering
are often very different. They can also be insanely detailed. For a computer
development shop, for example, the proposal may ask how many engineers
you have and what languages they work in. This detailed set of questions, by
contrast, may ask about specific versions of software, database schemas, traffic levels, and such.

Whereas you may have five to ten prefab components to a proposal, over
time you may have specific answers to hundreds of these questions. They are
best kept in some sort of simple database. When a proposal comes in, have the
head of the specific department (or you, if you're small!) answer those questions the first time, *then save all of the answers*. Over time, you will simply fill in
the answers you already have to the questions you receive, and have the department head check over the answers you've already completed, and add the new
ones. You will then update the old stock answers and save the new ones.

This can seem labor intensive, but I assure you it is the most efficient
approach. Nothing can be more stressful, for both parties, than for a five-page
detailed questionnaire to land on the lap of your VP of Engineering, and her
being told she has an hour to complete it, when she is already slammed with
work.

It's generally okay if one or two of these answers are slightly out of date or
wrong. This is expected. You're shooting for a B/B+ on those forms.

DOG AND PONY DECK

After the proposal template, a dog and pony deck is probably the most important thing your company needs. This is a basic PowerPoint/Keynote deck that talks about your company, its skills, its talents, and its past work. This deck needs to be awesome. It needs to be constantly updated. And it needs to be constantly distributed to every member of the company who may be going out and speaking about the company on your behalf. All of this is logistically harder than it sounds. It's easy to use the same deck for *years*, having it age and become out of date. It's also tough to make sure that your entire sales team is using the most current version. Build a process around this.

Here's one that worked for me. I wrote the initial deck. I got the design team to design it. I sent it around to four to five people on the new business team and in the leadership of the company and solicited feedback on the deck. I incorporated the feedback. I went out and did a dog and pony show myself with the deck a couple times and made sure it covered all of the bases. I then posted it on the corporate intranet and told everyone to download it.

Over time, the new business team informed me of places where I was missing a slide—something on a specific capability or past experience in a specific industry, for example. Those slides were then built. I put them into an appendix of the deck. The main deck itself stayed lean—maybe 20 slides—but the appendix grew to be a library of slides that covered 90 percent of the situations in which our sales team found themselves. They rarely needed to build a new slide. When they did, I would take it, get it properly designed, and then add it to the main deck.

CASE STUDIES

Case studies of past work are also monumentally important. You will use these in proposals, as well as in several other places. If you do things well, the standard pitch deck with some relevant case studies can go 90 percent of the way in winning a job. Case studies are also often sent along to clients— including preexisting clients—who are curious about a capability of your company that they've not yet used. For example, you may be doing a lot of design work for a company, but now it are also curious about your user experience chops.

You will want to develop, in advance, case studies for many of your past projects. These can be your most famous and successful projects, definitely, but also look for solid projects that have something unique about them—an industry in which you haven't done a lot of work, a package of software tools, a specific tactic. These aren't just your "greatest hits." Your case study library should include prewritten case studies in all areas in which you hope to win work. We had case studies for specific industries, software, marketing techniques, consulting engagements, and so forth.

VIDEO CASE STUDIES

A case study is really two components: the content and the medium. Distinguish between the two. The content may be presented in several ways. Most commonly, there is a single-page, printed case study layout that is useful for appending to proposals, and a slide-format version that is useful for appending to dog and pony shows. Additionally, more and more we are seeing the rise of well-produced video case studies placed on your website. This wasn't much of a big deal in the past, as so much of new business was word of mouth, and landed on the ground. These days, however, people actually *are* looking for services companies more and more by just poking around on the Internet. Having a few well-produced videos about some of your best projects can be effective. The downside is, of course, those production costs. The good news is that there is a growing number of talented filmmakers out there whose bread and butter is to make exactly this type of work for relatively low budgets. Look around on the Web for viral or demo filmmakers in your area. Chances are you will find a company that can do this for you, if it's not the sort of work your shop can do in-house.

CUSTOMER RELATIONSHIP MANAGEMENT (CRM) SOFTWARE

You'll need to develop a working CRM system. CRM systems can go from simple spreadsheets to massively complex enterprise-level software as a service (SAAS) systems costing tens of thousands of dollars a month. You won't need anything that complex, but it's important to have something.

Very early on, get a system up and running. Inexpensive, small business-level systems are available for purchase as an SAAS model from companies such as SalesForce, SugarCRM, and many others. When your entire sales team consists solely of you or your partner, this will feel less necessary. But over time, as your client services team, new business team, other partners, and others are all pursuing potential leads, this will be incredibly vital for two reasons. First, it's important to make sure that leads are properly assigned to the right people and that no one is stepping on each other's toes. Second, this will become a vital tool in projecting potential future revenue and managing your business.

When viewing the use of the CRM system through the eyes of deploying a hustler, CRM can be a double-edged sword. The hustler may talk to literally dozens of people a day, and it can be massively time consuming for the hustler to enter every potential contact and lead into the CRM system (unless they are already a CRM devotee or have an admin). Additionally, a hustler is intrinsically optimistic, and it can potentially wreak havoc on your financial projections to have every potential lead in the system, with the hustler insisting that the deal is "definitely gonna happen." A balance needs to be struck. I've found that requiring the hustler to enter projects into the CRM only when he has gotten to the point of talking with a potential client about a specific project—with a specific goal, budget and time line—is a good threshold.

Another nice feature of CRM systems is the ability to assign the likelihood of winning on jobs. Enforce this rigorously with your team. Ensure that every job has a budget placed on it, and a percentage likelihood. At TBG, we built our CRM system in-house, rather than use something like SalesForce. I found this a nice approach because I could customize it for our industry—for example, many low-end CRM systems have trouble with the concept of holding companies and different divisions. BBDO Minneapolis, for example, is a different billing entity from BBDO New York, but both are owned by Omnicom. This was useful for us to track.

COLD CALLING

Will your shop need to cold call? Hopefully not. It's a rarity in the marketing world, and it's not recommended. It makes your company look desperate, and it is incredibly hard to build trust from a cold call contact in this industry. People hire marketing services vendors relatively rarely, and it's a big decision for them. Cold calling typically works in industries where the buyers are buying frequently and from many people, such as media agencies buying ads from web properties. It's not particularly applicable in our industry. Far better to focus your efforts on networking. Have your hustler hit the trade shows, mixers, meetups, and industry parties, start talking, and start asking people out for lunches and drinks.

PROCUREMENT HELL

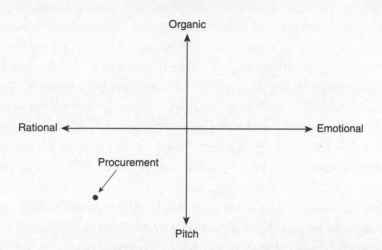

And here we come to the crappiest part of the advertising ecosystem: the procurement process. When Mike Parker was minted as McCann Erickson's new chief digital officer in 2002, *Digiday*'s Brian Morrissey asked him what he liked least about advertising today. He replied, "The least favorite [thing] is more and more the involvement of procurement and the commoditization [of] what we do that turns it into a calculus rather than focusing on the ideas and the value we can bring."[2] Talk about an understatement.

On its own, in the context of a large firm or organization, procurement can be fairly interesting. Large companies buy massive amounts of stuff. If I were buying 120,000 Herman Miller chairs, I would want a discount too. If you're the kind of person who likes negotiation, it's no doubt a perfectly fun job.

There's a difference between procuring pens, however, and buying creative services. Good procurement officers know this. But, astonishingly, many do not.

The problem, of course, comes when you need to negotiate for what is, essentially, a consultative or creative service. In a 2010 procurement roundtable for *Advertising Age*, Intel's VP-director of materials, Craig Brown, made a telling offhand comment: "Left alone these guys go wild on creativity at any cost and we try to get more accountability in there about meeting all the vectors of success."[3] I find this to be representative of the procurement mind-set: we "creatives" are irresponsible, and will "go wild" if left alone. And it is up to procurement to stop us.

More companies are migrating to a centralized procurement department and process, with SAAS platforms that all vendors, from the coffee seller to the ad agency, are required to use and fill out. They treat creative, consulting, strategy, and planning as commodities. The work suffers. A typical scenario goes something like this: you get a call from someone at a brand or from a search consultant. You're invited to partake in the pitch for Brand X, a brand you always wanted to work with. The brand's annual spending is projected to be $3 million. Usually, they flat out tell you this, which is kind of maddening later on down the road. Occasionally, you infer the spending amount from some media spending data publication that someone like *Kantar* or *AdAge* puts out.

You get excited. You put your best people on the pitch. The whole company chips in (because, like a good manager, you consciously decided this is one where you have a chance, and applying extra effort is worth it). You eventually have two to three killer ideas, an amazing presentation, the most charismatic team imaginable, awesome comps, and a brilliant leave behind, with the price breakdown all worked out conveniently to show that everything you are doing, you can do within budget. Your pitch is killer.

It's a heated battle. You're in there, following the script. You kill it. You go home. You wait two weeks. Then a third. Sometimes a fourth. In this particular instance, you are blessed. You're actually going to receive an answer.

And so you do, in the sixth week, you hear you won! Woooo!

Champagne is broken out. Whoops are yelped! "We won! We won! Woooo!" It feels good. The moment that you live for in this job. The winning of the big account. "We're unstoppable!" you think. You're excited that your genius, also-happens-to-be-doable idea was chosen, and you can't wait to get the team going on building it, because you know it will change the world, or, at least, be cool and sweet and awesome.

Then reality sets in. The account manager was the lucky one who got to take the call that your firm won. This is probably the best part of being an account manager, actually, come to think of it. But then the account manager mentions, "We won, but they didn't love our rate card, and we need to deal with their procurement process."

Many people on the team have never had to deal with this part of the process. They do, however, wonder why they won, but nothing's really gotten going yet. Larger firms can offset this by just going for it and starting work without a contract on faith. Indeed, in the later years, once we were big enough, at TBG that's what we started doing. It burned us once or twice when procurement negotiations didn't pan out—and this happens more often than you would think—but by and large it was generally better to get the team going. If it's a really large account, and you need to hire for it, this is all the more true.

When you're smaller, however, this isn't an option.

And either way, you're going to have to deal with procurement eventually. This typically means the account manager, your finance guy, and one senior executive.

And you.

Some stats. Procurement is on the rise. The Association of National Advertisers (ANA) studied procurement trends and found that for three-quarters of marketers, procurement plays a "significant part." More marketers report that the entire pitch is led by procurement—47 percent—than marketing goals—28 percent.[4] How screwed up is *that? Digiday* also reports that the ANA found that "the bigger the client, the more likely procurement is going to be in charge. Of those reporting annual marketing budgets over $100 million, 67 percent said procurement led the negotiation of agency fees. Over a quarter said they want to reduce agency fees in the next year or two."[5]

First problem: 10 percent.

Procurement basically wants to save at least 10 percent off of everything. Sometimes higher. This is how they prove they are good at their job. It's a miserable charade, but a manageable one. You didn't win this pitch on money—because, remember, the client already said they had $3 million. Everyone. Already. Knew. That. We're supposed to pretend we don't, but we know. So mark everything up by 10 percent before you send out the pitch, and then knock it off on the first wave of negotiations with the procurement officer. This may seem questionably moral, but, honestly, it's your company and you can charge whatever you want for your services.

Next: procurement officers work on benchmarks, or a list of roles with "industry standard" rates that they are willing to pay. So. Flash. An hour of a Flash person. What does a staffing agency charge for an hour of a Flash person's time? What would I pay for an hour of a Flash person's time on Craigslist or Behance or eLance? $50. Wait. What? You charge $120 for a Flash person? A junior Flash person? You mean a senior one is $200?! That's insanity. "An artist? A genius? I don't need an artist, I don't need a genius, I need an hour of a Flash developer's time at a benchmark rate."

"Okay, great, but we did not win the pitch because we promised boring, workmanlike Flash design."

"Well, then you can have your artist, but I am only going to pay benchmark."

I cannot tell you how many times I have had conversations like this. Line by line. Each role.

"What's this $300 an hour for consulting? That's way off benchmark."

"Okay, great, that line item says consulting, but you guys actually specifically asked for the CEO of the company to be in that role, and that's what he bills at."

"Well, he shouldn't be billing us for his time. That should be included in the cost."

"There is an amount of his time included in the cost, but you are asking for more."

"Well, we shouldn't have to pay for it."

Or: "$200 for a developer? That's ridiculous. I have developers benchmarked at $90 an hour."

You will go through this for every role. "Why do I need a user experience consultant and an information architect? What's the difference?"

"Well, our client wants to do a little research before we design the interface. The UX consultant does the research. The information architect designs the page from that research."

"Why can't they both be the same person?"

"Well, I suppose they could, but then I'd need to hire someone with a larger skill set, and it would cost even more."

"Why do I need two account people? Actually, why do I need to pay for account people at all. Isn't that customer service? Just built in?"

"Why do I need two developers. Can't I just use one?"

"Why do I need QA? You're building this. I expect you to build it right."

"We do too. And to do that we need QA."

"Wait, what's QA again?"

It's a nightmare.

There are two ways around this. When you're a small shop, the trick is to do the procurement yourself. You will be the only person in the entire negotiation who might actually make or lose money on this, and it gives you the moral high ground that is hard for procurement people to get around. "I can't do that. Look. I literally can't afford to do that. If I took that pricing, I would lose money and lay people off. If that's the best you can do, then we can't do this job."

And this is important: *you are probably the only person who can walk away. This gives you tremendous power.*

The secret truth about procurement officers is that they can hardly go back to the chief marketing officer (CMO) and say, "Oh, the vendor decided to walk because I was too hard on them." There are times you *will* have to walk. Like I said, this happens more often than you think. Right now, you need that procurement officer to go back to the CMO or brand manager—who's half the time in a completely different part of the company, doesn't report to him or his superior, and really does not give a rat's ass how much this costs at this level of granularity.

In any case, when the going gets tough, you need to give your potential new client a heads-up that procurement is being a little difficult, and you're just a tad concerned because you thought the client wanted something special, something great, something that will move people, win awards, and get your client promoted, and, really, it's not like your prices are any different from anyone else's, just go check the original pitches. Lay this groundwork, then go back to the procurement officer and tell them you're just not sure. You might have to walk. The procurement officer will then go back to your potential new client and gauge its reaction to this possibility. This, actually, can be a nice gut check to see how decisively you won the pitch. If all goes well, your client will whip the procurement officer into shape for you, and they'll come back slightly amenable. If not, pull the "I can't afford it" trip again, talk about how this is your livelihood. Remember: this money is fake money to everyone there but you. Play that card.

Wash. Rinse. Repeat.

The other approach is to mark up your fees a little bit more, and make your chief financial officer (CFO) handle the whole thing. They're not going to do as good of a job as you—I mean, don't get me wrong, my CFOs have been some of the best negotiators out there—but generally that whole moral high ground of its being your livelihood thing is removed, so they're not quite as incentivized to do as well as you are. When taking this approach, it's best to focus on how much more free time you have in your life and how your blood pressure has gone down, rather than focusing on the fact that you just gave in to a pointless, miserable system that does no one any good and lessens the ability for an vendor to effectively deliver to its client the best creative and most effective work, which then impacts how much that company might sell, its revenues, its profits, and, thus, its procurement department's zeal. Aspire to this.

In my experience, the best relationships are when the brand manager and the services firm are aligned in getting through procurement unscathed. This takes advance planning, collusion, and a shared understanding. The procurement process is an early warning of how you will work with your client. It's often best to discuss all this forthrightly, in advance, before you begin the procurement process.

Otherwise, you're in for a grim ride.

PART IV

THE PEOPLE

15

ON PARTNERS AND PARTNERSHIP

The act of choosing a partner is a peculiar ritual. Basically, you're choosing someone with whom you will spend as much time as you would your spouse, and often you're doing it on little information. You may have just met them. You may have only ever hung out with them in social situations, and never seen them under pressure. Yet you throw our lot in with them, with little more than a hope and a prayer, and try and build something lasting and beautiful with someone that, very often, whom you barely know. You consciously give up some measure of control to this person, making yourself less omnipotent in the process.

WHY HAVE PARTNERS AT ALL?

So why a partner? Why not go it alone? You may have gotten by up to now on your own, or with a constellation of employees and freelancers. This may point to the answer. You may now have an employee whom you've grown to trust and admire, and can't live without. Perhaps that employee is either looking for some sort of increased recognition, or debating leaving and starting their own thing. This can be a situation where making someone your partner is necessary. You literally can't imagine your company without them. More broadly speaking, none of us are perfect. We all have strengths and weaknesses. Hopefully this is self-evident to you as well. Choosing a great partner is a matter of choosing someone who complements your strengths and weaknesses, and gives your organization increased talent in an area in which you may be deficient. And let's suppose, for a moment, that you actually *are* good at all of it. The fact of the matter is that if you are on some sort of growth plan, there will be more work than any one person can handle. I don't mean more work like "more work than you can do in 40 hours a week, but could probably hustle through and do it all in 60 or 70 hours a week." Two hundred, three hundred hours a week wouldn't be enough to do all the work. The blunt truth is that you need bodies in the room. There is way too much work for one person. We had six partners, and there were times when there was *still* too much work to do.

Ask yourself: do you love all aspects of running a company equally? Do you love finance just as much as creative? Do you love selling? Why not bring someone on who truly *loves* the parts you are less than thrilled about?

You could, of course, hire people to do the work and not make them partners. And for some of these roles, this will indeed be the case. But let me introduce another benefit of partners: they are working for equity, in full or in part, and not just salary. You don't necessarily have to pay them, or pay them as much, as you do someone who is just working for the cash. This can be hugely productive. It could be argued that that factor alone was one of the things that made The Barbarian Group an early success: we had so much low-cost manpower in the forms of dedicated, intelligent, hardworking partners.

PARTNERSHIP MECHANICS

You may hear the term "cofounder." This isn't a legal construct, but rather a more descriptive title, reflecting that not only does this person have equity in the company but they were there at the beginning. We will use partner and founder interchangeably in this book. Someone can be a "limited partner"— as in own a portion of your company—but not do anything day to day. We're not talking about that here. What we're talking about is an active, or "general," partner.

These individuals are distinct from outside shareholders or employees who may own small chunks of the company. They are your business partner, like your spouse is your life partner. Major decisions are made with your partners.

You can have more than one partner. The Barbarian Group started with six partners and rapidly took on a seventh.

THE NAME ON THE DOOR

In the old agency world, primary partners had their "names on the door." This still happens. Droga 5 is named for David Droga, yet there are also other partners. The trend in naming services companies, however, has moved away from naming them for people. The Barbarian Group had no one named Barbarian, and last I heard, there was no one named Spaceship at Big Spaceship, though it'd be awesome if Michael Lebowitz changed his name to Michael

Spaceship. Over time, names on the door evolve, or the agency becomes so recognized for its name that it keeps the name even after the founders are gone. Arnold Rosoff hasn't worked at Arnold for a long time, leaving well before the agency became a national player. George Batten, Bruce Fairchild Barton, Roy Durstine, and Alex Osborn haven't worked at BBDO for a long, long time either.

The name on the door can become an incredibly contentious thing. Not-withstanding the endless mockery the new breed of shops receives for its funny names (Strawberry Frog, Hard Candy Shell, Naked), there is a very practical upside to this: the name on the door will never become a bone of contention. People are delicate flowers of ego and neurosis, and the name on the door can matter to them. Hell, even the order of the names can be debated.

CHOOSING A PARTNER

Your partner should be as monstrously talented as possible. Someone who is wonderfully, sublimely good at their job—a real pleasure to watch work. They should be a team player. They're going to be around for a long time, and you're going to be working incredibly closely together for years, making all major decisions together. It's not a role for absolutes, and it's not a role in which you want someone who doesn't know how to compromise. You and your partner should be able to change your minds, and be able to handle debate and criticism.

An underrated additional characteristic of a partner is that they should be a good person. Much like your spouse, your partners will see you at your best and at your worst. You need people around you who are supportive and understanding. This is not a role for the vindictive, at least not in your company.

Paul Graham speaks of the virtues of finding cofounders from within your circle of friends and personal network. "Being friends with someone for even a couple days will tell you more than companies could ever learn in interviews."[1] I second this. All of my partners at TBG were people I knew before we got started, and it allowed us to go in with an increased level of confidence and understanding.

In the old days, people found their partners at their previous job, with most of history's famed agencies being breakaways from larger shops. BBH started from a bunch of people leaving Publicis. In 1933, when BBDO bought the Minneapolis agency Harrison Guthrie, two key executives, Ralph Campbell and Raymond Mithun, left to form their own agency and "took every account in the Minneapolis office with them except Hormel," says *AdAge*.[2] DDB was founded when Bill Bernbach, Ned Doyle, and 13 other employees from Grey left and formed an agency, merging with Maxwell Dane and his small agency, Maxwell Dane, Inc.[3] The list goes on.

There are benefits to this approach, and if done well, it can be remarkably effective. You've presumably been working closely on tight deadlines with your current potential partners. You may spy an opportunity that is potentially big for you, or big down the road, but too small for the large agency to notice or pursue at this time. A word of caution is in order. A poor breakaway from a larger agency can foster untold resentment, both with the parent agency and potential clients. Stealing clients from the parent agency is even more fraught with peril. These days the most effective breakaways happen with the consent of the parent agency. This was the case with The Barbarian Group.

The act of agency founders breaking away from a traditional agency is becoming less common. More and more, I talk to would-be founders who were user experience designers, product managers, web designers, animators, and the like. They have come from tech or the freelance world, not agencies. It's a sign of the changing times, as the Internet continues its inexorable course toward the complete disruption of past marketing practices. The challenge here is that you'll want to get someone with some sense of the marketing business side. You may not have a ton of these people in your personal network. So look for people who have worked at small but successful shops.

Good partners can change your life. They can mean the difference between a mediocre shop and a great one. They can be some of the best friends you ever had. They can be incredibly rewarding. I liked nothing better than to throw my arm around one of my partners and shout "partner!" It feels very '50s. It feels very business. And the joy of seeing someone truly talented do their job brings you daily moments of joy and admiration.

I've never known someone to kill it in this business without partners. For a few years, yes. But to get to the top of the heap? Nope.

16

THE TEAM

The small shop is all about flexibility. Everyone does multiple things. As services firms grow, the trend is toward increased specialization. If you are excited about the prospect of only being a graphic designer, for example, and look forward to the day that all of the other job functions have someone else in charge of them, then this will dictate what kind of team plan you develop (though I question why anyone who *only* wants to be a graphic designer started their own company. Know that you will never 100 percent succeed, given the entrepreneurial path you have set upon). If, however, you view yourself as more of a Renaissance person, then think about which areas of the company you'll need to keep a hand in, and which you will not.

The trick here is to look for parts of your job that can be peeled off and, with clear instruction, given to someone else. Parts of the job that do not feel like they are core to your being. Parts of the job that you'll feel some relief about when they are handed off, or, if you're a control freak, at least you won't feel like they are ripping off parts of your soul. Think long and hard about which ones to peel off. The decisions you make now, early on, are not easily undone. If, three years from now, you find yourself missing the selling game, and you have a team of four dedicated sellers by that point, it will not be without substantial pain and difficulty that you reinsert yourself into the selling apparatus.

People have to know where they stand. People have to know who reports to whom. Creating an org chart will provide clarity. It provides a career path. It helps clarify thinking about what works and doesn't work in the company. These charts don't rule the entire company, but it does need to exist, to provide a rough guide.

Think of it as a map—as you hire people, you should know what they are going to do, to whom they will report, and what tasks they may take off your plate. Sketch one out early on, and keep it updated.

WHAT KIND OF PEOPLE ARE YOU LOOKING FOR?

For all of the additional members of your team, you're going to need people of a certain ilk. Talented people who also happen not to be evil. Friends work well early on. Kindness and empathy matter. So do passion and dedication. In terms of their skill sets, you are looking for people who have a specialty at which they excel, but are also comfortable shouldering other burdens.

Is it better to hire department heads first, or ground troops first? You don't *have* to make someone the department head because they were the first person you hired, or the first person you found. Use your intuition, common sense, and their experience and talent as a guide. You could hire a head of tech first in tech, and just a lowly junior designer first in design. If you do so, don't make the junior designer "head of design," as some day you may want to actually hire a proper head of design.

There is also the question of whether to hire junior or senior people. Here, too, a good mix is the order of the day. Talented juniors are phenomenally powerful, wonderful, and useful. Let's not forget cheap. They may never have been given responsibility, and may bloom under the increased remit they have within your organization. They can be hard workers, and they haven't formed the poor habits that an aging company may have imposed upon them. Senior people, by contrast, bring deep experience with them and can guide you through myriad rookie mistakes. They may also bring clients. Some of them may require a larger salary, but I've found that many of the best senior people know a good opportunity when they see it, and will try and make things work. In the famous words of Google's former CEO, Eric Schmidt, "If you're offered a seat on a rocket ship, you don't ask what seat. You just get on."[1] Hire a good mix of talented juniors and one or two senior people. Shops that rely too heavily on one approach or the other tend to have increased growing pains.

THE MAKERS

The first team members you'll want to think about are the those that round out your core offering. To clarify: you may be a graphic designer who is starting a graphic design consultancy. This means that the one and only thing your shop is offering, as it gets started, is graphic design. Since you're a graphic designer, at the beginning you will have someone to do all the work—you. Over time, you may need more people to do the work, but at the get-go, you have someone to fulfill the role of the person who does the work. However, you may be a graphic designer who is starting a full service web design and development shop. In that case, you're obviously going to need people who can handle the other skills that you are offering: front-end development, back-end development, and perhaps a dedicated user experience or product person.

Whether they are partners or not, the same rules that apply to partners also apply to finding the first person who will be responsible for one of the core offerings of your company. Hiring them as employees rather than as a partner simply means that there is a slightly increased margin for error in your selection—it's easier to let an employee who isn't working out go, than a partner. You'd rather this not be the case, however. Therefore, the same hiring advice applies here as it does for partners. Look for someone with whom you can see yourself working for a very long time. Someone of monstrous talent, who isn't a monster.

THE REST OF THE TEAM

After you've got the people who can do the work, you're going to need people who can handle your business. In addition to your co-makers and the new business peeps, whom we've touched upon before, you will need

- a money person,
- a technology person,
- a time person,
- a client person.

You probably can't hire three more people right away. But over time, these are the roles that are going to need to be filled. In the interim, they need to be *assigned*. Early on, these roles can be doubled up. Maybe you or your graphic design partner are good at one or more of them. That's okay. Do them for now. But you're aiming your growth toward getting people to individually fill these roles as quickly as possible. Barring extreme cases, you want one of each of these people before you start doubling up.

A word of caution. There have been innumerable experiments over the past decade around combining two or more of these roles into one person permanently. When we started, we had no client service department—this was handled in the production department, with some help from the partners. Production, however, was not dedicated by client, but rather, logically enough, focused on project type. This worked well enough, early on. Yet over time, we found that when our clients had a new job to give us, they eventually had no idea whom to call to get it started. Lord knows how many jobs we missed out on before one of our clients happened to tell me in a bar one day, "I literally don't know how to even give you my work." That was an eye-opener.

Beware of the unintended consequences of these assignment decisions. Any nontraditional assignments you have in-house may not be readily apparent to your clients, and you can't expect them to conform to your processes. If you find your clients are resisting your team structure, it may be time for a rethink.

WHEN TO HIRE WHOM

The most important people to hire first are the other builders—the other makers. The people on your team who will make up your core offering. If you're a full service web shop, this may mean, for example, one engineer, one designer, and one user experience designer. Consider making the most important of these people partners.

After this, the next hire is the person who's good with money, as they will help you accelerate your growth and, hence, the additions of the rest of the team. Following that, if you don't have one yet, bring on someone who is good with tech, and then someone who's good with time, and, finally, someone who's good with client service and new business.

A MONEY PERSON

The nitty-gritty financial details matter. Part of me thought they were irrelevant on a high-growth company path—that revenue mattered above all else, growth was the important thing, and the details were irrelevant. It turns out this is untrue. The little things add up. A bunch of small, overlooked spending line items can add up to enough money to hire another person, who can fuel growth. Over time, this makes a huge difference. Yet it's hugely time consuming to pay attention to these little things, while carving out room to do your "actual" job. It may not play to your strong suit. Someone will be need to be negotiating every single deal, paying attention to cash flow, paying attention to collections, paying attention to how much you're spending on soda. If you're not careful, you can end up spending a ton on soda. Twenty-six dollars-a-square-foot rent is very different from $28-a-square-foot rent. Three months' free rent is way, way better than two. A seemingly minuscule difference in interest rates on your line of credit can make a massive difference.

Cash flow can literally make or break your business. Collections. Planning when the checks come. Relentlessly calling clients to make sure the checks will come on time. Knowing when bills are due. Paying your vendors on time, which allows you to maintain good relations with your favorite and best vendors. There is nothing more humiliating and miserable than the freelancer you desperately want and need telling you he won't work for you because you still owe her $3,000 from that last job three months ago. This part of the business requires constant, constant attention.

Some business owners love this micro-management of funds, keeping track of what goes where. Some do not. Over time, you may learn that you have a keen head for business and love it more than actually doing the skill you started the company offering. A good approach, if you're into the idea of getting better at business, is for you to take it on, and hire a part time accountant. Over time, make that accountant full time, and then slowly grow them, along with your business, into a CFO.

A TECH PERSON

Depending on the sort of firm you are starting, this may or may not be obvious. Regardless of the exact type of shop you're running, having someone who has a deep, passionate, profound, and up-to-date knowledge of technology is vital.

I do not necessarily mean someone who "knows how to code." A technical person will have a profound understanding of the trends of technology in our lives and in our work. This is vital no matter what type of company you are starting. Technology is one of the profound drivers of change in our times, especially in the communication industries.

More to the point, as more and more of our clients' industries will be disrupted by technology in the future, and regardless of the exact role we play, we will need to be aware of and conversant in these trends. The tech revolution is the context in which we all live, and your company needs to be comfortable with it. The act of hiring a design shop without technical chops, for example, will stratify into the ultra low-budget, mom and pop commodity shops, and the ultra high-end, five best designers in the world. Everyone else in the middle—where we will almost certainly play—will need technical chops. Do you have one of those friends who has a great idea, and within a day or two has a beautifully designed website up and running? You ask her, "How did you get that done so fast?" And she starts talking about Squarespace or Tumblr or some other tech or website you know nothing about. And to you it seems like magic that she got it done so quickly, so effortlessly, so beautifully. Find someone like that. *At the minimum.*

A TIME MANAGEMENT PERSON

Time is money. Every day you are late is a day you have wasted, a day you are no longer getting paid. It's a day that could have been available for another client or another internal project. How many people are on your team? How much are you paying them? Calculate their costs for just one day. Now, take that amount out of your bank account. Burn it. That's what being late is.

Your money person can control other expenses, but he can't control project timing—which is your single largest expense. In an organization of ten people, the ability to keep your deadlines can easily add a million dollars to your bottom line for the year. The other day, I took a walk with the owner of a small design firm. I asked him his number of employees (fewer than ten) and revenues. He told me. The number was nearly $800,000 a year higher than most shops his size. I already knew that his shop was a supremely prompt one. I also knew his billings, costs, and rates. There was only one explanation for that excess revenue: rock-solid schedule management. The dude could buy two Ferraris a year, crash them, and still be more profitable than his competitors.

The only way to be prompt is to be organized. The challenge of this increases exponentially as your team size grows and the number of projects grows. These organizational challenges very rapidly surpass the resources of a part-time manager. Almost from the get-go, you are going to need someone to be responsible solely for this.

This person has various names. Project manager. Producer. Project lead. Product manager, often, in tech firms. I was the project manager at first, and then I handled these organizational duties with a team of young interns. Eventually, we hired one of the interns for the job, whom we then trained over the next ten years.

Your producer can be young and doesn't need a ton of past experience. Estimating the specific time needed for a job is the one tricky part of the job, and experience matters there. You can help them with that in the beginning, since you know how long your work takes. The rest of the job requires organization and persuasion, not experience. If you're a shop that has a more complex offering, lots of custom work, intense, large-scale web development work, or things are done differently on each project, then maybe you're going to need someone who's got more experience, but otherwise, this isn't too necessary. Look for someone eager and cheap, who displays the qualities of assertiveness, perkiness, and organization, with, perhaps, a dry sense of humor.

A CLIENT PERSON

Your first aim in your client relationships is to do great enough work, at a reasonable enough price, that you have built up a well of goodwill between you and your clients. The goal is a default relationship in which they like you.

In doing this, you are essentially building up a karma bank—a store of goodwill that you can borrow against when you need to be a bit of a hard ass to your client. They've loved you enough in the past that your relationship can withstand a hit now and again when you need to put your foot down. A good shop will be building up a karmic savings from the get-go.

Yet inevitably all karmic bank accounts trend toward depletion—either because the clients begin to take you for granted, or you take them for granted. You may not even see it coming.

This is why we have client service. Client service is an insurance policy against karmic bankruptcy by putting in place a team and processes that ensure the organization as a whole mitigates and minimizes any individual's antipathy toward the clients, and vice versa. They are the Allstate against clients throwing up their hands and saying "screw this, I don't need your prima donna attitude anymore, you've gotten old and there are a million stunningly talented kids out there dying for this business." Because, though you may have forgotten, there are. It's also an insurance policy against your client giving in to temptation and thinking, "I can get better work from someone else," even if it's not true.

Happy clients are vital, and client service is the institutionalized, consistent development of happy clients. They are also, over time, a powerful profit center.

It's understandable that you might doubt the need for client service in the early days. It is tempting to say that the client's needs can be attended to by someone you already have hanging around on the payroll. And indeed, as we've said before, this is possible, for a time. But ultimately, the conflict within an individual who must to attend to the needs of two masters slowly becomes untenable. Eventually, the client will need its own representation on the team.

Once an agreement has been made for you to undertake a project—a journey—with a client and the mutual terms have been agreed upon, there should be no reason for someone to "take sides." It can seem reasonable to view the presence of a client service representative as lopsided. Why is there a client service representative when there is no *company* representative? Because *within your company, the company's viewpoint is pervasively, institutionally dominant.* The existence of one client service rep on the team does not create an imbalance toward the client; rather, it goes a small way toward righting the existential balance toward your company. In order to protect your company from becoming an organization that, at its core, takes its clients for granted, this small nod toward balance can help mightily.

The existential need to protect your company from getting too insular is a de facto reason for the necessary existence of client service. It is an important reason to split client service off from production: so the conflict is between two people who speak out loudly, and not in one person's head. When the client service exec and the producer are one and the same, it's often the case that the dilemma at hand isn't even spoken out loud. Yet it still exists. If there's a tension between the needs of the client and the needs of the company, it's vastly better if those words are spoken out loud for all to hear, so that a decision may be arrived at out in the open.

Speak to the value of your client service team to the rest of your company. Many people make the mistake of instituting client service within their company, then going completely hands off with the whole regime, so as to maintain their esprit de corps with the rest of the organization, and to keep their own creative judgment from getting clouded by business considerations. It's important that management explains to everyone why you have client service, and represents them as a valued part of the team.

Make it clear that client service doesn't run the show. They speak to the needs of the client, but they are not the law. Encourage all parties on a team to reach consensus on their own. But if they can't, don't let either party "win" (a word to be discouraged) all the time. Implement a process by which there is some sort of "tiebreaker" to whom all parties will need to appeal (often this is you).

Consider the incentive structure of the account department. The account department can become a powerful revenue center—after all, your current clients are one of the best sources, if not *the* best, for new business. You want to implement a system in which the talented account exec is rewarded and compensated appropriately, but is not incentivized to make inappropriate sacrifices. This means that account people should not be rewarded with sales commissions. Develop a bucket of metrics that aligns their goals to the organization at large—perhaps not just revenue but also margins, adherence to timelines, creative merit and, if you're feeling totally crazy, ultimate efficacy of the project with the end consumer. Then, after that, reward effective account people like there's no tomorrow, promote early and often. Get the best ones to the top as quickly as possible.

Account service is a skill learned on the job. Unlike many other disciplines, there aren't really schools for it. Look for MBA students who are interested in marketing, and not banking. Also look to advertising graduate programs, such as the Virginia Commonwealth University's (VCU's) Brandcenter Creative Brand Management or Strategy tracks. But, really, the most successful account people have learned on the job. And if you are so lucky to have a prodigy in your ranks, who has picked up the skills quickly, it is vital you give them the additional responsibility and reward that they crave, or they'll go somewhere that will.

17

EMPLOYEE RETENTION

In terms of human resource matters, we can broadly break things down into two categories: employee retention and employee departures.

HR VERSUS RECRUITING

In tech, HR is often equated with "recruiting." I have seen many tech companies hire people in HR whose only job is to recruit. This is a mistake.

Depending on your specific discipline, recruiting may be a breeze or a pain. The odds are, in the early days you will do most of it yourself. Hiring a recruiting firm or a dedicated internal recruiter probably won't make sense until you're around 100 employees or more. Leverage your personal network, your clients, and your employees in the early days. Set up an incentive system, rewarding the employees for referrals that lead to a hire.

But above all, don't confuse your recruiting efforts with your HR efforts. As your company grows, a real, dedicated HR capacity will become vital. The tipping point is between 20 and 30 people. Once you have some employees, especially if they are performing well, it's easy to "set and forget" them. That is, it's easy to focus on the problems in your company and not pay as much attention to the things that are going well. When the thing that is going well is a machine or a process, this can work. When the thing that is going well is a human, however, over time, "set and forget" can lead to problems.

It took us a long time to figure this out. We were good about giving raises and praise. But beyond that, in many ways, I see now, we took our good employees for granted. What I eventually came to learn is that if we are trying to make employees feel invested in the future of the company, we need to invest in our employees.

BE THE GROWN-UP IN THE COMPANY

You own a company now. This means that you are far, far more incentivized than you ever were at a previous job. You know this. This is what drives you.

This is why you own your own company. While your company may be great, the incentives you feel are far, far more weighty than those of people around you. They are, almost by definition, not as vested in the fortunes of the company as you are. It may hurt to hear this, but to some of your employees, even some of your best employees, *this is just a job.*

Secondly, you are now privy to the thoughts, lives, activities, ailments, and foibles of every person in the company. Unless you're starting your company and you have a background in HR, this was probably not the case at your previous company. Some people have real problems. I had one employee—a great employee—whose child was born with an incredibly rare condition that was severely life threatening. *Of course* we made ample exception of the rules for her. Sometimes life's problems pile up. Sometimes an employee had a hangover, yes, but then the next week their mother died. The two may or may not have been related. But this person can still be a good employee. You don't need to make an example of them.

Some of your employees will ask for things that seem ridiculous. They may not even know they are ridiculous. This may literally be their first job ever. As tempting as it may be, it's important not to treat them like children. Your job is to assist, guide, nurture, and help them grow.

Police the outliers. If you have a lax work-from-home policy, and 95 percent of the employees do not abuse it, let them be. Do not let the 5 percent ruin it for everyone.

REVIEWS

Employee feedback is invaluable. They are a vital source of information and ideas on the welfare of your company. It's true that at any time, employees can come and tell us, as managers, what they think. Whenever I talk to managers about employee feedback, this is often their approach—they are passively open. But there's a big difference between being able to speak up and someone asking you what you think, and caring about the answer.

THE BASICS OF A REVIEW PROCESS

I see this dynamic failing all the time in my consulting: employees are massively disgruntled and have no one to talk to about it. I do what I can and strongly encourage them to take their concerns to their managers. But every time, I am forced to concede that, yes, that boss should be talking to them regularly, asking them how they are doing.

Regular reviews are not just worthwhile but also absolutely necessary. At the very least, set up a process in which you talk to every employee every six months. It takes about six months for someone to quietly realize they are unhappy in their job, decide that leaving is the best course of action, and begin looking for another job. If you check in every six months, you can usually catch them before they act.

Set aside an hour. You'll often use less time (but you'll just as often use it all up, and there's nothing worse than abandoning an employee for another meeting when things get intense).

It would be lovely if every employee came up to you and said, "I am unhappy and thinking about leaving." Many do. But not all. Not even most, I'd wager. The reasons are mixed. Some view the fact that you haven't come and asked them how things are going as evidence that their unhappiness is justified. Some are not even aware of the possibility. Some just don't think it's their place.

Whatever the reason, know this: it is much, much easier and cheaper to retain an employee before they have begun looking for another job.

Sometimes the employee will just sit there. Sometimes they'll be not a big talker, and be happy as a clam. Some of them will wonder why you're having this one-on-one at all. Don't sweat it. Just say it's important for the company to make sure they're happy, ask how they're doing, ask if there's anything that can make things better. Even though they didn't necessarily say anything, or even understand why this is happening, the process is still doing its job. If that person later becomes disgruntled, they will know they work somewhere where they can talk about it, and that fact alone will go an incredibly long way toward their not running off and seeking a new job without consulting you.

If you do nothing else, set up a system in which this happens.

A MORE ADVANCED REVIEW PROCESSS

As your company grows, which means that you cannot be in on every review, a more robust process will need to be implemented. Establish two review types—the informal check-in, described above, and the formal review, where raises and instructions are given. Map it to the actual job description. Rate the employees on each factor of their job description. Not only does this ensure that the employee understands the specifics of their job, it allows both parties to redefine the role if it has changed significantly.

There are four components here: the superior's review of the employee, the self review, a peer review of the employee, and the employee's review of management. All are important. Until you're over about 60–70 people, you or another partner should do this yourself or be present. Don't pass it off until you absolutely have to. Once you do pass it off, insist on something written from all the parties and read every single review. Look for differences between the peer review and the manager review of the employee—this is a good way to spot an underperforming manager. A well-designed review will offer insights about you and your company, and it can be profoundly useful.

Make it a point to tell employees they can't *expect* a raise or a promotion at a review. These are earned by achieving excellent marks against the actual work in the job.

There exists an eternal debate in business America about whether you should do all the reviews in the company at once, or do them scattered throughout the year. I do them scattered throughout the year. The downside to this is that as you grow, you'll find yourself doing a review every week, and eventually more, which can take a lot of time if you do it right. Pass off the formal reviews before you pass off the informal check-ins. Hang on to those as long as you possibly can. Besides, it's nice to go grab lunch and check in with employees.

RAISES

Broadly speaking, here is the economic arc of your company. In the early years, people will leave higher-paying jobs to jump ship to your company for greater responsibility and, sometimes, a greater title. Over time, your company will slowly evolve from the underdog into one of the big guys. If you have kept your cool image in the marketplace and your employees are working on rewarding projects, you can keep salaries lower. If you haven't, the salaries are going to have to rise.

For early, great employees, as the company can afford it, you will probably have to make a series of repeated large raises for a few years until you get their salary near something approaching market rate. In the early years, our raises averaged 18 percent a year.

Then the raises will slow down.

As you grow and hire people at salaries closer to market norms, your raises for those people will be smaller.

Over time, once you've normalized to a sustainable rate and no one is grumbling about being underpaid, you can set expectations for raises in the 3 percent to 5 percent annual range. No guarantees.

Sometimes, someone will be about to leave, and you'll need to offer a large raise to keep them. Sometimes, a person will come in and demand a larger raise to stay. This is annoying, but it will happen. Take a judicious approach. I was okay giving big raises if someone was important and not too threatening. I would even, occasionally, submit to the pressure of someone about to leave, if I felt it was important and necessary. Sometimes, however, I would simply say, "No can do. You will be missed." Basically use your best judgment.

TITLES

Titles shouldn't matter. Titles are just window dressing. No one who's truly good should care about their title. Titles are just frippery. Employees would be a lot happier if they didn't have to worry about them. Let's just give everyone the same title!

This line of thinking is tempting, but misguided. The act of downplaying or even completely negating job titles within your company sounds like a kind and egalitarian act. But in reality, the only person who truly doesn't care about job titles in the company is you. Because you have the best job title in the company.

Telling the story of their company on their wonderful home page, the partners of digital services firm Teehan and Lax recall going through the same wringer:

> Internally, we were a mess. We had prided ourselves on having no titles....This worked great for the first chapter of our company. People who joined, couldn't care less about titles, they just wanted to do good work. But by the time we had grown to 35 people, this structure was just too loose. Employees didn't understand how their career advanced.[1]

WHY TITLES?

There are two main reasons titles are important: employees value them, as seen in the anecdote from Teehan and Lax. You plan on staying at this company forever, but your employees may not. This is okay. Your goal is to keep them through the company's having a great culture, but some will eventually want to leave. You still need them now, and to retain them now, they may need a title they can be proud of.

It's easy to become dispirited about your employees' title ambitions. But people care about titles for a host of valid reasons. Maybe they want to impress their parents, their spouse, or their high school buddies. Do any of these motivations mean they aren't a team player, a good culture fit, or talented? I don't see the correlation. There's no correlation between talent/culture fit and concern over titles. That is, just because a great person cares about a title does not make them "un-great."

Secondly, as the organization grows, people need to know who does what. This is easy and obvious early on, but as the company expands, it becomes more difficult. Newcomers coming into a 50-person company, or even a 30-person company, where everyone's title is "ninja" and "guru" is massively confusing and a waste of time. Remember, your org chart (guide map) is populated with both job functions and titles.

TITLES = SALARY WITHOUT MONEY

Early on, sloppy titles might be a *good* thing. Early on, your company doesn't have a lot of money, and a larger title is a tried-and-true way for a small and scrappy company to lure someone away from a larger competitor. We made much use of this in early Barbarian years, and I wouldn't have given up that arrow in my quiver for anything in the world.

What I realized at the time was that *a larger title is equal to a larger salary,* except it's free. When money's tight, this insight is immensely powerful. Employees like to see career progress, and an improved title, along with commensurately more responsibility, is one of the single most popular motivations for employees to leave their cushy, well-paid jobs at large companies. You will, of course, have to fix all of this later in the company's life (and it will not be easy), but in those early years, when every penny matters, and the addition of VP to a title can make or break the snagging of a key employee, just go for it.

LEAVE ROOM AT THE TOP

I would caution using C-level titles for anyone but partners in the early years. Simply put, you need to leave room at the top. There are some great people whom your company will truly want, but whom you won't be able to get early on. But as your company grows, as your ability to pay more improves, as your client base improves, and as your reputation spreads, they may eventually realize that your company is a rocket ship they want to ride on. This is a good thing. Thus there will come a day when you need to hire someone *above* the recently hired VP-level employee. And if you've already filled up your C-level titles, this can be an exercise in absurdity and misery (why is my title the same as this kid I am managing?). Far easier never actually to use C-level titles at the beginning.

FUNNY TITLES

I hate funny titles. I am convinced it took Mark Zuckerberg years to live down his first business card, which said, "I'm CEO, bitch." I loathe titles with the word Ninja, Sensei, Guru, Rock Star, and so on. "Dude" is probably the worst. Being a creative guy, I get it. Yes, they're funny. They can be a good time. In extreme cases, such as a Zen-like great employee who does one specific thing that is not client facing, and who wants nothing more than to do that one thing the rest of their life, such titles might even be useful. Other than that, avoid them. They'll make no sense to clients. They'll look ridiculous on an employee's résumé, and the employee may come to resent it. Wacky titles have a tendency to get more and more extreme and ridiculous over time.

TITLE NORMALIZATION

Once a company reaches a size where titles are also representative of the organization, you will need to go through the somewhat harrowing process of "title normalization"—retroactively reassigning job titles to be logical and coherent within the company, and giving everyone a promotions path.

What, then, does the process look like? At TBG, we developed *title tracks* for each department. It might go something like this: associate producer -> producer -> senior producer -> associate director of production -> director of production -> senior director of production. We also kept the same paradigm (associate, normal, senior, director, senior director) in each department, as best we could, to allow easy cross-departmental comparisons. We then wrote job descriptions for each of these roles, and what would qualify someone for getting to the next role. Next we developed salary ranges for each job.

We then assigned each employee to their appropriate role. For many of them, this was not a problem—it mainly meant adding "senior" or "director" to the title, since our titles tended to be non-level based in those days. But for the ones that might appear to be a demotion, we talked to the employee, explained our rationale, and made clear how they could obtain the next title.

It could be awkward, but because we took the time to talk to everyone, there were no major problems. In one or two extreme cases, we let a person keep their more-senior title, but explained to them they needed to grow into it, laid out the steps how to do so, and informed them it would be a while before they saw another promotion.

Was it fun? No. Was it worth it? 100 percent. Almost immediately after the dust settled, we noticed a marked turn in many of our employees, who now understood what they were working toward, not just in the company, but in their own career.

PROMOTIONS

Let's talk about the "Peter Principle." The term comes from Lawrence J. Peter, and his unsung cowriter, Raymond Hull, in their 1969 book, *The Peter Principle: Why Things Always Go Wrong*, which is sort of a Far Side/Dilbert-esque book on business and life. Colloquially put, the Peter Principle states that "employees tend to rise to their level of incompetence." Basically, employees are promoted, so long as they know how to do their job and do it well. A well-designed promotions process protects against these pitfalls. It's more than just a title. It's important that any promotions process guards against the forces of encroaching mediocrity in your organization. Goals, accomplishments, skills, and qualifications must be laid out in advance for a promotion. Promotions should not be given willy-nilly. They're not guaranteed; rather, they are earned. Lay out a system for what that means in each department and let your employees know this, all the time. Getting a promotion isn't about their doing their current job well. You expect that. That's why you hired them. It's about being qualified to take on more responsibility.

In our system, if an employee didn't achieve a promotion at their review, clear guidelines and goals were laid out for the next review cycle. If these goals weren't met in the next review cycle, we would first try and guide problematic employees toward an exit, rather than firing them. In extreme cases, however, we would have to let them go before other people quit around them and it harmed the organization permanently.

TRAINING

As your company grows, training your employees will become more and more of a concern for you. At first, this need may well not be obvious. The type of people you hire into your company at first will probably be highly talented in their skill sets, young, eager, and very technically capable. "Training programs are for the oldz," you might think. "My gang knows what is going on." This is probably true, at first.

Over time, however, this will change. Suddenly you find yourself hiring someone who doesn't know how to use GitHub, and you'll be annoyed. "WTF?" you may think. "We are the new school of marketing. We aren't a bunch of oldz who don't know how to use a computer."

So what's going on?

The advertising and marketing industries have gone through radical transformations in the past decade, with more to come. Much of this has been driven by technology. As your company grows, you will come to understand that there are areas in which you'll need increased expertise. You may also find yourself winning clients who have high client service requirements. They may have hired you for your creative chops and innovation, but quite liked the level of client service they had from their old agency, and if it's not too much bother, would you consider hiring Jane? We really loved her. These people are going to be painful to introduce into the company. They may not know what you and the rest of your team know, but they have a purpose. The best approach here is to explain to those people that it's perfectly okay that they never got around to learning these things, *but it is time for this to change.* Get them trained.

CHANGE IS CONSTANT

Different job roles have different levels of minimum technical proficiency. These levels are changing, and are going to very much change some more. Good people, talented people, have worked at companies that haven't necessarily understood this. Here is a concrete example. I believe that over time the account/client service people in services firms will need to be able to understand agile development and be an active stakeholder. This means they'll need to learn things like Pivotal Tracker, Sprintly, GitHub, or Trello. Is this going to happen any time soon? No. Am I bitter when I hire a stupidly talented account exec who doesn't know these things yet? No. I make them learn them.

Things will change tomorrow. Things will change next month. The number of things that have changed in digital and marketing since even the beginning of the 21st century has been staggering. We have to keep up.

As you get older, your industry is going to change around you and your employees. It isn't quite a full-time job to stay abreast of this, but it sure can feel that way. New innovations will come along. You may have built the foundation of your company on a rock-solid, world-class iOS development shop. This work may go away. You may be a great social media agency. Social may coalesce back inside the client company. Who knows. In my time at The Barbarian Group, we went from doing Flash Minisites, to viral marketing with YouTube, to more robust platform sites, to social marketing via Twitter and Facebook, to app development, to content marketing and products. New trends emerged every 18 months. You and your employees will need to keep up, even if you are all insanely busy. Training helps.

So, then, what to do? In the old days, your company taught people, either with a robust in-house education system or by paying people to go to college, or both. Ogilvy is particularly well known in the industry for its long-term dedication to training. David Ogilvy himself was hugely proud of this, and the legacy exists to this day in the form of the Ogilvy Digital Marketing Academy.[2] But the fact is, Ogilvy's training prowess is not what it once was. Financial pressures from conglomeratization have gutted in-house training budgets around the world. Increased competition has piled on, making it very hard for companies, which all operate on razor-thin margins, in a competitive environment, to justify spending such money. Some companies—notably Google—still keep up training. Paying for outside training is also less of an option than it used to be. We are not in the same employment environment as we forty years ago. People don't stay at the same job their whole life. It's much harder to do this kind of formalized in-house training in today's work environment.

So, then, what to do?

It is vital that you institute a culture of personal learning. This should be a criterion for hiring. Beware anyone who does not express a desire to learn. Ask people how they like to learn. Ask them about something they recently learned. Self-training should be made part of the job description, and should be included in the reviews.

Recently, I was talking to a 24-year-old, highly intelligent grad student of marketing. I commented how it was interesting how few people in her class used Tumblr or Foursquare (including her). She proceeded to launch into a critique of the apps, and what she did and did not like about them. But she did this *as a consumer.*

To me, this is akin to a 50-year-old ad executive ranting about how much they don't like hip hop or Taylor Swift. *It doesn't matter what you think yourself.* You are here to understand, leverage, and predict cultural forces. You can only do this by experimenting with and experiencing them.

Beyond the hiring process, the company itself can learn from within. Weekly seminars on topics—any topics—that one employee teaches another are hugely beneficial and free. With the conclusion of each major project, the team should present the project to the rest of the team and talk about their experience from it.

In terms of apps and technologies, one or two people can lead this for the rest of the company. Some people should be formally or informally charged with keeping abreast of new apps and technologies, and writing up reports or teaching people about them. *Everyone in the company should be expected to be downloading and registering for new apps.* Your technology advocates can be the first, and then they can invite the rest of the company. Once you've grown large enough, a full-time or half-time technology investigator/evangelist can be hugely powerful. As you grow, more formalized programs can be developed by the HR department, which can bring in interesting speakers. Young people who are doing new, interesting things in design, technology, and so on are more than happy to come talk to some cool shop about what's going on. A wiki, or some learning center, should absolutely be made for the company on its internal intranet. Tape everything. Put it online. Have someone take notes. Put those online too.

There are also great free or cheat courses on the Web or available through sites like the Apple Store. Thinkful, Skillshare, and so forth are hugely valuable here. This environment is hugely in flux right now. There are radical changes in how people learn afoot here in the early 21st century, and these can be very powerful for your company.

A basic list of requirements for each role should be made, with links to the appropriate courses. For example, an account executive should be required to learn Pivotal Tracker, Google Apps, email, instant messaging (IM), Keynote, and whatever spreadsheet app you're using. Links should be provided to courses for each one. A planner may be required to be on every social network ever. They may be required to know Keynote, a spreadsheet, Google apps, Pivotal Tracker, and IM. You might even require them to know some coding basics.

In addition to in-house programs, there do exist five or six organizations whose explicit mandate is to educate people in advertising about the latest trends in technology. I would specifically point out to you the VCU Brand-center, HyperIsland, Boulder Digital Works, and the Miami Ad School. All are very good.

It's important to think of creativity as something that can be learned and trained. As your company grows, you should pursue this more and more.

18

EMPLOYEE DEPARTURES

Now let's turn to the sadder side of HR—employee departures.

DEPARTURES

As sad as it is to admit, there will be a time when good employees decide to leave your company. This is going to be inevitable. And it will hurt.

THE EASY ONES

Of course, there will be the times it doesn't hurt. You may have secretly been hoping for a while that one particular employee would leave the company. There have been times I've been so happy, so pleasantly surprised that someone was announcing their departure, that it was difficult to contain my enthusiasm.

There will also, of course, be the person who comes in with the fake threat of departure, but who is secretly angling for a raise or a promotion. These people have overplayed their hand, and it's good of you to illustrate this to them, but illustrate it kindly. Don't be too tough on them. It's actually quite difficult in this world to have a fair and balanced, and accurate sense of self-worth and value to a company. "Yeah, we can't do that promotion right now. We will be sad to see you leave. Thank you so much." Show them the door. These are the easy ones.

The tough ones are when it is someone you love. A great employee. Someone you see as valuable to the team.

GET TO THE CAUSE

The most important thing in these situations is to get to the root cause of *why* the employee is leaving, because if this is a good employee, you may want to do something about her departure. And the first step in that is finding out whether anything can be done.

Indeed, sometimes there isn't. They may be switching careers entirely—I had one employee (two, actually) who wanted to become a landscape designer. They may be moving to Timbuktu. They may have just married a billionaire. People leave for all sorts of reasons. Some of them don't have to do with you.

Yet some of them do. They may not be getting along with another employee. They may be fed up with the work they are doing. They may feel underpaid or underappreciated. They may not like the direction the company is going.

Whatever the reason, get to the bottom of it. Let them talk. Don't be defensive. Listen. Get them talking. Often an employee, when faced with a difficult work environment, will feel like they've already attempted multiple times to remedy the situation, and now the quitting is just a formality. If they are clammed up, beg them to talk to you. Tell them it's important that you learn from this, tell them that even if you can't make things right for them, you want to work toward fixing these problems in the future. If you know definitely that you want the departing employee to stay ask them outright: "Is there anything that will make you stay?" Get a firm idea. This is vital, as later on, when you present your package (if you do), you don't want this to turn into a negotiation.

Don't act just yet. Once you've gotten to the bottom of the reason, and know whether there are any specific acts on your part that would convince them to stay, thank them for their candor and ask them if you can talk tomorrow. Don't take any rash actions here—especially if you have partners. Tell them you want to think about all of this and that you'd love to get closure by talking again tomorrow. There are, of course, individual cases in which bold, immediate action is necessary, but these should be the exception.

RETENTION ATTEMPTS

Your most pressing decision is whether or not to attempt to retain this person. First and foremost, know that no case is a completely lost case. I have retained some employees who, on first blush, seemed like impossibly lost cases. Don't give up hope.

Next, though this is probably not the time to rub it in, this needs to be said. *The hardest time to retain an employee is when they are walking out the door.* Unless this employee got cancer or married a billionaire, honestly, you never should have gotten yourself into this situation. You should have been talking to the employee regularly. You should have caught this in advance.

I realize it is painful to hear this at this particular time. But if this is a preventable departure, it is vital that you learn from it and don't let it happen again.

You should have some sense of what it would take to retain this employee after your conversation with her, so you should now be able to weigh the benefits of keeping the employee against the costs. If the cost is a simple raise or promotion, and this person is a good employee, I'm usually happy to do it. But, again: if I got myself into a situation where a simple raise or promotion is all it takes to retain a good employee, and I'm learning it as they are walking out the door, I have probably done something wrong. These are the clear-cut cases, and they are the easy ones..

The fuzzier cases are where the employee is *pretty* good, but what they're asking for is excessive—a raise that they do not really deserve, yet. You're going to have to make a call here. The hardest situations are when an employee is very good, but the problems they identify are dead on and ridiculously hard to fix. "Yes, I love you, but until you fix these major fundamental flaws in the company, I can't see working here." You may even agree with them. But it might take months to fix the problems. Some of them will never be fixed. A frank conversation here is often needed. If things are fixable, but not for six months, ask the employee to give you six months to make it right. Put it in the calendar. If it's something that cannot be fixed, look for workarounds, things that can alleviate the employee's pain. Or, put it in perspective. Every company has problems. Does the employee know for sure their next place of employment is less messed up?

Whatever course you decide, meet with the employee again the next day and present your package for retention. They may or may not take it. There shouldn't be too much back and forth if you got something concrete out of them in your last talk. If it's fuzzier, some negotiation is in order. Get it worked out in this meeting, and don't linger. They can take a day to think about it, but do everything you can to avoid turning this into an endless cycle of back and forth negotiations.

If, in the end, it doesn't work, tell them, "Well, I am sad we couldn't make that work, but I do hope our offer and our attempts to keep you show how much we care about you and will miss you."

Conversely, if you have decided not to retain them, tell them that you can't make anything work, but you are grateful for their feedback and it means a lot to you, and you hope they find some comfort in the fact that you will now work to fix these problems. Tell them they have made things somewhat better for everyone else.

These negotiations and the outcome should be kept confidential, and the act of doing so should be a condition of the deal. If one good disgruntled employee is ready to leave, others may well be thinking about it. If they see that walking into that room and quitting is the only way to get things done in the company, they may resort to it. Once you're in this cycle, things are doomed. If this cycle of lots of employees quitting starts in your company, institute a new review process immediately, and start it by meeting everyone *right now.* It's still gonna be hell to get out of this, but that's the only way to even start.

It can be painful when a good employee departs. They may feel like family to you. You may care about them deeply. You almost certainly rely on them in some capacity. You might consider them a friend. The rejection can feel profound. This is not often discussed, but it's absolutely worth mentioning. In the same way it's bad for a worker to burn their bridges when leaving an employer, so too is it bad for the employer to do so when a worker leaves.

LAYOFFS

Regardless of how well you've been managing your company, there may well come a time that you will need to lay some people off. Here's the thing. Growing your freelance business into a real business, with a goal of actually making it worth a substantial amount of money, is an exercise in rapid growth. It puts growth at the front. I'm not shy in advocating rapid growth as your primary goal with your company (while maintaining quality, of course. Style points matter. We've driven this home by now, I hope).

When everything works well, this strategy works well. When things go south, though, so too does this strategy. What does "going south" mean? It means two things: either there has been a massive, structural change in the economy, or there has been a massive change in your company's prospects and its ability to sell in the marketplace.

The first of these situations is pretty much beyond your control. In 2008, the entire economy imploded, and everything changed. It's entirely conceivable we'll have a major economic meltdown in the next ten years and then another ten after that. You can survive a major economic meltdown if you move quickly. And moving quickly entails layoffs.

The second scenario is bleaker. If your work is good, you've been maintaining consistent quality, and you've been following my advice on PR and marketing and new business—if all is going well—you should be a fairly hot property with your clients, who really want to work with you. But there are times, however, when the zeitgeist changes and suddenly you find the unsolicited RFP well drying up, or a major client leaving you. Regardless of why this happens, the most important thing is to act quickly. Figure out the root cause and act accordingly. Is it because you're too expensive? Is it because the technological trends have evolved and suddenly no one wants Flash minisites anymore, and they all want HTML 5 or viral videos or social or mobile? Is it because you turned over the new business process to a new employee who's not half as good as you are at pitches? The odds are you know what the problem is, and you will need to fix it rapidly. This may entail firings of problem employees. That is a separate issue. Layoffs are different. Layoffs are the collateral damage.

If you've caught the problem quickly and you can resolve it quickly, you may not need to lay anyone off. However, at a company that is a sinking ship, the solutions are long term, painful, and structural. If that's the case, you're going to need to buy some time. And buying time entails cutting costs. The same is true of a recession. You need to cut costs, batten down the hatches, and weather the storm. You need to save your money. And in both cases, your largest cost is employees.

LAYOFFS SUCK

Let's be clear. Layoffs suck. They are miserable for everyone involved. You may well lose some friends out of this. And the psychological impact of people losing their jobs is incalculable.

If you're at all a good person, your first instinct is going to be to try and avoid layoffs at all costs. This will most likely turn out to be a mistake. I nearly sank our company—thus putting way more people out of a job—by initially trying to get through the 2008 recession without any layoffs. It was one of my largest mistakes in running the company, and one that nearly cost us the entire company.

In hindsight, if we were going to end those jobs anyway and put those people through that pain, we should have done it earlier. We would have been able to offer them substantially more severance. In the end, we were able to cobble together two weeks of severance. This for some people who had been working for us for years. It was slap in the face. Six months earlier, wiser counsels were telling us we should consider layoffs. We ignored their advice.

HOW DEEP TO CUT

It's often the case that your first instincts are to cut as little as possible. This can be misguided, though, as it's often not enough. It is extraordinarily detrimental to go through several successive rounds of layoffs. You want to cut deeply enough that you have solid, profound confidence in the company's prospects for at least six months out, preferably a year. Numerically, 20 percent to 25 percent of total salary is probably where you need to be. The situation may get worse. How much would you need to cut then? Cut it now. You want to be able to get up in front of the company and tell people, when it's over, "This is over. You made it. We should be good now." The wording, of course, must be chosen carefully. "We do not plan to do another round." "So long as things don't get worse, we should be fine," or "We aimed to do this once and once only and get it over with." No promises.

WHOM TO LAY OFF

The choice of whom to lay off is sensitive one. There are some concrete numerical challenges—typically the most junior employees and the newest employees are the most easily cut. But typically they also don't cost you nearly as much money as more senior people, and thus more of them would need to be cut to make the same impact. When it's a decision between one $300k person and six $50k people, that $300k person starts to not look so sacred.

Many companies are unapologetic about cutting the worst performers in a round of layoffs. Some companies do this routinely. If you've been running your company well, you probably don't have *tons* of bad apples lying around. If you do, then they will go first. Yes, you're going to take job performance into account when you choose whom to lay off. But you should be explicitly laudatory toward everyone, both in the layoff process and afterwards. These were good employees. They should be honored and remembered. Yes, everyone will know a couple bad apples were let go in the process, but it should not be spoken of, and should be actively discounted in order to keep the reputations and spirits up of all the employees let go, bad *and* good.

Apple veteran and tech guru Guy Kawasaki advises to "whack Teddy." "Most executives have hired a friend, a friend of a friend, or a relative as a favor. When a layoff happens, employees will be looking to see what happens to Teddy. Did he survive the cut or did he go? Is it cronyism or competence that counts at the company? Make sure that Ted is dead."[1] This is invaluable advice.

If your company is comprised of over-50ish people, you may need to work with department heads to figure out who's getting cut. This may be necessary, but it is also insanely risky, as it will radically increase the chances word will leak. Do it quick, give the department heads one day to decide who to cut, and give them either head count targets or monetary targets.

HOW TO DO THE DEED

When the time comes, follow these steps. If you've spent any time with HR execs, you'll find they have a lot of rules and can seem paranoid about following these rules, even though many of them are not required by law. This is one time you should follow their instructions completely. People do sue. People do complain. The risks are real. They almost certainly will happen to you, eventually. Reduce your risk by protecting yourself legally. If you have an experienced HR exec who has done this before, you can do this without a lawyer. If you don't have one, consult with your lawyer before you do this the first time.

Many people advise performing the layoffs on a Friday, because the surviving employees have time to decompress and process. While this may be good for your current employees, for the laid-off employees, it's actually worse. Someone laid off on a Monday is more likely to dive right into job searching on a Tuesday. We owe them this.

Ben Horowitz advises not to delay. "Once you decide that you will have to lay people off, the time elapsed between making that decision and executing that decision should be as short as possible. If word leaks (which it will inevitably do if you delay), then you will be faced with an additional set of issues. Employees will question managers and ask whether or not a layoff is coming. If the managers don't know, they will look stupid. If the managers do know, they will either have to lie to their employees, contribute to the leak, or remain silent, which will create additional agitation."[2] If your salary is high, consider taking a cut yourself. If you have kept it low, let them know you don't make more than the rest of them. Seeing the leaders spill blood with the troops is only fair, and can be a massive motivator.

Do the lay offs all at once. As quickly as you can, in rapid succession. One by one. If you have multiple offices, make sure you do it at a time when all the offices are at work, and do them at the same time.

Do them in person. I'm sorry. This is a must. As companies grow, into the hundreds and thousands of people across multiple offices, this becomes much more logistically difficult. Too bad. The employees are owed this, and you should do it.

Don't perform the layoffs alone. Two people should be present for every layoff. This is vital. One of you can participate if extensive travel is required or you're doing this across multiple cities. Bring them into a closed room for a meeting. When starting the meeting, come right out and say it. The first words out of your mouth after the greeting should be something along the lines of "we're going to have to let you go." Let them know it's a layoff and not a firing. But don't prolong their agony with small talk. Don't lead them on. Don't say anything along the lines of "if things pick up, maybe we can get you back." Do not get into the *why me*. Don't bring it up, and if they bring it up, say it is not relevant. Again, yes, you may have thought about job performance—*along with myriad other factors*—in choosing which *batch* of employees to let go, but you should never, ever talk about why *this specific* employee is being let go. The company is in dire straits. Cuts are being made. If you're canning a whole department or job level, for example, you can talk about a group of employees being let go for strategic reasons, but *never the individual*.

Have some release documentation ready for the employee to sign. Work with HR and your lawyer to prepare this. The vast majority of employees will just sign it. One or two will not. Some will threaten to sue. Be ready with answers regarding applicable law, as prepared by your lawyer or HR exec. Someone—probably your HR exec or your lawyer—will need to work with them, talk to them, guide them toward the inevitable conclusion that they should just sign the damn paper. Eventually, most will. You will, occasionally, get sued, even if you've done everything right. Therefore, document everything. Doing this with two people will allow for a witness to dispute any claims of threats or lies about what you said.

Most people, however, will get through the process with as much dignity and grace as they can muster. Some will cry. Some will be relieved. Some will be mute. Some will be robotic. Some will be angry. You see every human emotion in this situation. Treat them all as professionally as possible. Tell them to gather their things and say you need them to leave the office quietly now and that you'll set aside a time to let them get their belongings privately, or you will ship them. Spare them the indignity of the walk out with the box. And when you're done, I recommend a shot of whiskey.

At this moment, do a few things. Give IT the all clear to turn off the email accounts of these employees, change their passwords, secure your IT infrastructure, and so forth. You can ask the laid-off employees in the meeting if they have a forwarding address they'd like their email to go to if you're that kind of company. More often, you can have their email forwarded to their superior or another manager or IT worker who can then forward personal emails.

Next, email everyone in the company saying that the layoffs are over. Call a company meeting for later that day. Then explain the situation as best you can. Why it happened, who got let go if you're small, or which departments/how many if you're large. Lay out where the company's going from here. Rally the troops. It won't be easy. But it needs to be done. Above all, take responsibility.

Be visible. Horowitz again: "Be visible. Don't leave this to hatchet men, or if you do, be walking the halls. The urge to stick your head in the sand will be massive. Fight it. Your employees need to see you right now."[3]

THE AFTERMATH

If you did all of this right, you will notice positive effects within two or three days, as soon as the shock wears off. The remaining employees should be energized, knowing they escaped alive and are wanted, and if your speech and plan to get the company out of its hole were sufficiently rousing (and *make sure they are sufficiently rousing*, for God's sake), they should be extra motivated.

It's also slightly uncouth to talk about this, but laying people off can have a massive detrimental effect on you, the management who has to do the deed. It is emotionally exhausting. Many of these people were your friends. The feeling of failure can be profound. Find someone to talk to.

After the first round of payroll without the severance, you'll notice massive positive effects as your bottom line expenses radically drop. This will be when you start to breathe easier.

FIRING

There will come a time when you need to fire someone. If this is your first firing, that time probably will come well before you know it.

Most management gurus these days advise to "fire quickly." This is not terrible advice. The costs of a bad employee are immense. The longer you delay, the longer your other employees resent you for it. And once they start leaving, in lieu of the bad apple, your company is severely, horribly damaged. The minute you go down the path of the bad employees' staying and the good employees' leaving, you are dead.

If someone's been performing well for a long time, and things have changed suddenly, find out why.

Employees who are suddenly underperforming may have something going on in their personal life. Don't discount this possibility, even if you don't know of anything specifically. People keep a lot of things to themselves. Sit them down, tell them their performance is becoming a problem, and ask explicitly if it's anything in their personal life. Get them the time or help they need. This is what decent people do for people who need help. There are, of course, personal situations where all may be lost: hard-core drug addiction, alcoholism. Be the company that tries to get them help. Over time, you may have to quietly let them go. But do what you can to help keep their insurance coverage for as long as possible. Basically, make sure you've done everything you can to help before you take the last, drastic step.

PROBATION

When people say, "Fire quickly," they are really saying, "Start the process quickly." Through the years, I've tried a million different permutations on waiting, not waiting, giving people another chance, putting people on probation—you name it. What I've learned is that *you never know*. I've given someone three kind, clear warnings to change one easy thing, and they've failed completely. I've gone through these motions with an employee who everyone thought was a lost cause, and they pulled it off, turning into a fantastic employee.

Never fire anyone without giving them a second and, generally, third chance. Not only do *you never know*, but there are legal issues as well. Today's modern HR environment is a legal minefield, and you don't want to fall into it. This advice is, I admit, controversial. I stand by it.

Sit the employee down, and tell them they are on probation. Explicitly tell them that they are in danger of being fired. Tell them this can be avoided by performing the following steps. Tell them you will check in in two to four weeks (or some appropriate time frame), but regardless of how that turns out, they will be on probation for a full six months. If that check-in goes well, you will map out other goals.

One of four will happen after this conversation.

First, the employee might wise up, know they're not up to the job, and quickly quit or find another job. This is always nice. Broadly speaking, I am a big fan of guiding people out the door of their own free will, provided it can be done quickly.

Next, the employee will slack, try and cheat, or laze their way through the goal, or half-ass it and pretend you're like a ref in an NFL game in which there's some higher authority like the instant replay ref or something. They'll come to the meeting and say they hit all the goals, when they didn't, and you'll say they didn't, and they'll say that's no fair, blah blah blah, you can't do this to me, blah blah, I did what you asked, blah blah. It's almost certainly the right call to fire them right on the spot. If you do choose to give them another round, make it clear that attitude is part of it, and it can't be faked.

Third, the employee will hopelessly come nowhere near reaching the goals, in which case you let them go.

Or, magically, fourth, the employee may actually shape up. Again, it does happen. God knows why. Could be any number of reasons. An honest misunderstanding about the job requirements. Who knows? But it happens.

DOING THE DEED

Compared to layoffs, firing is a breeze. It's only one person, there's a reason, and provided you've gone through the probation period above, it's probably not your fault. Still, it can hurt for you, and it can hurt even more, obviously, for the person being fired. It absolutely must be done with professionalism and respect, even if you are absolutely dying to shout, "You're fired! Get out!" in front of the whole company.

The actual act is pretty similar to a layoff. Never do it alone. Have a package ready for the employee to sign. Turn off their IT access immediately. Make them give you their laptop, and make a backup. Ask them to quietly leave immediately and arrange for the in-private delivery or collection of their personal belongings. If malfeasance or a crime has been committed, escort them out.

There's no need to make a public announcement. If their supervisor was not already aware of the situation, fill them in. But it should be a rare occurrence that their direct supervisor is uninvolved. If the person you're letting go has direct reports, talk to them. Let them know what's going on and to whom they now report.

SOME ETHICS

A couple more notes before we leave this topic.

First, play fair. Friends are great, friends matter, but if you work for a friend and they are not pulling their weight, you need to fix it. Employees will ultimately think less of you if you don't do this. Good people will leave, and your company will suffer.

Next, take sexual harassment seriously. It's terrible that I have to say that in the twenty-first century, but I do. I attempt to assume positive intent in everyone in my personal life, so I understand the right intentions that lead to poor decisions when it comes to sexual harassment in the workplace. I also understand the salty jokes that can come with long hours, and know that both genders willingly and happily make off-color jokes. I also know culture changes over time, and as a company grows up, these things need to evolve. Take every complaint seriously.

Third, don't make "you're fired" jokes. We used to joke around, saying, "You're fired" all the time. People thought it was funny. We thought. Until they didn't think it was funny. Cut it out. Be sensitive. A massive amount of American's self-worth is wrapped up in their job, and it's not kind for you to toy with that through pointless humor. We made an effort to ban it, and it worked wonders, once a few employees opened our eyes to it.

BREAKING UP WITH A PARTNER

It's tempting to think this will never happen to you, but the odds are good that at some point in the course of your company a partner will leave. Hopefully all went well in your operating agreement drafting, and the process is clear. Remember that it's always an option for the company and the departing partner to agree to do more or less than the operating agreement stipulates, should all parties agree. The operating agreement should be viewed as the bare minimum, and generally only be leaned on if things get acrimonious.

Should you find yourself needing to fire a partner, make sure that you have a clear majority—ideally unanimous (save the departing partner). Next, do anything you can to ease their transition and keep them from being too disgruntled. You don't want them going around saying bad things about your company. All parties should sign nondisparage agreements upon departure. The goal here is to negotiate with the partner to agree to an amicable departure, and sign airtight documents agreeing to the terms of the departure.

Remember that in the American legal system, minority shareholders have rights, and their equity has value. It cannot be legally voted away from them. Just because 90 percent of the company votes to fire the 10 percent owning partner does not mean their ownership can magically go away. It must be compensated for. This means you need to either follow the terms of an operating agreement to which they originally signed on, or they need to agree to new terms.

It's often the case that the company cannot afford to pay out a partner to the amount that they feel is reasonable. It's therefore important to distinguish between *employment* and *ownership*. It may be feasible to let the partner retain their equity stake, but quit working as a partner. This would mean you don't have to buy them out. This may be an option in certain situations where all agree and money is tight.

If your company is relatively large, and they are fully vested, you may find yourself owing millions of dollars that you cannot afford to pay. You may need to explain to the departing partner that an insolvent company is not one from which he or she can get *anything*. A bit of brinksmanship may be in order. This can be incredibly harrowing, wildly emotional, as the departing partner feels like they are being cornered or, worse, blackmailed.

Calculate the value of the partner's shares per the operating agreement. Offer as large an upfront payment as can be reasonably handled. Offer to pay the rest at the rate of their current salary. Include a sunsetting provision that allows for the payment of the balance of their shares immediately, prorated, in the event of a sale of the company. Throw in health insurance. This gives the partner some financial breathing room in their life—it's hard for anyone to turn away the chance to not have to work for a year or two. It also includes some accommodation for the fear the departing partner may feel that as soon as they leave, you're going to turn around and sell the company for more than they are receiving. You may find this fear absurd, but I assure you it's quite reasonable.

One final note: even if the partner is a deadbeat or, worse, has done something criminal, treat them with respect and fairly. Make sure the signatures are all locked up. Make sure they feel okay, or at least have made peace with the terms.

PART V

MONEY

19

BOOTSTRAPPING

So maybe you started your company in your living room, or you rented an office share in a communal work environment. But now you aspire to a real business, an agency with your name on the door. What about our office? What about those sleek desks with the dashing receptionist and the Eames chairs? What about the rows of gleaming MacBook Pros?

All of that can wait, my friend. You're going to be bootstrapping.

Advertising is not an industry that lends itself to early investment. Investors traditionally don't look at professional services firms in the same way they look at tech start-ups. It's virtually unheard of that two or three young, scrappy entrepreneurs will get a $500,000 check from some venture capitalist to start a services company—that a larger-than-life fairy godmother will say, "Go make me rich." Fat chance.

Now, I make a distinction here between institutional investment and your own personal investment, or that of friends and family. You and your potential partners may have some savings they are willing to put into your new enterprise. And you may have some friends and family who are willing as well.

I advise caution, however, in you're even considering taking money from friends and family. Mixing friends and business is always fraught with peril. When money is involved, these considerations get infinitely more complex, and while you can choose your friends, you can't choose your family, and you'll need them around for a long time. Secondly, you'll find that these people may well view themselves as "partners" and have opinions.

Then there are the purely financial considerations: why take investment and give them a chunk of your company when it is not 100 percent necessary?

But the final reason is the most important reason: if you're good, you won't need it. TBG is living proof of that. You should be able to get a gig without investment money, and you should be able to start collecting checks without getting an investment. Getting set up, through investment money, in offices you can't necessarily afford yet or with fancy chairs and computers, can set expectation levels unrealistically high, when you have a few years of slumming it ahead of you.

BOOTSTRAPPING 101

One of the great things about starting a marketing services company is that you don't necessarily need tons of money. We started The Barbarian Group with meager personal savings (let's say under $10,000 each), and a borrowed $500 we took from our friend and financial cofounder, Brian Costello, who footed the bill for our business license and registration paperwork. We paid ourselves as we got work. We leased an office once we won enough paying work to afford it. In those early days we didn't take any investment from anyone (Brian's $500 was a loan), and we were proud of it.

This is called bootstrapping.

I truly believe that this is one of the great things about advertising agencies and consulting companies: anyone with talent can make a go of it. You don't necessarily need anything more than the clothes on your back, a little bit of hustle, and a beat-up old laptop—you could probably start with nothing more than a used iPad. It's my view that this characteristic of the services model is a noble feature, a pathway to potential prosperity for Americans who weren't born in the right city or to the right family or couldn't afford the increasingly exorbitant cost of a college education in this country.

If you've got some savings, great. You're going to need it. Probably best to keep it in your own bank account and prepare yourself to live off of it for a while. Typically, you are going to start your shop with partners. And the odds are you all have varying levels of personal savings. And these levels of personal savings do not necessarily correspond with your ownership level, your financial needs, your talent, or your responsibilities at the company. Traditionally, agencies all had capital buy-ins, which meant that founding partners put up their own capital for a stake in the firm. That capital was critical to securing office space, equipment, and the funds to create and print gorgeous pitch material.

This is no longer necessary, as you can now set up shop in your own bedroom and create a stunning and clever pitch from your own desktop. At the early stages, it's vitally important that the shop stay as trim and lean as possible. There is massive price competition in this kind of work, and one of your key tools to winning work will be your ability to undercut your more established competitors.

(This can be a depressing thought. Later, you will be one of those larger competitors with more expensive prices. And somewhere along the line, you'll have to risk pissing off your clients and increasing your prices. That's okay. For some reason, the whole thing seems to work. Don't sweat it.)

Since you need to stay lean, you should start lean. Having extra money in the beginning just means you will spend it. Taking investment that makes your company too bloated at the beginning will only dull your ability to act like the shark you will need to act like.

The first days of a new services firm are not unlike the opening launch of the *Hunger Games*—you are panicked, you are running around like mad, you need to get supplies and make some kills. You take what work you can, and you rope in whomever you can to do the work. This is an intense time. You'll be relying on your wits, your hustle, and the innate talent of the people you have around you.

The goal here is to develop relationships with clients that can keep giving you work, either through solid relationships or, if you're extremely lucky, retainer accounts. Focus on the clients that will keep on giving. One-offs can be good if they are high paying or creatively amazing, but you'll not get out of the frenzy until you have some semblance of repeat customers. There may be one or two large companies in your region that have in-house marketing or brand departments. Get to know them. Think twice before passing up any work at all.

The goal here is to birth your company. It is to fight, rail, and shake against reality, explaining that this company is worthy of some of the energy in the universe coalescing around this particular enterprise and giving it some stability. You know those scenes in science fiction flicks when a new alien life form is teetering on the brink between existence and nonexistence, and the humans in the spaceship are doing everything they can to help the new life form wean itself off of their warp nacelles and begin existence as an independent, nonparasitic entity? That's your firm. It doesn't necessarily need to take flight yet, but it needs to be able to stand and breathe on its own.

The quicker you get out of this phase, the better. If you're still in this phase after a year or, worse, in two years, I would rethink things. Something's not clicking. Maybe it's the team, maybe it's you, maybe the work isn't good enough, maybe a potentially nurturing client has turned poisonous. I can't say for sure, but I can say you probably have a hunch what it is. Fix it. Fast.

But if all has gone even mildly according to plan, eventually your enterprise will begin to become self-sustaining. You'll notice a small uptick in your bank account. You'll slowly shift your thinking from "if" we get another gig to "when" the next gig comes in. You'll start thinking about where you want to take this thing, which means, in some way, you'll start thinking about growth.

Important note—this will be true of almost any shop, *even the ones that don't want to grow that large*, since at the beginning you won't even be paying yourself. Presumably you aspire to have some salary in your life, one or two employees around you, the ability to pay rent, cool and meaningful work, and clients you like.

Before too long, you'll get the hang of this. You'll have some income, and a million different things that you want to do with the income, and only enough real capital to do one or two of the things to improve the business. Maybe you want to hire another person. Maybe you need a new printer. Maybe you need a new office. Maybe you need to pay yourself something. Maybe it's time to splurge and get everyone health insurance.

I should pause and reassure you that this will be the standard operating procedure for at least the next few years. Many of the CEOs I advise feel like maybe they're not growing fast enough, that a few years in, it is still a slog. There's still not enough money to go around.

Repeat after me: *there will always be more things to do with the money than there is money.*

This is a good time for two quotes. The first is from one of my personal heroes, Bill Drummond, founder of the pop group KLF and author of a book called *The Manual: How to Have a Number One Hit the Easy Way*. He eventually left the industry in a spectacular fashion by literally setting a million English pounds on fire.[1] In *The Manual*, he writes,

Money is a very strange concept. There will be points in the forthcoming months when you might not have the change in your pockets to get the bus into town at the same time as you are talking to people on the telephone in terms of tens of thousands of pounds. Some of the following might seem contradictory, but in matters of money they often are...

Nobody wins the pools. There is no such thing as a fast buck. Nobody gets rich quick. El Dorado will never be found. Wealth is a slow build, an attitude to life. I'm afraid that the old adage that if you look after the pennies the pounds will look after themselves is always true.

That being said, you must be willing to risk everything—that's everything you haven't got as well as everything you have got—or nothing will happen.[2]

When we were in the middle of our bootstrapping cycle, employees often asked whether we could buy X or spend money on Y. We were obviously a growing company, and yet there never seemed to be any money around. In May of 2008, this led to an email from me to the company that laid out the bootstrapping challenges. After quoting the same Bill Drummond passage above, it went on,

Before the partners even get paid, that leaves maybe $2–3 million to finance everything. Everything.

Salaries. Rent. And, most importantly, new hires. New Hires so you guys aren't so over worked. New Hires so we can do all of the things we want to do.

At any given time, we have about 20 plays we could make if we had the money for it, so if we get the money for 1 or 2 plays, we'll make them, even if it means we ourselves don't get paid (which has happened on several occasions, though not in the last few months). We take risk. We are aware that we take the risk, but like Bill Drummond said, you've got to be willing to risk everything.[3]

If you're trying to grow your company to 10–20 people, achieve stability, and then just groove out for the rest of your career, you will still have to face the cash flow issue for a long time—long after you've achieved your head-count growth.

But if you are on the path of growing your firm as much as possible for a potential sale, this will be your path forever. Get used to it.

BUILDING A CASH RESERVE

Before too long, you will have noticed that while *jobs do not come in regularly, the money goes out regularly*. Every month you need to pay rent, employees, health care, electric, leases, Internet bills, and so forth on specific dates. And the checks from the clients? They come in when the clients feel like sending it. This has no bearing on when you actually completed the work, mind you.

The only way ever to get a handle on this is to build up a *cash reserve* in your bank account. Typically people think of this in the number of months of the company's operations that can be funded from the cash reserve, if checks don't come in, or, worse, new work doesn't come in.

When I go talk with other service shop owners, there is some debate about how much cash reserve *should* be on hand—most say 6–12 months, though I've known some people who are constantly shooting for 18 months. There is more consensus around the fact that there is always significantly less than that actually in the bank.

The question is how much to spend toward growth versus your cash flow and your safety net.

Three months is a good number. Any more, says Modea CEO David Catalano, "is a huge opportunity cost."[4] Capital equals growth. And you need to be growing.

In our case, the fact of the matter is that for more than five years, we had maybe one month of cash in the bank. We pushed it as far as we possibly could—and often too far. Every penny we could take and put toward growth or improvement of our company, we did so. There were times when we were hours before payroll was due and didn't have it. There were times we were late. There were times we bounced checks.

These will be fundamental questions you will need to answer: how much of a cash reserve, in months, do I feel comfortable with? How fast do I want to grow? A more conservative cash reserve will come with costs. It will mean slower growth, and it will mean taking that much longer to get where you want to be.

EFFECTIVELY SPENDING THE CASH YOU HAVE

Whatever your balance, the excess cash needs to be put to work in growing your company.

More importantly, you'll need to learn to prioritize which of the many expenditures you have on your to-do list is the one that gets the money.

Some of the money can be spent toward growth—new hires in fast-growing, highly profitable, or potentially new sectors of your business.

Some of it can be spent on maintaining creative quality—more or more talented designers or art directors who will give your current employees breathing room and, thus, time to flesh out ideas better. Some of the money will need to be spent on culture. You want a great workplace. You will have to balance all of these. This is more of an art than a science.

Pretty soon, the art of rotating through the various business needs and applying funds to each area in a sequential rotating manner will get to be second nature.

20

"I WANT TO GET RICH"

For all the reasons that people think about starting consultancies, getting rich seems to be one of the more popular ones.

If you're starting a services firm because you want to get rich, and you believe it is the best way for you to get rich with your skill set, that is totally okay. Just know this: you'll never get, like, "Bill Gates rich" off of the affair. It can be a good living, and small fortunes are there to be made.

Our society has a funny relationship with money, and you will probably lose a friend or two if you go around telling everyone you want to get rich, but at least be honest with yourself and your partners about it. Or you could change whom you hang out with to people who aren't ashamed of wanting to make a lot of money, but I don't recommend it, as a room full of those people can really suck your soul. It's best to hang out with them in small doses.

But we should talk about being rich.

So there's rich, and there's *rich*. Actually there are probably three shades of rich.

There's the "I don't really think twice when I buy a $100 dinner out" rich.

Then there's the "I need to think twice when I buy a Ferrari, but I still pay cash" rich.

Finally, there's the "Oh, I bought a jet? Weird" rich.

A services shop will get you to the second level. But almost never the third.

THE HAPPINESS AND SCIENCE OF BEING RICH

Fact of the matter is, that after $75k a year, you aren't any happier with extra money. A study from Princeton University's Woodrow Wilson School finds that "people say money doesn't buy happiness. Except, according to the same study, it sort of does—up to about $75,000 a year. The lower a person's annual income falls below that benchmark, the unhappier he or she feels. But no matter how much more than $75,000 people make, they don't report any greater degree of happiness."[1] Another study finds that "53 percent of those worth $5 million or more were 'very satisfied' with their job or previous job. That compares with only 21 percent for those worth $100,000 or less."[2]

Perhaps money does buy happiness.

INCOME VERSUS NET WORTH

We should talk about income versus net worth. Simply put, income is a non-rich person's game. When nonrich people think about being rich, they think about how much money they would need to *make*. A Gallup poll found that when asked how much they would need to *make* to be rich, the median answer in America was about $150,000 a year.[3] This would probably put you in the "I don't really think twice when I buy a $100 dinner out" camp of rich.

Now, it's quite easy, with some hard work, diligence, and a bit of luck, to make a solid six-figure salary in advertising or marketing before too long without starting a company. You could do that. It's pretty easy to get to the "I don't think twice when I buy a $100 dinner out" rich simply by getting a good job in the industry. Most people get there before too long. If this is what rich means to you, take a good long look at your motivations for starting a shop of your own, as opposed to working for someone else. Because if you start your own, it'll be a while before you're making a mid-six figure salary again. Much quicker to get there through someone else's firm.

Then there's the "I need to think twice when I buy a Ferrari, but I still pay cash" batch of rich, and the "Oh, I bought a jet? Weird" cabal. These people don't think about income nearly as much. They think about *net worth*. When people were asked about net worth, the same Gallup poll found that "About 26 percent of Americans say they would need a net worth of at least $1 million to consider themselves rich, of those 14 percent say they need $5 million or more."[4]

One million to five million. That's a big range.

WHAT IS YOUR NUMBER?

You're going to need a number. How much net worth are you going to need? Because there is only so much net worth to be made from a marketing services company.

Maybe you just need enough money to be financially secure. To *feel* financially secure. Science has increasingly found that this is more or less an unobtainable goal. Boston College has been undertaking a study of the super wealthy—165 respondents, 120 of whom have assets over $25 million. So far, the study has found that "Most of them still do not consider themselves financially secure; for that, they say, they would require on average one-quarter more wealth than they currently possess."[5] Indeed, in many cases, they find themselves *less* happy.

Getting rich in advertising will only get you so far. Say $1–5 million rich, maybe $10 million if you're lucky. You'll feel rich compared to your nonrich friends, but if you're not careful, you'll end up hanging out with people much richer than you. This can be stressful, and can diminish the rewarding sense of accomplishment with what you've done. Robert Frank finds in his 2007 book *Richistan* that fully 20 percent of the people in this range of wealth spend all of their money keeping up with the Joneses.[6] There's really not much point in killing yourself making this kind of money if you're just going to blow it on keeping up. Have a plan.

EARNING IT VERSUS KEEPING IT

Then there's *hanging on* to your money. In a think piece on the growing young tech elite in the Bay Area and their spending habits, Ellen Cushing in the *East Bay Express* points out several alarming statistics: "nine out of every ten lottery winners goes through his or her winnings in less than five years; according to *Sports Illustrated*, nearly 80 percent of NFL players file for bankruptcy within two years of retiring."[7]

It seems to me that there's a sweet spot between $1 and $10 million of net worth that increases happiness, but sidesteps the guilt-ridden complications of the super rich. Provided you don't get caught in the trap of keeping up with the Joneses, this might speak highly of a target area of wealth accumulation. In that case, perhaps starting a marketing services company is a good idea—that's exactly the range you can hope to make in your endeavors, and it would put you on the high end of your peers (assuming you don't get new, rich friends). Thus you would not feel compelled to blow your money in keeping up appearances.

WHY MAKE SO MUCH MONEY AT ALL

Pursuing wealth, greater wealth, takes a toll on the soul. There should be a good reason for it. There are times the whole thing will feel like a zero-sum game. The psychic cost of the accumulation of the wealth will seem almost as if it's too high to be worth it. Indeed, many right-thinking, rational people have concluded that the cost is, in fact, not worth it, and have declined to pursue this path.

Money opens up possibilities to do other things. What those other things are, is up to you. I strongly recommend making an effort to ensure that the bulk of those other things benefits other people in some way. If you accumulate a ton of wealth and spend it on nothing but yourself, you will be miserable.

Take heed from ad legend Rosser Reeves, chairman of the Ted Bates agency. "My kids claim they never saw me until they were about 25 years old."[8]

GETTING RICH FROM THIS MEANS EVENTUALLY SELLING

But let's assume you have your reasons. You're going to go for it. "Screw that," you think. "I want to start a company." Okay, Okay, I hear you. You have read my warnings. We shall move on.

So. Getting rich. From a marketing services company.

Can you get rich running a consultancy? Yes, you can. Concretely, with a decent intellect, some hustle, and some discipline, you can get, like, $1–5 million rich. Maybe if you're a complete badass, you can get, like, $10–20 million rich. Can you get Mark Zuckerberg rich? No. Can you even get "that kid started his company two years ago, sold it to Facebook, and made $30 million" rich? No, probably not. This is not a tech start-up.

To achieve this, it will almost certainly mean selling your company. You may have aspirations of making a product and selling that product off while keeping your company, or having the product spin off tons of cash. It's conceivable, but it almost never happens—we'll get to that later. It is phenomenally unlikely you will get "Oh I just bought a jet? Weird" rich. To even get to the $20 million point, you'll have to be pretty cutthroat. You'll have to become a banker, basically, and spend your life thinking of ways to screw over the people around you. You'll probably have to delve into ad tech and start talking in miserable sentences about things like "conversion rates" and "monthly actives," and use the word "optimize" a lot. Unless you're a complete math nerd, it won't be fun. Be warned.

And there are some august ad men of the last generation, flush with extra cash from the profits of their agencies, who have made wise investments with that money in real estate and other businesses that have lead them to substantially augment their services firm-derived net worth with outside profits. But really what they're doing is just wisely investing the excess portion of their fat salaries. If that's the approach you're going for, what's the point of starting the shop at all? Climb your way up the corporate agency ladder to a $500k salary and learn to invest.

Boring, you say. We're starting a services company. We. Are. Starting. An. Agency. Stop asking why. Okay, okay!

THIS WILL DRIVE EVERYTHING ABOUT YOUR COMPANY

A final warning about wanting to get rich with your services firm. This will drive everything you do. Your company will need to grow, and grow constantly, to achieve your goals. Every year, every day you are not growing, is one day further away from your goals. This does not mean the work necessarily needs to suffer—I believe absolutely that growth and quality of work are not mutually exclusive, at least at these levels. It does mean that occasionally you will have to do great work for lousy clients. It does mean that you will occasionally have to take a job just for the money. Even in these situations, you should still do great work, but often you'll do it for less than stellar clients, who may be incompetent or unappreciative. Though you should keep it to a minimum, it will also mean that occasionally you will find yourself doing work for asshole clients.

Think of growing your company in order to get rich like a cross-country drive. If you hop in your car and start driving, you can get across the United States, from New York to LA, in about 40 hours without stopping. Every time you stop—for a bathroom break, to sleep the night, to check out the Corn Palace, for a detour to see your sister—you are delaying your journey. Some of these delays may be useful, even necessary, but every delay is a compromise from attaining your goal as quickly as possible. And some things are no longer options at all, if your goal is to drive to LA. Stopping in Denver, buying a house, getting married, and chilling out playing XBox for the next few years is completely incompatible with your goal of getting to LA.

So it is with services firms. If your goal is to get rich, then having a small, lovely shop that only does one or two of the coolest jobs in the world each year, does a lot of awesome pro bono work, and spends whole weeks on making a robot that makes you peanut butter and jelly sandwiches are antithetical to your goals.

I am not saying that's not an absolutely wonderful shop to work for. But it is not a shop off of which you will get rich. "But people will pay more for quality! If we are famous and do amazing groundbreaking work, people will pay more for us!" Yes, they will. But you still can't get rich from it without growing.

If you want to get rich, your shop must grow.

21

ON GROWTH

I often talk to people who have grown their freelance business into an agency without quite understanding why. They're not sure why they ever went beyond freelancing, other than some vague belief that it would be cool to "own their own company." If you want to run what is called a "lifestyle" business, then by all means go for it. If you want your business to outlast you, want to make a dent in the world or culture, or want to make a decent amount of money, you're going to need to grow your company.

It's interesting how much of our world is predicated on the concept of growth. As humans, we grow up. Plants grow. Animals grow. In society at large, all of economics is concerned with growth. Growth is often an unspoken given. The world economy needs to grow. Is it right or wrong that so many companies on our stock exchanges are expected to grow constantly? Is it okay that capitalism requires growth? Why is the world like this? What does it mean? Why can't we chill?

This is not a book about taking on capitalism. In fact we are, in essence, writing a book about becoming a capitalist in the classical sense. You will no longer be a laborer.

There are, of course, different types of economic growth. There's the endless growth of the world economy—globalization and all that. There's economic growth in your city or region, which feels a little more real and vital. There's the growth of the enterprise itself—from your small business to the largest global organizations.

When it comes to companies, it's sometimes difficult to believe that behemoth corporations need to get any bigger. Share prices and the relentless quest for "shareholder value" are easy targets for criticism, if you're someone who has antigrowth tendencies.

And within your own company: How big is too big? Are 20 people too many? A hundred? Two hundred? A thousand? These are all very valid questions. If you are someone who loves the day-to-day work, do you even *want* to get too big?

If you are holding this book in your hands, I believe the answer is yes. You will need to grow. Growth is inevitable. Make your peace with it, so you can own it and control it. Find a way to embrace it.

For me, being comfortable with growth has been about job creation. I found great nobility and pleasure in providing jobs—good jobs, jobs that people loved—to people. The more jobs I could make, the better. The more people who loved their jobs, the better. Growth facilitated that.

I believe that there's a secret underworld of "style points" in how you accumulate wealth. If you do it without hurting other people, that's good. If you do it and help other people along the way, that's even better. You could just become a banker. You could make your money in toxic chemicals. Instead, you have chosen marketing. There are worse things.

HOLDING COMPANIES AND GROWTH

In your period of running your shop, you will often come across people who just assume you want to grow. When you start keeping an ear out for it, it's often amazing just how many arguments about a specific course of action have at their core an ironclad belief that you want your company to grow. Often, when I was considering selling my firm, I would listen to the potential acquirers talk in euphemisms for reasons we may want to sell to them. In the back of my head, I would think through their motivations and logic. It always came down to growth.

"You should consider joining up with Agency X. We could put an outpost for you guys in every office they have around the world," says Mr. M&A man from big agency holding company.

"Why on earth would I want to do that?" I'd ask.

"Well, you want to grow. You have to grow. This would facilitate growth."

"Why do I want to grow?"

Blank stare.

I don't blame an investment banker at WPP or Omnicom for being concerned with growth. These are publicly traded companies, and their stock lives or dies according to the growth of the company. They have to grow. This is why they are constantly acquiring agencies.

If your goal is to get rich from your company, it will need to grow. Again, you will have no choice. If you're an intellectual individual, the moral conundrums of growth and advertising may well percolate up here and there on your path to personal wealth. This is a good thing—evidence that you still have a conscience. Besides, if we lived in a world without growth, much of the advice in this book would be moot. That would be a shame, since starting a services firm is one of the relatively viable avenues for the poor, the disenfranchised, or the nonconnected to pull themselves up by the bootstraps.

Does everyone just *think* that growth is required in business, and that since consensus makes reality, growth *is* required? Well, yes. In this case, consensus makes reality. You can spend a good amount of time warping your brain on these paradoxes of growth, consensus, and reality versus perception. Take it up as a hobby. It's sadly irrelevant here. Growth is the religion taught at business school, and many people do not feel comfortable questioning their religion. Growth is the name of the game, it is what they are expecting, and if you are in this world, or want to enter it, let that existential stuff go and dive in.

A SIDE NOTE FOR THOSE WHO AREN'T IN IT FOR THE MONEY

If you're one of those people reading this book with a goal of something other than getting rich, this still pertains to you. You may well dream of running a little boutique shop, and being well respected for said work. A worthy dream. But growth will still matter to you.

The reason is that this whole company is going to be, essentially, your savings account, your IRA, and your home equity all rolled into one. The very act of founding a company from your successful freelance career dictates it. Otherwise, you're a freelancer with an IRA.

And life happens. Maybe you need to pay for your kid's college. Maybe you need to own a house. Even if none of this happens, you are going to retire one day. And even if you managed to start and grow a company AND save a bunch of money in an IRA for your whole career, what are you going to do? Just close up shop? *Not* sell off your most valuable asset? You will, eventually, sell. Unless you're going to go out of business.

And once the buyers get their hands on your shop, once you've retired, they will grow it. Unless they deem it so worthless they just shut it down. And then, honestly, what would you rather have as your legacy? A growing shop or a closed one?

Better to control it.

22

BANKS AND FUNDING

After a few years, if everything is going well, you'll start to notice something. You'll notice that *at all times the primary constraining factor of growth is the number of people on staff.* You'll realize that if you had more people *now*, you could get more work *now*. If the company's humming along according to plan, eventually you'll be able to predict with a pretty high degree of confidence exactly how much more revenue you could bring in with X number of additional people now. It will seem very obvious, and mathematical. Growth is constrained only by head count. Head count is constrained by your cash balance.

Once you've reached this "stable growth" phase, there is a potential solution for acceleration: an infusion of capital. Not at the beginning. Not before things have matured. As a cheaper source of revenue than venture capital or investment, it's probably worth thinking about a bank as your solution.

After all, a bank does not, generally speaking, take equity in your company. Working out a deal with a bank to finance your growth may be a smart move, if you can pull it off and you can stomach your bank.

Getting financing from a bank can be hugely daunting. Even learning the banking landscape can be difficult. Writing in the *New York Times* about small business lending, small business finance expert Ami Kassar sums up this confusion: "The processes are confusing and overwhelming. If you type 'small business loan' into Google, you will find a myriad of options but little help figuring out which ones make sense for your company's particular situation."[1] Raising money for small business has been, as *Rolling Stone* journalist Matt Taibbi eloquently puts it, "a severe pain in the ass for quite some time."[2]

At the beginning of your business's life, it can be nearly impossible. This is why the best time to talk to a bank is once you've mastered the slow and steady art of bootstrapping—when you've learned the ins and outs of winning work, balancing the books, and balancing growth against saving for a rainy day.

Banks like your company to reach a certain size before they will consider lending you money. The magical number seems to be 20 employees. The National Federation of Independent Businesses (NFIB) found in 2010 that "just 41 percent of those employing fewer than 10 people currently have a credit line while 68 percent of those employing 20 or more people do."[3] A more recent report finds some modest improvement in these statistics, but the essential truth is still there.[4] Banks like to see that your business is more than a personal consulting firm.

Hopefully after reading this chapter, you will have a good grasp on the basics. I'll walk you through the various types of traditional small business lending. We'll go through which types of banks may be more likely to lend to you and why. I'll also walk you through the basic workings of the US Small Business Administration (SBA) and alternative lenders.

Finally, I'll explain to you exactly what you and your company can do to make your agency more lending-friendly. There are several simple steps, and some not-so-simple steps, that you can take.

If all goes well, you can have a warm, productive relationship with your bank. If you succeed, I will envy you. I have a good relationship with the banks in my business life—now. But it took me nearly ten years. The journey was riddled with tears, rescinded credit lines, cancelled credit cards, and frayed relationships. Some of this was our fault, but some was not.

LOANS, CREDIT CARDS, LINES OF CREDIT

There are three types of financing mechanisms that banks typically offer to small businesses: credit cards, loans, and lines of credit.

PERSONALLY BACKED CREDIT VERSUS COMPANY BACKED

There are two different ways you can guarantee any sort of credit mechanism for your business: personally or through the company. A personal guarantee means that you, the individual, are guaranteeing all loans. If the company goes belly up, you're responsible for the loan. Your company guaranteeing the loan, assuming you're an LLC, means that should the company go bankrupt, you're not responsible for the balance on any outstanding loans.

Obviously, a personal guarantee is much safer for the bank. If you guess that this is easier to obtain, you are quite correct. It's important in your business to establish whether or not you are aiming to have the company's loans guaranteed by the company, or personally. Partners may complicate this. Often, each partner has to personally guarantee the loan. This was not an option for The Barbarian Group, so we worked hard to establish the company in and of itself as a credit-worthy entity. Some companies don't bother with this distinction.

CREDIT CARDS

Credit cards are a major force in small business lending. Nearly every small business has a credit card, according to the NFIB, 79% percent of small businesses had at least one credit card in 2012.[5] It is by far the most common credit source for small businesses. Credit cards offer two services: credit and "transaction convenience"—that is, the ability to easy complete a purchase and have a record of it, without issuing a purchase order. Transaction convenience is a far more common use of credit cards by small businesses than use of the credit facility. Only 20 percent of small business credit card holders use their credit card for lending.[6]

Credit cards are one of the most widely used credit facilities for businesses with fewer than ten employees—a circumstance of the relative difficulty for the very smallest of businesses in getting credit. You may well find yourself using a credit card's loan function for your business in the beginning. However, take caution that you will not be funding your business through your credit card for too long. "Transaction convenience" is one thing, but if you're using your card as a loan function, and your company is pushing 20 people, it's time to consider another lending source.

One thing to watch out for is the balance you keep on your card: the NFIB reports that small businesses with over $10,000 outstanding on their credit cards were almost completely unable to obtain loans or lines of credit from their bank. If you have used your personal credit card to fund the launch of your business, pay it down completely before you even think about turning to the banks for any lending.

BANK LOANS

A bank loan is exactly what it sounds like: a one-time loan from a bank. This is more or less the same mechanism you encounter when you buy a house or a car: your company puts up some collateral, agrees to terms, and the bank gives you a check. You then promise to repay the bank on a regular basis according to the terms of the loan.

Typically loans are issued to small businesses for specific endeavors that have a new cost-benefit analysis, for example, the opening of a new factory or retail location, the purchase of a car, or the acquisition of another company. This is a step that's a little different from personal lending. With your car or your house, the cost benefit analysis is a pretty straightforward prospect: cars halve their value when they leave the lot, and then slowly depreciate after that. So as long as your down payment and monthly payments are enough to off-set these losses, the bank is good to go. With a small business loan, however, more work is needed. Each business idea must be weighed against its own merits, with calculations made for the prospective return on investment for the endeavor. This can be a difficult endeavor: will this new location increase revenue and profits by X percent in Y years or not? Small business loan calculation can be highly subjective. Therefore, in reality, most small business loans are made purely based on the creditworthiness of the small business and the collateral put up: if everything goes bust with this loan, this person still seems willing and able to repay the loan.

> You would think, then, that if the bank were looking primarily at whether or not the loanee can pay back the loan, it wouldn't care *what* the loan is spent on. This is not the case, banks still like to know exactly what the loan is being spent on and how this might be a good investment. This is borne out by the data. Banks appear unwilling to offer loans for multiple purposes in one loan.[7]

Given that the financing needs of services firms typically revolve around funding growth, loans are not usually the approach these companies need to take. The money you need will be used for all sorts of things—hiring people, equipment, accounts payable float.

LINE OF CREDIT

This brings us to the most important funding mechanism for services firms: the line of credit. This will be your lifeline. If done right, and negotiated correctly, this will be your friend. Lines of credit are the lifeblood of the relationship between start-up and mid-sized service firms such as ours and banks.

Simply speaking, a line of credit (LOC) is a set amount of money that the bank allows the small business to draw against, as needs require. For example, you may have a $1 million line of credit. It may sit untouched. Then, one day, you may need \$100,000 to finance a purchase. You will *draw down* the line of credit by \$100,000, and the bank will transfer the amount into your checking account. You may then spend the money as needed.[8]

This gives your company two advantages over a traditional loan. First, you are only paying interest on the part of the LOC that you have drawn down. In the example above, you will only be paying interest on the \$100,000 you have drawn down, not the balance of the LOC. Secondly, the line of credit offers greater flexibility on how you spend the money when compared to a traditional loan.

On paper, this could be exactly what your shop needs. It can be the fuel for your growth. It can be the bridge that crosses over the chasms of slow payment by your clients. It can also be a crutch, one you come to rely on that glosses over harsh realities about your business and fogs your glasses to a reality that is less rosy than you think. It is important to tread with caution.

FACTORS IN CALCULATING A LINE OF CREDIT

There are four factors you should care about—the size of the line of credit, the interest rate, the collateral demands, and the drawdown requirements. The size is obviously the most important factor. The interest rate is much like an interest rate on a credit card—if you manage the line well and pay it back regularly, and keep the amount drawn down to a minimum, there is room for flexibility on the interest rate. If you plan on having a large amount of the line drawn down, this will matter more for you. Interest rates across banks do vary, so it pays to shop around.

The collateral demands are tricky. You may be young and have nothing to offer as collateral. You may have a wife who does not find it too keen to have your house as collateral on your business LOC. You may have partners with wildly varying creditworthiness, which can make it difficult for everyone to offer equal amounts of collateral. You may well find yourself in a situation where one partner is putting much more on the line to secure the line than another partner. These things will need to be worked out internally. At our company, those who were creditworthy enough secured the original LOC, while those who weren't, didn't. There was definitely a little lingering resentment about this, so I recommend talking frankly and honestly about the additional sacrifices and risks involved, and perhaps finding other ways to offset or mitigate them. As your company grows, it may be possible to secure the line of credit without personal guarantees. It pays to continue shopping around, maybe after a year or two, to see if this guarantee can't be shifted to the company itself.

Drawdown requirements regulate the amount you can take out of the loan at any one time, and for what purpose. Pay attention to these, as they will matter. Most LOCs in the sizes we are talking about are fairly flexible in this regard, and you should seek one that has fairly benign drawdown requirements. The last thing you want is to explain to some banker why you need to cover payroll, have them ask for accounts receivables tables, and whatnot. Or, worse, explain to them why you absolutely *need* a new TV projection system, video conferencing rig, and X Box. You make content for it!

HOW MUCH CREDIT?

How much credit should you take on in your credit line? The short answer is as much as you can. There is no obligation to use the whole line of credit. Provided the collateral demands aren't onerous, it's good to have as much as you can, for a rainy day. At minimum, a line of credit should cover three months of operating expenses for your company.

Take care, however. If your company is on a path to grow as much as possible as quickly as possible, the growth needs are, for all intents and purposes, infinite. And you will find yourself viewing your credit line as fuel for growth. It can be easy to end up spending the whole line of credit on growth. This can make a lot of sense. If, as we've discussed, your business is a pretty well-oiled machine by this point, you have a firm sense that growth is only constrained by credit, and you have companies beating down your door to hire you, you may be tempted to spend the whole line of credit on growth. That is what we did. The risk you take on with this, however, is that if something bad *does* actually happen—a client defaults on a payment, for example, or, you know, the entire economy grinds to a halt—you won't have any dry powder in the keg to keep things going. I cannot stress this enough: *these things do happen*. In a perfect world, try and keep *at least* one or two months of operating expenses handy on the line of credit or in your bank account. Unless you like to gamble. *Advertising Age* calls taking out a line of credit "a dangerous step."[9] And indeed it is. Don't say I didn't warn you.

THE SMALL BUSINESS ADMINISTRATION

If you're looking for financing for your small business, the SBA may pop into your head. It popped into mine. "Hey, Jay!" I asked our CFO in 2002, "Can't we get an SBA loan?" I wasn't quite sure what one was, but I knew we were a small business, and I wouldn't have minded getting a loan.

"Hrm," Jay said, thinking about it a moment. "Probably not. But I can try."

Well, that was optimistic.

Turns out, Jay was right. We did try. And we did not get an SBA loan.

What gives?

The SBA is a federal government cabinet-level (for now) organization the remit of which is to "to maintain and strengthen the nation's economy by enabling the establishment and viability of small businesses and by assisting in the economic recovery of communities after disasters."[10] It does this through three mechanisms that people refer to as the "3 C's"—credit, counseling, and contracts.

This is an important point right off the bat—SBA loans are actually a small part of what the organization does. Counseling and contracts make up a large part of it. For example, 23 percent of federal contracts to the US government are through the SBA. This is probably not particularly useful to us as marketing services firms.

(Yes, these contracts do exist, and you may find yourself, from time to time, solicited by various branches of the government in taking on work for them. This can be a monstrous bureaucratic burden. Generally, we avoided these contracts, though you may have better luck. Mileage will vary. And in any case, it is, obviously, but a drop in the bucket of the spending of the industry as a whole. If you're pursuing some government-focused agency, good luck to you. I am sorry I can't be more helpful.)

The agency also has some good educational resources—some of them will seem quaintly rudimentary if it is your expert field. That the online SBA resources teach companies about marketing and advertising is adorably quaint if you're an advertising pro. Yet other resources can be very useful to your small business—there are wonderful tutorials on the basics of accounting, for example, along with payroll, taxes, and whatnot. It's a fun site to spend a leisurely evening reading on your laptop on your couch. Honest.

MADE THROUGH BANKS BIG AND SMALL

When it comes to the third C, credit, the SBA does not actually issue the loans itself. This may be obvious to you, but I am a bit ashamed to say when I was dreaming of obtaining an SBA loan, I didn't know this. I pictured it as being something like getting your passport—going into some big old dilapidated government building, waiting in line, and delivering your forms, and some clerk stamping them with an "approved" or "denied" stamp.

Turns out they don't actually do this. Rather, the SBA works much like Fannie Mae and Freddie Mac—they guarantee the majority of a loan that is actually made by a regular bank. So if you go to a bank and get a small business loan for, say, $100,000 the SBA will guarantee up to $90,000 of that loan. This is meant to increase the bank's confidence in lending to you, because the odds are much better that you will pay at least $10,000 back of your loan compared to paying the full $100,000 back. You'll notice that $90,000 of $100,000 is 90 percent, and since 2008, under the *Small Business Jobs Act*, the SBA has been backing up the banks to the tune of 90 percent of the amount individual loans.

The NFIB notes that large banks and small banks handle SBA loans differently. Large banks, knowing that the bulk of the loan is backed by the federal government, tend to use algorithmic approaches, paying particular attention to loan compliance with SBA guidelines and some modest collateral guidelines. The business model is not generally super important. Smaller banks, by contrast, tend to lend in the more "old-fashioned" way, sitting down with the business and working through the business plan. You know. Doing things. Therefore SBA-backed loans tend to mirror the larger trends we've seen in the differences between the lending habits of small banks and large banks.

ALTERNATIVE LENDERS, RECEIVABLES FINANCING, AND SO ON

All of this may be enough to make you wish that you didn't have to deal with banks at all for financing. You are not alone. A whole array of nonbanking financial lending instruments has been developed in the United States. These are called, broadly speaking, "alternative lending."

The temptation to use these is strong: alternative lending can provide a more sympathetic means of obtaining financing for your company. Additionally, these people will probably start coming to you. Many alternative lenders are voracious marketers.

There are many types of alternative lending, ranging from reputable to flat out usurious. The landscape can be confusing. Kassar comments that "Many small-business owners find dealing with these companies painful, but in many cases they feel they have no choice."[11]

To me, alternative lending is a path of last resort. Still, when you have $2 million of accounts receivable, with no hope of collecting for months, and a payroll to meet, then perhaps it's worth it. The main types of alternative lending are leasebacks, peer-to-peer loans, cash advances, nonbank loans, and receivables financing. For our purposes, receivables financing is the most viable, but let's go through each one real quick.

Leasebacks involve a company's buying your equipment from you for a lump of cash, then leasing it back to you. This typically works great with large pieces of equipment and real estate—buildings, large fabrication machines, and the like. However, given that the primary asset of a services firm is the people, this is often not a really viable option for us. Small agencies probably lease our offices (though if you happen to own it, this may not be a terrible approach), but all we really own are a bunch of computers, which aren't really valuable enough to make this worthwhile. While he primarily used his bank for such funding functions, agency owner David Catalano finds thinking about this in a methodical manner somewhat useful. "In the early days when we started growing faster and bought computers and (gasp) SteelCase desks and chairs, we would wrap up equipment purchases every few months into 2 year loans at ~6%. That freed up capital to grow the business."[12]

Peer-to-peer loans are a new kind of loan that makes capital more accessible to a larger group—these are the new burgeoning world of loans made by groups of individuals to businesses. There has been a remarkable blossoming of this sort of financing throughout the world in the last decade. This could include the micro-lending work of people such as Nobel Peace Prize winner Mohammad Yunus, with his Bangladeshi micro-lending institution Grameen Bank (now expanded into the United States).

Then we have new, digital peer-to-peer lending companies such as Kiva, Prosper, Lending Club, and Zopa (who were our upstairs neighbors at the TBG SF office). These generally require a good credit score, but more relevantly, the loans are often pretty small—the maximum at Lending Club is $35,000, for example.[13] These loans are great for small, small businesses, but are generally not quite enough to handle the financing needs of a shop over, say, 20–30 people.

We also have the new batch of indie lending sites, most notably Kickstarter and Indiegogo, which are blazing trails in the world of group-sourced financing. Typically, however, these sites are used to fund *projects*, not *businesses*, and thus are not super useful to our type of company that may be suffering liquidity problems. If you are making some cool new piece of art, or a lab project, however, these may be useful. With the introduction of the *Jumpstart our Online Business Startups (JOBS) Act*, the regulatory environment for these companies has been loosened. Passed in April 2012 with bipartisan support, the act includes an array of provisions that are primarily more useful for tech start-ups than services firms. However, one provision loosens the regulatory environment for group funding of a business up to $1 million, and we may soon see a growth in websites catering to these needs. For now, however, it's still not quite ready for prime time for service firm needs. Kassar confirms this: "Unfortunately, crowdfunding hasn't taken off yet....It will take time to iron out the kinks and figure out how to make it work—how to strike the right balance between helping companies and protecting investors."[14]

Cash advances aren't quite as nefarious as they sound. We're not talking pawnshops here, but rather loans against the daily take of cash-intensive businesses, such as bars or restaurants. It's a pretty awful system, with loans rates sometimes exceeding 70 percent,[15] but, luckily, it's not really for us, so we can just skip that whole miserable world. Ugh, they give me the willies just thinking about them.

Nonbank loans could seem, on paper, like they might be good for us. This is just what it sounds like: a loan from someone other than a bank. These generally fall into two groups: commercial and nonprofit. The commercial entities tend to focus on small businesses with "high profit margins," a rubric under which your firm may or may not fit, but quite possibly won't, especially in times of high competition. Interest rates can exceed 20 percent. Warrants for a percentage of your company may also be issued.[16] To me, the cost of these seems unacceptably high, but maybe in your situation you can find something tolerable.

The majority of alternative lending to services-type businesses, however, falls under the category of receivables financing. This is when a company loans your business some money against how much money other businesses owe you. For example, if your account receivables amount to $1 million, you could borrow a sum less than that, say $800,000, receive the money now, and turn over the commensurate amount, along with a tidy fee, of future incoming checks to the receivables financier.

On paper, it can seem like a dream, and I am the first to admit I picked up the phone and chatted with receivables financing companies more than once. The cost, however, is substantial—enough to give me pause. The monthly fee can be 4 or 5 percent, with an effective annual fee of 20–30% percent.[17]

Still, many businesses believe they have no choice. It can be, literally, your only hope.

MAKING YOUR BUSINESS A MORE ATTRACTIVE LOAN PROSPECT FOR BANKS

You'll recall that this whole giant banking chapter started with my commenting that maybe, by now, your business has 20–50 employees and you've gotten a real sense of how much work there is out there, gotten good at managing your finances, and know exactly what you would do to turn on the growth spigot with additional funding. That remains doubly true today. If you've not gotten this basic stuff sorted out, there is virtually zero hope for you to go to a bank.

So what can you do?

While banks are not your friends in reality, some day, if your agency is any good and you're on any sort of growth plan, you're going to deal with them. There are some concrete steps you can take to make your life better down the road.

WAIT UNTIL YOU HAVE ENOUGH EMPLOYEES

First and foremost, there is no point in applying for credit until your company is big enough.

The employee statistics mirror my advice that it's virtually pointless to go to a bank until you have 20–30 people. Grow your company to over 20 employees: "Just 41 percent of those employing fewer than 10 people currently have a credit line while 68 percent of those employing 20 or more people do."[18]

LIVE IN THE RIGHT STATE

Your geography is something you may or may not have control over, though if you have flexibility in this area it's worth considering moving to a more prosperous region of the country. Hell, if you're thinking of starting an agency and you can go anywhere, this is generally good advice, even ignoring the increased lendability factor. Certain states are statistically less likely to offer credit to small businesses. These states are the ones hit hardest by the great recession: Arizona, California, Florida, Georgia, Michigan, and Nevada. Obviously, moving may not be an option, but know that in these states, your path may be even more challenging.[19]

MAINTAIN YOUR CREDIT SCORES

When talking about credit scores, there are two scores to consider: your personal and your business credit score. Most of us are familiar with our personal credit score—same sort of thing that rules our life when it comes to cell phone plans, credit cards, home mortgages, lease applications, car loans, and everything else.

The relationship between the two can be a bit fuzzy, and may not always be obvious to you. You're a limited liability company (LLC), right? Your business is a different entity from you. It should have its own credit, and yours should be unrelated. This is true on paper, but in reality, banks focus intensely on personal credit. The NFIB states that "theoretically, the financial worth of an owner's residence has no business implications. A person (with their home) and a business are two separate financial entities, particularly incorporated businesses. Practically speaking, nothing could be farther from the truth. The individual and the business are intimately tied, incorporated or not, meaning that the owner's personal finances, including his home, have implications for the business and vice versa."[20] If you're a solo entrepreneur, your personal credit history will very much matter, as will whether or not you hold a mortgage (or a second one). Many business loans to solo entrepreneurs are generally glorified second mortgages.

If you have partners, however, things are a bit more complex. We talked about this earlier, but the odds are that different partners will have different credit ratings. The banks will focus on the ones with good credit ratings and home mortgages, and push to have them personally guarantee things. Your partners may be cool with this, or they may not. This will need to be negotiated.

In terms of business credit scores, what people are generally looking at is your Dun & Bradstreet (D&B) number. Your company will need to build up a credit history, the longer the better (note the NFIB says that older small businesses fare better than new ones). Register for a D&B number right away upon founding your business, to begin accruing a business credit history. This will make it less necessary (though probably not completely unnecessary) to rely on your personal credit down the road in a few years when it's time to deal with banks.

Next, it is vitally important that you pay your bills on time. The bills that matter most are your credit card bills and payments you owe to large companies and financial organizations. Credit cards are particularly important, as the use of a credit card for credit, as opposed to payment convenience, is another indicator of loan worthiness. Only 20 percent of small businesses carry a balance on their cards (a credit function vs. a payment convenience function).[21] If you're in that 20 percent, that's a warning sign, and your bank will notice. The NFIB further starkly comments that "credit card holders maintaining balances of more than $10,000 after monthly payments are virtually never able to obtain additional credit."[22]

FOCUS ON SMALL BANKS

Statistically speaking, small banks are a better bet than large ones for your credit needs. The NFIB has found this to be true in its surveys time and time again. You may think this might have to do with the quality of the borrowers at smaller banks. Not so, the NFIB finds: "a review of D&B's PAYDEX credit scores indicates no difference between the two sets of customers or even a slightly higher average rating for those whose primary institution is a large bank."[23]

Develop a close relationship early on with a small bank. When you're setting up your business, consider working with a smaller, local institution for your checking and savings needs right from the bat.

ASK LOTS OF BANKS

Another interesting finding of the NFIB studies is that it actually helps to ask a lot of banks for credit. This might seem counterintuitive, because in our personal lives, for example, asking ten credit card companies for credit can actually worsen your credit score. Yet the studies found that "Little difference appeared in the frequency of attempts to obtain a new credit line by the size of the primary financial institution patronized."[24]

DEVELOP A RELATIONSHIP

Catalano speaks with what can almost be described as love for his bank: "I have a relationship with a manager who knows me and my team. Better yet, I know my manager's boss. I even meet once a year with my relationship manager's boss's boss. I view them just as I would a board member. I tell them what I'm going to do, and then share the results. This builds confidence. I am a big deal to my bank. They tout me having me as a client and use me to win other business."[25] That is great. In short, find a small bank, and develop a relationship.

Seek out a bank with experience in the ad industry. This is nigh on impossible in some localities, but if you're in a city where advertising is a larger industry, it's best to find a bank that's dealt with agencies before. Ask the bank outright whether it has such experience.

RUN A TIGHT SHIP

The best thing you can do to help your shop maintain a good relationship with its bankers is the obvious one: run a tight ship. As a creative company, it's easy to be lax about these things, especially early on. We'll devote a whole section of this book to this topic, but I cannot express enough, here, how vital it is. Banks may be soulless machines relying on inhuman algorithms, but they also have deep experience in this area, and those algorithms were developed for a reason. They focus on the most important financial indicators of your company. It's vital that those look good.

Accurate accounting is vital. The service shop world has a lot of murky terminology about billings and sizes of accounts. Billings and revenue are different things when media buying is taken into account. And if your shop spends a lot of money on freelancers, this, too, needs to be clearly indicated. Keep an eye on large expenses. Keep rent down, keep compensation low. Focus on key employees and make sure they are happy. Do what you need to keep them, but don't go crazy. Keep your own salary low. The wealth comes later. Sacrifices need to be made in the early years.

This will sound like common sense, but it's amazing how many agencies don't follow it: make sure jobs are profitable. Work up a calculation of everything that the job cost you—include nonsalary items like real estate, utilities, administrative support, shipping, and so forth. Individual jobs need to be profitable at a healthy margin. If you have an unprofitable client, fire it.

Key to all this, of course, is knowing what to charge. It's vital that your company charges the right amount for each job, and the banks can clearly see that every job, or almost every job, is profitable.

PART VI

OPERATIONS

23

STARTING UP

From a legal standpoint, the first order of business is to turn your freelance business into a real business entity.

SETTING UP A LEGAL ENTITY

When you were a solo freelancer or an agency stiff doing freelance on the side, you didn't much have to worry about this. You could just use the regular Internal Revenue Service (IRS) form 1040 and fill out a schedule C, as a self-employed individual, using your Social Security Number (SSN) as your tax ID number.

When you're an independent contractor or a freelancer, your SSN serves as your identification with the federal government for tax-related matters. With businesses, though, SSNs are not used. Instead, the IRS recognizes individual businesses by an Employment Identification Number. You will need one of these. You can file these online (ignore the misery of the user experience of the site) at www.irs.gov/uac/tools. You will need this number often. Memorize it like you did your SSN.

In a business that has employees and partners, there are several different forms a business can take, and selecting one can be pretty complicated. I am not a lawyer. Your business may have special needs or circumstances, and your region may have special laws. But broadly speaking, in the United States, you're looking to set your business up as an LLC.

The main reason an LLC exists is seen within its name: limited liability. As a company grows beyond the individual sole proprietor, liability becomes an issue. It is important that you have protections against the obligations, debts, and liabilities that the company may incur. There will be times where you need to sign away this liability protection and personally guarantee things such as loans and credit cards; therefore, it's important that this default liability protection exists. Even if you do not plan on having partners right away, if your company is going to have employees, liability protection is paramount.

The LLC was created to give small businesses some of the advantages of large ones, including liability protection.

Another important aspect of LLCs is the tax regime under which they operate. LLCs can be operated as a *pass through* entity, which means they do not directly pay taxes themselves. Rather, the individual partners of the LLC receive a schedule K-1, which they file with their 1040. This allows the entity to pay only one set of taxes, and each partner pays taxes according to their share and their tax rate. There is flexibility here, too, as you grow, allowing the business to file as an S-corporation. In the tech start-up industry, LLCs are sort of pooh-poohed as being insufficient. This is because many tech companies issue stock, and issuing stock isn't something that works well in an LLC.

You will no doubt find many people encouraging you to set up an S-Corporation in Delaware for your new business, and if you see yourself creating the next Facebook, then may that is a good strategy. Personally, I don't think this is necessary. At the beginning, you're looking to get your business set up as a legal entity with as little hassle, paperwork, and legal fees as possible. The best way to do this is simply to register as an LLC in the state in which you reside. This can be done with a minimum of hassle. File a doing-business-as (dba) certificate with your city, write some articles of organization for your LLC, and file an LLC certificate with the state. You can find out online how to do this in most states.

If you're looking to go the full do-it-yourself approach, a gentleman named Michael D. Jenkins has published a series of books available on Amazon called *Starting and Operating a Business in State X*, X being any state in the union. These are useful for learning all the quirks of filing in any individual state. I'd recommend hiring a lawyer for this process. They'll know all the legal requirements of your region, be able to point out whether there is any compelling reason to file as another type of legal entity (though get a second opinion here if they do), and file all the paperwork.

Remember that you can change your business form at a later date. While lawyers are expensive now, later on, when you're bringing in a couple million a year, the costs to reform your business will feel minimal. For now, the order of the day is getting set up as a legal entity *that will suit your needs* as quickly and cheaply as possible.

DESIGNATE A TAX MATTERS PARTNER

The next thing to do is to designate a "tax matters partner." This is an IRS term designed to let the IRS know which partner to bug on matters regarding the finances. The IRS will also want to know, and many states require, this identification when you file your LLC form. And it will be the person who is required to sign your tax forms, such as the Schedule K-1s. This sounds cut and dried, but is actually a cipher for various roles and responsibilities in the partnership. If you're a majority partner, this may well be you. If you have several equal partners, this is the time to designate which one you think should be responsible for the finances.

THE OPERATING AGREEMENT

Your operating agreement is an incredibly important document. This is the document that spells out exactly how the partnership will be run, and what responsibilities, rights, and expectations exist for the partners. It's important that you have a solid operating agreement and that all expectations are aligned from the get-go. While one of the benefits of the LLC is that the operating agreement can be changed at any time, it is an incredibly useful tool for going through issues of major importance with your partners at the outset. Operating agreements have a tendency to become increasingly set in stone over time. Various partners come to rely on various terms, and the legal system in the United States makes it difficult to amend an operating agreement without a *supermajority* of votes—perhaps 70 or 80 percent—not just a majority. It is not good business practice, and quite often not even legal, for a majority to remove the rights of the minority by vote.

There are several issues that you want to address as you develop your operating agreement. While any individual decision can be undone, it is best to approach the initial operating agreement of your company with care. Many of the issues are hypothetical, and hard to imagine at the outset. Developing a good operating agreement can be uncomfortable in the same way discussing a prenuptial agreement can be in a marriage. This is a time of excitement and celebration, why are we spending too much time talking about death, dismemberment, drug addiction, and breakups? Some partners may well resent having the conversation at all. Some may not pay sufficient attention to the ramifications of their decisions, which will take on increasing import throughout their life at the company.

It's important to *have a guide*, preferably in the form of a lawyer, who can walk you and your partners through each of the decisions you're making, telling you various common approaches, and pointing out any pitfalls of the approach you and your partners are considering. Secondly, *birth your company in good intent.* It may be tempting for you to jockey for terms more advantageous to you. It may be tempting to realize that one of your partners doesn't understand the ramifications of what they are about to agree to, and to capitalize on that "to your advantage." Avoid these temptations. Otherwise, there will eventually come a time when the partner realizes what you have done to them, and enmity and resentment ensue. Let's go through some of the major and common provisions within an operating agreement.

ALLOCATING PARTNER EQUITY

When a partner joins a company is the primary factor in determining a fair share of the company. The partners who start with you from nothing will deserve, and will probably expect, a much larger stake in the company than those who come later. These initial partners, too, are starting from nothing, and the value of the company at that point is zero. As the company grows, it begins to accrue value. It slowly becomes a more stable, sure thing. The people who are coming on to a company that's already up and running are taking less risk than those who joined when it was just a hope and a prayer. The further you take your company before bringing on more partners, the less equity you will have to give them. Make no mistake—adding partners is valuable. But there are equity differences between adding one at the beginning and one two years in.

Some people find equality noble. We did. We started with many partners, and we started with more or less equal shares. All for one and one for all. We loved the message it conveyed. This worked because we all took the plunge into nothing at the beginning. Each person played a vital part. There were, of course, inevitable disagreements about pulling your own weight—when people have the same equity share, it's easy to compare their relative levels of hard work and importance, and resentment can creep in. Beware of this. Find other ways to offset it—perhaps by varying salary.

Sometimes one person is manifestly the most important person in the company. They may be a rock star, someone with personal renown. They may be someone bringing a ton of clients to the new enterprise. These things are okay, and should be accommodated with different levels of equity. It's totally okay for one partner to own 30 or 40 percent, and the others to own 10% percent.

The negotiations in this realm can be very sensitive. People have a tendency to equate their proposed ownership percentage with a numerical indicator of your value of them as a person. This needs to be carefully managed.

VESTING

While I remain happy with our all-for-one, one-for-all equality-based partnership levels, I profoundly wish that someone had taught me about vesting before we started our company. Vesting, in a nutshell, is the act of allocating partnership equity over time. For example, if I am given 20 percent of the company, this will vest over, say, four years, which means that every month, I acquire 0.416 percent of the company. If I leave, I stop vesting, and that's my ownership level. So in this example, if I leave (or am fired) after two years, I will leave with 10 percent of the company. The rest of my potential ownership stake will revert back to the company. Finally, many vesting deals have what is known as a *cliff*, which means that up until that moment, if I leave, I don't get *any* of my shares. In this example, let's say I have a one-year cliff, which means that if I quit (or am fired) after ten months of employment, I don't get any shares. If I leave after a year, I get a quarter of my 20 percent equity stake, or 5 percent. Typical vesting deals also usually include a provision that says that everyone fully vests if there is a sale of the company. These deals also can have a provision saying that so long as you're at the company, you can vote your full 20 percent, regardless of how much you've vested at this point.

If you haven't brought up the issue with your new partners, now is the time. Suggest that each and every partner —including you, if it is a brand new entity—follow the same vesting schedule and cliff. What this is, exactly, can be up for negotiation. Perhaps some equity is vested at the outset. Perhaps there is no cliff. There is room for negotiation. But now is the time to work it out.

HOW DECISIONS ARE MADE

The next order of business is to decide how decisions get made in the company. There are four basic approaches: unanimous consent, a supermajority, a majority, or any partner can make a decision on their own. Additionally, you can approach these based on equity—a partner owning 20 percent of the company gets more say than a partner who owns 10 percent—or based on a "one-partner-one-vote" system.

Start with the big decisions—what kind of vote would it take to sell the company, close up shop, go bankrupt, or purchase another company? Then move on down the list. Can you open another office? Rename the company? Fire your largest client? Fire a small client? Take on a giant piece of business that would completely transform the company? Hire? Fire? Hire directors?

Fire the receptionist? Make a purchase of $1 million? $100,000? $10,000? Many companies have cascading permissions, where smaller things can be done by any partner, and larger ones require more votes. Even if you own a majority of the stock, this is still a worthwhile exercise to ensure your new partners that you, too, will operate within the rules you have all agreed upon. You may want to agree to some things being unanimous consent, supermajority, or one-partner-one-vote, even if you legally own the majority of the company, to foster camaraderie among your partners.

Ideally, your partnership should have few enough partners that the vast majority of decisions can be made by consensus, not votes—especially the day-to-day operations of the company. What we're looking at here is how major, company-changing decisions get made, and the fallback rules for when consensus cannot be reached and a vote must be taken.

PARTNER EXITS

Partnership exit agreements have four components: the voluntary departure process, triggering events, the involuntary departure process, and the buyout calculation and process.

VOLUNTARY EXITS

A voluntary exit is when a partner quits of their own free will. Does the partner lose everything? Keep the ownership portion of the company that has vested over time? Get bought out automatically by the buyout calculation? It's up to you guys, and now is the time to decide. This is very hard to change later.

TRIGGERING EVENTS

A "triggering event" is an event that happens in the real world that triggers a specific provision in an agreement. You will want to develop a list of potential scenarios in which a partner might have to leave the company for reasons in their personal life that would not qualify as a voluntary exit. These could include fatal illness in the partner or a debilitating disease that impairs the partner's ability to do their job. Triggering events also exist to protect the partnership from the troubles of a specific partner. These could include bankruptcy, substance abuse, a major lawsuit found against the partner, theft, sexual harassment, or the committing of a felony.

In both cases, some of these are very clear cut, such as bankruptcy, conviction of a felony, or the death of a family member. In other cases, more subjective measures might need to be taken. Work through these. Some may require evidence of a specialist such as a doctor, while some may be decided upon by a supermajority vote, such as a case of substance abuse.

In all cases, the death of a partner should be treated as a triggering event.

It will be horrendously, miserably unpleasant discussing all of this. Warn the partners in advance that you are going to have a session that involves talking about a lot of unpleasant things. Ask everyone to approach the issue as professionally as they can. One possibility is to distribute a list of topics in advance, with some ideas or options, before coming together, so partners can get their initial emotions out of the way before discussing the issues at hand.

BUYOUT FORMULAE, RIGHTS OF FIRST REFUSAL

The trigger activates the buyout formula, which is a calculation of how the company goes about compensating the partner for the shares of the company and the shares are repurchased by the company. Remember: minority shareholders have rights—rights that a majority cannot vote away. By unanimously agreeing upon a buyout formula in your operating agreement, and clearly spelling out the triggers, it is more difficult for a partner to claim in the future that the majority is abusing the minority.

If a partner is leaving the company and they must sell their shares back, the company may want the first chance buy them. If the company does *not* buy them, then someone else can. This is a "right of first refusal." This also allows flexibility. If the company does not want to buy the shares, it can pass, perhaps allowing an individual partner to buy them. Work through the right of first refusal chain with your partners. A typical one is "partnership first, individual partners next, then anyone whom the partner wants." With the actual dollar amount determined according to the formula.

It's important to keep the shares within the organization. By instituting a right of first refusal chain, the partnership can ensure that a departing partner does not go sell their shares to some random individual, thus foisting upon the partnership a new person whom they might not even know, with the same rights as them. Consider, too, whether you want an exemption in the event of partner death. Are you comfortable with the partner's spouse being a partner? Are you comfortable with the spouse owning shares, but not being an active partner? Or would it be the strong preference of the partnership to purchase back all shares on the event of death at a fair market price?

After you have worked out your rights of first refusal chain, you need to figure out a mutually agreed-upon formula for buying back the shares of a departing partner. Think of this as the "worst-case" scenario. This is what you fall back upon if no other agreement can be made among the partners. You can always institute a rule saying "unanimous consent can override the buyout formula." If times are great, and the partner is leaving under amicable terms, and the company is flush, the partnership can vote to buy out the departing partner at a dollar amount higher than the previously determined buyout formula. Conversely, if the partner isn't fireable, but everyone wants them to leave, and yet the buyout formula is too low for the partner to be willing to depart, the partnership could unanimously vote to up the purchase price. This formula is what you fall back upon when agreements cannot be made.

What is a fair calculation? There are several different methods: You can use a formula tied to the financial books of the company—known as an accounting method. You can use an appraisal method, employing the use of an appraiser to put a fair market value on the company. You can make a list of agreed-upon values by date—one year equals $100,000, two years $200,000, and so on.

Because the value of consulting companies is a fairly fixed value, It's not necessary to use the services of a potentially costly appraiser. Generally, 2x annual revenues is the high end of what a consulting company goes for (you could also use an EBITA approach, but I don't think that is necessary here). Making a formula that is conservative, but nods to this, such as 1x or 1.25x, is a reasonable approach. At The Barbarian Group, we used 1x the last calendar year's revenues. This was a good balance.

PAYMENT TERMS

Paying a partner, in full, per the buyout formula at once can be a devastating financial hit to your company. And since the amount paid out grows as the company grows, this is a risk that will never go away as you grow. Be sure to include a payment terms schedule in your buyout formula that ensures your company can bear the burden. We found that agreeing to pay out the departing partner at the same rate of pay as their current salary ensured that the company did not take an undue financial hit. For example, if the buyout calculation yields that a partner is owed $400,000 for their shares upon departure, and they are paid $150,000 a year, you will continue paying them their salary for 2 years, 4 months.

EMPLOYMENT AGREEMENTS

There is a distinction between being a partner of the company and being an employee. At the moment, you are going to be both. But some people will one day be employees and not partners, and there may eventually be partners who aren't employees. Spell out the distinctions between each. This also allows for differing salaries among partners based on role. Make the distinction, and write up an employment agreement for each partner along with the partnership documents. This also has the benefit of keeping you on the same page as your employees.

PERSONAL GUARANTEES

Somebody is going to need to guarantee some things against their personal finances. This seems strange, on the face of it. The whole point of an LLC is to shield the partners from liabilities in their companies. The problem is that many banks and landlords know that this is the exact point of an LLC, and know they are incurring a huge liability by lending, unsecured, to LLCs. Therefore, they may ask one or more of the partners to personally guarantee certain financing instruments and leases. You can choose to avoid this, but it will hinder your growth. Someone is going to need to sign them. It is best to have this worked out in advance. Having this discussion, along with the operating agreement discussion, is useful.

DEAL WITH THE ACCOUNTING

Next, figure out who is going to handle the actual bookkeeping. It may be the partner, an outside firm, a freelance or contracted bookkeeper, or a full-time hire. Over time, your bookkeeping will get more complex. You will need to grow this department, eventually bringing it all in-house. Hiring a bookkeeper is a good start. Eventually you'll also need to hire accounts receivable people, accounts payable staff, and the like. That comes later. For now, get your bookkeeping sorted out.

Finally, you will need a certified public accountant (CPA). This will be an outside relationship, like that you have with your lawyer. While you could probably handle filling out your own tax forms, having a CPA has several advantages. A CPA can handle what is called an "outside audit." This means that a certified firm, and not people inside your company, have audited your books and confirmed that they actually say what they should say. This is very important when we get into the world of lines of credit and financing. It adds significant credibility to your firm. It may not be necessary right away, but it's good to have an outside firm as early as possible, even if you try and tackle your own tax forms. They can still perform an audit, check the books, and be involved if anything goes awry with the IRS.

24

HOW MUCH TO CHARGE?

It's inevitable that in the early years of your company, you will be making up your prices out of thin air. Odds are good you're coming out of the freelance culture, where you could say things like, "Oh, I bill $150 an hour, and I think this will take 4 or 5 hours" and your client would say, "Whatever, that's fine." They are treating you like a freelancer, and they have a line item budget range. They can see your costs are probably going to fall within it, or close enough, and they don't need to worry about it.

Early on, you may well have clients who say, "Oh, thank god, you are literally half as much as our other bid." You'll wonder how on earth anyone could ever charge that much. Two or three years in, you'll find yourself sending proposals with costs you never, ever imagined that you could ever charge. Take advantage of being small and cheap while you can.

If you have great clients in the beginning, they'll often just tell you this: "I have $10,000 for this job." And you'll quite possibly find yourself doing some quick rough math in your head, adding everything up and saying, "Yeah, that works."

Later on, you will be taking on whole projects, which generally means slightly higher budgets. You will also, therefore, take on a whole combined budget line item—the project budget, not an individual contributor's budget. These are often more firmly set.

This can work for a long time. But as your shop continues to grow, eventually this too will change. Your growth will mean that you are often talking to new clients, who may not know you as well and need a little extra information from you. Your growth may also mean that your jobs are getting bigger. As a general rule, the more money involved, the more documentation required.

KNOW YOUR COSTS

When you are thinking about how much to charge, everything is based around costs. This doesn't mean that there won't be times that you are picking a number out of your head. This doesn't mean there won't be times when you can charge a client way more than cost. But it does mean that every time you do this, you know exactly what you're doing and exactly how it relates to costs.

Everything you create at your company costs you more than you think it does. It's easy to forget the cost of rent, and computers, and FedEx, and your Internet connection. Every job should bring in enough money to cover the percentage of rent and other "overhead" that it requires. This includes any non-billable people you have.

In the early years of TBG, I only calculated our costs once a year or so, whenever I got around to it. *Every single time* I did so, I found that we were radically undercharging, and in many cases we were actually losing money on jobs. It's vital to calculate your costs regularly. Even something as simple as looking at your monthly accounting, adding up all the nonemployee expenses and dividing it by the total number of hours all your employees work in a month is good enough for now.

PRICE DIFFERENTLY FOR DIFFERENT SERVICES

If your firm diversifies at all and offers various services, it's good for you to get to the point as quickly as possible where you charge different amounts for different services. The cost of design production, for example, should be lower than the cost for project management or user experience design.

Just because you know your costs, doesn't mean that there are some roles you can't price above that level. There may well be some skills that your business will be able to charge more for. These are typically the expertise that you and your partners are known for prior to starting your company.

Oftentimes there are multiple clients clamoring to "work with the genius." In our case, charging an exceptional premium for the supposed genius's time, compared to having our other employees do the same work, allowed the clients who *really* wanted to work with the genius being able to. Other clients also get a less expensive option. The great thing about this, then, was that many of them chose the less expensive option, received great work, and then grew to love the other employees, who slowly become geniuses in their own right. Everyone won.

There will be other parts of the project where it would be easier for the client to give that work to you—to give the whole job to you—but if you're too outrageously expensive on, say, front-end markup, they will have to go to someone else. In some things you can be competitive.

IN THE EARLY YEARS, ALWAYS BE RAISING YOUR PRICES

In the beginning, you may have developed a bit of a pride in your cheap work. You may have found yourself with a culture at your company that pooh poohs the giant bloat of the big guys. You may have thought that your small size and nimbleness were your advantage. And indeed, it was.

Over time, though, this will need to change. Your costs are going to always be going up. This is inevitable. Adjustments to stay profitable will be required. And if you're always raising your prices in small amounts, there will never be sticker shock as they jump significantly.

It will probably take you years to get your prices to where you want them to be. There will be times you'll need to raise your prices on a current client. Those are uncomfortable discussions, but you'll need to have them. Far more common will be that your renown for your past work will generate a continuous stream of new clients. New clients will be given the new prices, and wonderful old clients may stay on the older prices for a while. But if you're growing, your prices will need to be adjusted over time.

DISCOUNTING

Discounting is a legitimate part of your business. The first cardinal rule of discounting is the one related to the costs: *know how much of a discount you are giving.* Calculate the true costs and record the discount. Keep track of discounts.

Also, maintain control over who can give discounts. And track how many they give. It's vital that some sort of agreed-upon process for giving out discounts is established, and faithfully and truly maintained. At our shop, every discount had to be approved by one of three of the partners. The challenge, really, is in the client service and new business groups, once you have them. Price pressure is an extraordinary part of the sales process, and a "deal" is one of a salesperson's most powerful tools. Make a nice system in which one party calculates the cost, and another party is responsible for selling the project. This keeps the selling party from having any ability to succumb to pressure to change the costs to make it more appealing to the client. Then give the seller a range in which a discount is acceptable. Any discount beyond that range requires partner approval. Track every seller against how many discounts they give on average.

But, early on, things don't need to be that complicated. The basics are to

- *know your costs,*
- *know how much of a discount you're giving, and*
- *keep track of discounts.*

If, after doing all of these things, you find that you are not a profitable company, it should, at least, be fairly easy to see where the problems lie.

FIRE THE BAD CLIENTS

Unprofitable clients exist. Avoid them. If you have one, fire them. *Adweek* preaches the same approach: "if a client is still costing you money, end the relationship. You're better off with fewer clients, less staff and a profit, than with more clients and a money-losing firm....If it's a new client, after six months you should be able to assess whether it will be profitable.[1]"

Start by calling the client and saying, "Listen, friend, you are costing us money. We're going to need to charge you more." This works about half the time. If it doesn't, you're going to need to fire them.

LEARN TO TALK ABOUT IT

All of these tips require you to be a good communicator with your clients.

You will need to learn to deliver your price without a hint of embarrassment, and with an aura of its being not necessarily nonnegotiable, but more like a fact of life, like gravity.

The client can smell fear; they can smell a novice. You need to wash these stinks off of you. It will, of course, get easier with practice, and one day you'll actually laugh that you were ever scared about asking for $10,000.

Sensitivity and patience are required, and communication and honesty are key, but *complete* communication and honesty are not necessarily for the best.

There will also be times, if you're lucky, sort of, where some giant company may be considering giving you a giant contract. The wisdom of taking this contract is something we'll discuss later, but let's assume for the moment that you want it. This contract may come with some pretty excessive strings in the form of opening the kimono to the large company, which will want to review every aspect of your books, and poke, prod, and measure everything about your business. If you find one of these situations unavoidable, the best thing to do is to sit back, relax, and endure it, like any doctor's visit. Here, too, however, there's a little leeway. When the doctor asks you if you drink "more than 5" drinks a week, you don't need to volunteer that it's actually closer to 40, unless she asks. Same rules apply here. If they don't ask for something, no need to volunteer it.

DELIVERING PRICES TO CLIENTS

We've talked about the benefit of not showing your client the details of your pricing if you can get away with it. The advantages of this are many. The client can't drill down, looking for specific areas to cut. It makes it harder for the client to second-guess your approach. It keeps the client, basically, from asking too many questions.

Yet there is a difference between showing a single line item price, and not calculating the full price at all. As a general rule, you should show as little pricing information as you can get away with. But the calculations should still be done.

PRICING APPROACHES

When pricing work for clients, we usually calculated the costs of our projects based on the number of hours we thought they would take, and in the end we took that number and offered it as a flat fee for the client. If we got it finished quicker, we'd make a little extra money. If we had to do more work to get it done, we would have to eat it. I liked this because it had predictability, and incentivized our whole company to get things done quickly and well. Most of our clients agreed.

There were two other ways we priced jobs: the monthly or the quarterly retainer, and the agile/iterative approach. In both these situations, the client was paying for a team, to direct against certain work, by the sprint, the quarter, or the month. We still priced these in the same manner, putting a month's time of the whole team into the pricing worksheet, and then offering the total (with markup) as the cost for the team for each period. We then agreed on the number of weeks, months, or quarters that the project would go for. Extending the contract was handled with a simple one-page addendum.

25

SOWs, MSAs, AND IN-PROs

Now that you've pitched the job, gotten the proposal out, worked out pricing, and won the job because you are such a great company, with values and a vision aligned with the work you do, it is time to start the job. This means you need to get the client to sign something.

There are essentially three ways to do this:

1. a SOW, which is a job contract for a specific job
2. a master services agreement (MSA), which is a master document between you and a client in which you agree to general terms for *all* jobs, so each additional job may be started without a lengthy negotiation of terms and conditions
3. an in-production report (in-pro), also called a change order, which changes the terms of an existing job

Always get something signed for every job, no exceptions. Do this, preferably, before you start. There will be times with trusted clients when you start without getting something signed, but these times should be rare, and you should still get something signed ASAP. Don't do this for new clients.

STATEMENTS OF WORK

Our SOWs had the following sections:

- Project Description: This is a brief, layperson's description of the project. It is not overly technical, just a brief synopsis of what you're doing and what the goals are.
- Project Scope: This is where you get detailed. Make sure this is explicit and clear. What are you doing in this job? Are there things you are definitely *not* doing, or are not included in the cost? This is

not the time to fudge things. If you're not including photography, but are worried the client still might think you are, even though you've said you're not a million times, make it clear, here, that you are not including photography. If they only get three rounds of revisions on the comps before you need to charge them more, say so. The number of things that can go wrong on a project is infinite, and through the years you will find yourself adding more and more details as you learn where common areas of confusion are for your clients. Our scope section was a hybrid of the specific work being done for this job, and a laundry list of problem areas we'd encountered before.

- Team Organization: This is where you list the staff assigned to the project. Include their names and roles. If required, include the number of hours or percent weekly allocations. We generally bid our projects out on a flat fee, so we didn't include hours, but often the client required it. We usually did this in terms of full-time equivalents, or FTEs. If a person's on a job for half the week, that is 1/2 FTE. If you know the specific person, include his or her name and role. If you only know the role, list that. Work out how you're going to present this with your client beforehand, so it knows what to expect here.

- Technical Considerations: I find that a detailed technical considerations section in an SOW is a necessity for any job that requires coding. It should explicitly address any potential areas of confusion.

- Project Timeline: This lays out the timing of the project and the due date, or duration. Some of our SOWs say that the detailed timeline will come later, by a certain date. This is especially true on larger projects. It is also vital to mention that the timing is contingent upon the timely signing of the SOW. It can be frustrating watching a client not sign the SOW and still expect the project to be done the next week.

- Project Costs: This is the amount of money the project costs and the payment terms. We often include a table of payment due dates and amounts. Also include your company's accounts receivable information, mailing address, and bank wiring information.

- Terms and Conditions: This is the legalese that defines the contract. We'll talk about this in a moment.

- The Signature Lines: This is where each party signs on the bottom line.

TERMS AND CONDITIONS

Over time, your terms and conditions—or T&Cs—will grow increasingly complex. I strongly recommend that you work with a lawyer to draft a base set of T&Cs. They should cover project start, approvals, changes, delays, revisions, expenses, indemnification, what warranty and code compatibility guarantee you offer, intellectual property, contract termination, project promotion, nonsolicitation of employees, arbitration, ownership of the work created, and which state's laws you are signing the contract under (typically your home state).

I cannot and do not offer legal advice. I emphasize: get a lawyer to help you write your default terms and conditions. That being said, here are some areas I have found that will be contentious with your clients.

Intellectual Property. First, clients want to own everything. This is generally fine. You are working for them. However, in the course of being a developer, you probably have developed certain snippets of code, or tools that you need to use for each and every client. You may also be using open sourced code that you do not own. Therefore, these cannot be "given" to the client. You need to make it clear that some code you are using will stay with you, but in that case, they have a permanent, royalty-free, worldwide right to use the code. You'll also need to make it clear you use open source software, if you do, and that this cannot be transferred. Some shops find it to be an immense profit center to force a client to license code that they have made. If that is the case for you, it should be spelled out in the body of the SOW, under Scope and Technical Considerations.

This can often be a tricky discussion because you are dealing with people who do not necessarily understand technical topics.

The other area in which it is often necessary to have a conversation in advance is about promoting and crediting the work you do. Some clients want to pay you to do the work and not have anyone know you did it. That is not necessarily bad, so long as everyone is upfront about it and is compensated accordingly. However, your desires here and the client's can often diverge. For this reason, have a frank discussion about credit before you start the job. If the client is not comfortable with your promoting your work, this is the time to find that out, so that you may decide whether you still want the job or whether you want to raise your rates. Your T&Cs should reflect this conversation.

MSAs

Statements of work are common for smaller, one-off jobs, but eventually you may well find yourself doing several jobs for the same client, or engaging in a year-long project with a client. Your client may also not want the hassle of repeatedly negotiating legal terms with you over and over, since they have to send everything with legalese in it through their legal department. These associations are handled with the use of a Master Services Agreement (MSA). An MSA is essentially a SOW without specific deliverables and without a specific project. It is the legal language that dictates your relationship, the payment terms, and a time frame. With most MSAs, clients like to use their own documents as a starting point, as opposed to your default SOW, meaning the onus is on you to root out the provisions of their terms that do not work for you. And here, you need to be very careful. Pay close attention to the following areas:

- Payment terms: How long the company has to pay their bill.
- Intellectual property: Same deal as above. Make sure there are carve outs for code you use across many clients, and open source code.
- Credit & Promotion: Again, same as above. What you can and can't say about the client and the work should be spelled out in the terms of service.
- Indemnification, nonsolicit: Default MSAs often push to have these be *one way*. That is, you indemnify them (indemnification essentially means that you won't sue them or hold them liable for anything, and if other people do, it's all on you. Again, I am not a lawyer), but they do not indemnify you. Or you cannot steal their employees, but they can steal yours. Push to make these two way, which means both parties agree to play by the same rules.

MSAs are a pain because you probably don't have an in-house lawyer, and going back and forth on these can be expensive. We relied heavily on our CFO. For large, important, multiyear MSAs, it may be wise to put them in front of your lawyer, but often, you'll just have to wing it. No small firm can realistically afford a lawyer to negotiate all of these. Pay close attention, and have a couple different people look at it. Use a lawyer when it matters.

IN-PROS

It's impossible to always get everything right the first time, so there are, unsurprisingly, many occasions where the parameters of the job need to be changed midstream. If you're in an agile or a retainer contract, this usually revolves around team composition. The key here is to have a process to handle these changes, get them documented, and, most importantly, to get you paid for the changes. These are handled through in-pros. Other people call them, perhaps more sensibly, change orders.

This is essentially a document outlining the changes in deliverables, cost, and timing from the original SOW. It's a one-page form that just lists the changes and the impact on costs and timing, that states that both parties agree that the rest of the SOW still stands, and that contains signature lines.

A good client is always trying to get as much out of the project as it can, which means it is always asking for more. There is therefore a continuous challenge of keeping the clients reined in even when they are good clients. In-pros can, however, also be very profitable. Take care to manage the situation well. You can't bleed the client dry with a thousand charges for every little thing. Yes, we can make that change. It will cost X and take Y days. Or, we could not do it. Another option might be Z, which we could probably get in for free if you give us an extra day. A good client knows things are a give and take.

26

TRACKING TIME

Time sheets are a joke. They are an outright lie. They are, first and foremost, a massive fraud, contentedly perpetrated and affirmed by all parties in the ecosystem—the employer, the client, and the employees. Finance knows it. Your client knows it. Your client's finance department knows it. Your boss knows it. His boss knows it. Everyone knows it, but no one cares. There is zero accountability or incentive to discover the truth. Time sheets are supposed to perform one job—to accurately track time—and they don't accomplish this. People lie. People forget.

There's another major reason why time sheets are so awful—they kill creativity. They foster an environment of mistrust. It's sad that services firms spend so much time fostering creativity and giving their employees so much in terms of freedom and creativity, but almost all of them expect this ridiculous charade to continue.

A SIMPLE ACTUALIZATION PROCESS

Your shop lives invoice to invoice. If you undercharge for a job, you'll lose money, and you have no money to lose. You know how to estimate a job, but when the job is done, you need to make sure that it was profitable. This is called *actualization*. Actualization is part and parcel with knowing how much time people spent on a job.

Time sheets or no, you will still need some method of actualization. It would seem like time sheets would play an integral part of that process, but they don't, not just because time sheets lie (never, ever forget this), but because they inflate time estimates, and thus costs. This must be constantly, vigilantly guarded against, or your company will soon become comically expensive and two kids down the street will have taken your client.

Here's what we did. The team does the job. No one on the team really worries about how many hours they spend on the project. We pay them a salary, this is the project they're assigned to, and they do their job. They are treated with respect and manage their own time. Like human beings. If you are being paid for 40 hours of development time, but you pay a developer a salary, by the week, this is really the place to resolve those two different cost calculations. If the developer does the work in 30 hours, good for her. She is being efficient. If she needs 42, and she scrambled to work late, that's cool too. I still got paid for 40 hours, and she got paid for a week either way. It's humane. It's fair. It's civilized.

Of course, occasionally there are all-nighters, and there are some challenges when employees are assigned to two projects at half their time, rather than one full time project. So we have a resource manager. In a small shop, this is the person who's good with time management. She goes around, asks everyone how they're doing, and keeps track of things. Even without the resource manager, problems would bubble up—if two producers are using the same developer, and one project is eating up too much of their time, the other producer will usually say something. The resource manager is there to fix it, track it, and report it.

At the end of the project, the producer fills out a simple one-page form. How many weeks was this project supposed to go? How many did it go? Did it go over? Why? Did we get paid for the overage? How many people were on the team? Boom. Done. From this, we see that we estimated accurately and got paid. If we went over, we can see whether we got paid for it. If we messed up, we can see it, we can see why, how much it cost us (team size times costs), and we fix it for the future. Actualization doesn't need to be difficult, but you do need some system in place. Like all end-of-job processes, it's difficult to make sure everyone complies—everyone seems to want to move on to the next thing—but you, and your finance department, must police this heavily.

27

BILLING, COLLECTIONS, AND CASH FLOW

Collections in services companies face unique challenges. Recurring revenues are more and more rare these days. Advance bookings are rare. We rely on getting paid, promptly, for the work we do specific for a certain client. Law firms and accounting firms, most notably, rely on similar systems. Whereas the law industry has been billing by the hour for centuries, advertising agencies have only been doing it for perhaps 50 years, and in that time, they've been doing it in a few different ways. Established norms don't exist. What worked well with television advertising has not yet been replicated on the Internet. In many ways, you are on your own.

WHEN THE CHECKS COME IN

One of the most challenging aspects of your business will be that every two weeks, you have to pay employees, and every month, you have to pay rent, while your income is, essentially random. Checks come when they come.

You need to stay on your clients to pay on time. This requires constant communication with the client company. Typically, your actual day-to-day client will have very little say over when you get paid. What you need to do with them is have them introduce you to their payments team. Talk to them at least once a week during the course of the job. Get a date out of them when the check is coming. Be kind, be helpful, be professional. When the date is imminent, give them a call to be sure that they are sending the check out. Make sure there are no problems.

Develop a calendar to track when the checks are coming in, and an accompanying spreadsheet that lays out all of your checks and expenses. Do this early, before you start spending heavily on growth and things get tight. You want to make sure there are no surprises.

Next, embrace electronic transfers. This is becoming increasingly common, but many companies still pay by check as a default. Ask if they support electronic transfers. Get into the system early—well before you need them to send you money. Make sure the whole process works early, billing electronically for a small job early on. An electronic transfer can mean three to five additional days saved in getting paid. This will matter.

Finally, as much as it pains me to say this, and it will pain you to do it, if your client has a program to speed payment by paying a fee—typically 1 percent or 2 percent—enter into the program. Do what you need to do to get paid as quickly as possible. If you need to mark up the job for these clients, do so.

PAYMENT TERMS

Payment terms is essentially an agreement between you and your client regarding how quickly you get paid for the job. On smaller jobs, clients are more willing to sign your SOW, not worrying too much about the details, and thus accepting your payment terms. It's important to note that while they may have *signed* those payment terms, they don't necessarily have any intention of *abiding* by them. When working with a new client who's signed your SOW and your payment terms, you should immediately do two things: first, point out what the client signed, and tell the client you mean it. Secondly, ask to be introduced to its accounts payable department, right away. When you talk to the accounts payable team, be sensitive and courteous. They will probably immediately tell you that whatever the client signed isn't the way the company dos things. Figure out how it *does* do things. Figure out whether that's acceptable. If not, get your client to help you broker a solution.

THE FIRST CHECK

The Web is a Wild West frontier when it comes to standards and practices around project payment. I find that many, many clients have no concept of paying anything upfront.

It'll sign an SOW that says 50 percent upfront due at signing of the invoice and prior to the start of work, and it will literally have no comprehension you actually meant it. It will just assume that means that it will turn the invoice over to accounts payable, that the signature is enough, and that you can get started right away.

When you are small and cash is tight, not only will it be maddening but it will also be virtually impossible to handle a situation like this. And if you use outside vendors, this is even more true. If you succumb to this tyranny, you will often find that you are paying upfront costs, out of your pocket, on behalf of a much larger client, with no idea of when you'll be reimbursed.

In the early days, it is imperative that you endeavor to make it crystal clear to your new clients that "50 percent payment upfront prior to start of work" means exactly that. You won't always win this battle. But you must try. And you can't try in a passive-aggressive way. You need to explain all of this to the client upfront. You can explain that as you both get to know each other, there will be increased flexibility in this term, as you get to know the firm's accounts payable (AP) department. Once you know exactly how long a specific client takes to pay, and you've developed a solid relationship with its AP department, you can work that into your cash flow calendar and make a determination on whether or not you need to be insistent about the first check with this client any longer.

To this end, on every first project, I would walk my clients through the SOW and say something like this, "Now, just as a head's up, we mean this. We'll need the first deposit before we begin work. If you have an impending deadline, we should get this process started right now. Do you have a good relationship with your AP department? Should we talk to them?" If the client has a tight deadline, there are ways around this, such as making it pick a specific date, starting in good faith with the understanding that you will be paid on that specific date, and stopping work if the client hasn't paid. But until you've gotten to know a client, play it safe. No matter how nice your client is, this doesn't mean its AP department is as nice. As you grow, you will have a bit more flexibility in this regard.

BILLING

Send your invoices out immediately upon receiving the signature on the SOW or passing a relevant milestone that makes the next payment due. Deliver them electronically and by mail. Be sure they include the payment terms date, a contact name, phone number and email, a physical address for paper check delivery, and wiring instructions for electronic payment. You may also want to consider unilaterally including a 1–2 percent discount for electronic payment before a certain date. This works more often than you would think.

It is vital that you submit your invoices in the required manner, with the required information. This is where a healthy relationship, forged in advance, with the client's AP department comes in.

But most importantly, get the invoices out ASAP. It's astonishing to me how many companies forget to invoice in a prompt manner.

OTHER TACTICS

When all else fails, you may want to consider legal action or a collections agency. When you do this, most clients will wake up, face reality, and pay quickly, but there are expenses involved. Typically, the clients who aren't paying are small companies that are probably going to go bankrupt soon. It's often better to call them up and work out a settlement, settling for less than you would get if they paid in full, but more than you'd get if they go out of business. With the larger companies, suing them is almost always futile. The check will come, eventually.

Finally, above all, guilt-trip them. Call frequently. Let them know people are hurting. Let them know it's important. It really is true in this situation that the squeaky wheel gets the grease. Many companies don't care if the check shows up in 30 days or 90 days. You do. Let them know that.

28

WORKING WITH VENDORS

Depending on your disposition and specific industry, you may or may not make heavy use of freelancers. The use of freelancers is common at agencies of all sizes, including your size and is an important tool of effective agency management. In today's freelance economy, most clients understand that your company will be using freelancers for certain portions of the job. Nonetheless, many clients are absolutely firm that the leadership on the job—the top account, creative, strategy, and tech people—are full time and committed to the job. The exception is for certain high-level consultants, such as senior content strategists or information architects, whom the client understands are a different beast.

WHEN TO HIRE A FREELANCER FULL TIME

If you find yourself hiring the same freelancers over and over again, as we did, and you know with a fair degree of confidence that you are probably going to keep doing so, you should consider hiring them. The freelance-to-permanent journey is one that has many benefits, most notably that you are hiring someone whose skills you know and are comfortable with.

Freelancers are more expensive on a per-hour basis, but you don't have to pay them every week no matter what. The rate a freelancer would cost if you hired them for the whole year is about 1.5x higher than an employee would cost for the whole year, benefits included. (An employee, by the way, generally costs about twice their salary in overhead and benefits as a rough figure). However, the benefit is that you only pay them for the hours worked, and those hours are, presumably, paid by a client against a pricing sheet. You also don't have to pay for their overhead or benefits. Many of them will work from home. Many of them have their own computer.

However, also be aware of the intangible economic benefits of a full-time employee. They can work on spec work. They can work on "product," if you are going that path. They can put ten extra hours into a project on a weekend when they're bored, and you won't have to pay them for it. You don't have to pay them overtime. I know some of this sounds craven, and I don't mean it to. But these are the numbers.

If you feel that you will keep working with the same person, and if there is every reasonable indication that the amount of work coming into your company will stay the same or grow, you should hire the person. Remember: if everything goes wrong, you can fire the person. If the work doesn't materialize, or the employee turns from Dr. Jekyll to Mr. Hyde, you can let them go. You will know in two or three months, maybe four.

TREAT VENDORS WITH RESPECT

Negotiate with your vendors with humanity and respect. Pay them promptly. You should keep them informed about what's going on with projects. With vendors, showing kindness and respect is an easy way to keep them on your good side. If times get tough and you can't pay them for some reason, and you have a history of being a good payer, you can have a frank conversation with them and they will generally be helpful to you.

I took pride in our relationships with our vendors. However, as we grew, and my role in the company became less connected to the nuts and bolts of promptly paying our vendors, we lost a little of our mojo here. The vendors who'd been around a long time would give me a call when problems arose, and I could go run and fix it. Yety eventually I realized that while I believed we should treat our vendors with uncommon respect and prompt payment, this vision was not dissembled throughout the larger, rapidly growing company. For a while there, we lost our footing in this respect, and I am saddened by it. Eventually this was rectified. But this experience allowed me to witness, concretely, the perils of such actions. The day you desperately need a vendor for a job, and they won't take it because you haven't paid them in six months is a dark day indeed.

PRICING VENDOR COSTS

The traditional big agency way to figure out how much vendors are going to cost is to call two or three of them and get estimates. This is the notorious "triple bid." Use this only in a limited way, and don't be dishonest. Tell the vendor you're triple bidding it and looking for ballparks. Don't be false and pretend you plan on hiring them to get a more accurate proposal, only to leave them in the lurch. This breeds resentment.

If you *know* you are going to use a specific vendor, and you know the work is specific to them, by all means, talk to them and work out detailed costs with them. But if you're not sure whom you're going to use, don't leave a bunch of vendors hanging, angry and stewing. Arrive at an accurate estimate on your own. Sometimes your producers will get it right, sometimes they'll be over, and sometimes they'll be under. But you can track, through the actualization process, the accuracy of any individual producer and deal with the problem cases.

Often jobs have multiple vendors, and where one vendor category might be over, another might be under. The producer can manage this.

If you are not sure which freelancer is going to do the job, and all of your regular go-to freelancers are busy, consider doubling the freelance budget on this job. You can explain to the client that "the market's really tight right now and rates are high," and offer them the alternative of extending the project out. If you've already committed to an overall budget, perhaps this one freelancer line item is negligible, and they won't notice. If both of these fail, and it's an emergency, you can always consider cutting the margins to the company on this one job, and pass some of the savings on to the freelancer.

NEGOTIATING WITH VENDORS

Here are some pointers for negotiating with your vendors:

When you're small, do all the negotiating yourself. Even when producers estimate out-of-pocket costs, and designers say whom they want and what they'll do the job for, negotiate it yourself. No one else in the ecosystem is incentivized to do best by the company like you are.

When you're growing, establish a set of rules that keeps your creative director (CD) from telling his buddy the outside designer that "they have $20k for this one," when the outside designer would have happily done it for $5k. The easiest way to do this is to not tell your CD how much you have for the job. The producer sets the budget, and the CD recommends people. The producer does the negotiations. There are times when the *producer* will say, "We only have $20k for this one," but those are different times, and producers are tracked on money, while CDs aren't.

When you've become a larger company, consider centralizing vendor negotiation (but remember, instill them with a sense of humanity and respect for the artist), so that the producers don't just slide everyone the full amount they have budgeted. This, luckily, is a time-honored tradition and skill in the advertising world called "art buying." It's a far more humane practice than a normal company's procurement department. Hire an experienced art buyer and make it clear you are a moral company that believes in treating its vendors well. Yes, you will actually have to say this.

Work closely with finance to make sure vendors are paid promptly and that the vendors most in need or most important are prioritized.

FINDING VENDORS

At TBG, we were always on the lookout for new vendors, even in the early days. As the company grew, this became something approaching a full-time job. Online portfolios were scoured. Networking events were relentlessly attended to. An internal database was set up of potential vendors, and all people in the company were encouraged to add to it any of their friends or acquaintances who might make good vendors. We regularly attended the recruitment days of the major design, tech, and advertising schools. We found people when we were out drinking at awards shows. We kept a listing on our site at all times, welcoming people to send in their portfolios. It's imperative that your stable of freelancers is deep enough to handle all the work you might conceivably win at any given time. When your company is hit with three major wins at once, the last thing you want is not to be able to take all the work. And freelancers will be your buffer to handle it.

29

EMPLOYEE EXPENSES

Your employees are going to need to spend money. This is necessary. You will also need to closely account for this money and keep this spending to a minimum. Here are some tips.

COMPANY CREDIT CARDS VERSUS EXPENSING

There are two broad ways employees will pay for things: with corporate cards, or by using their own credit cards and then filing an expense report. Broadly speaking, the corporate cards should be kept to a minimum, given to key employees higher in the organization. As you grow, you can expand the number of people who have corporate cards, perhaps going one rung lower in the org chart, or assigning one to every account service person.

Know this: *expenses are much, much higher with people using corporate cards than expensing things from their own cards.* To clarify, spending is not increased simply because employees have increased responsibility once they get a company card, and thus have more to buy. Nor am I talking about how when five people are out for dinner, the person with the corporate card will pay the bill because the accounting is easier, though both of these things are true. I don't know why it is, but even accounting for both of these things, corporate card holders spend more money than those using their own card.

EXPENSE REPORTS

At least once a month, employees should fill out an expense report. List the expense, state the client (if there is one), and attach the receipt. The employee should get their supervisor (or supervisors, if, for example, they are a client service exec on multiple accounts with different producers) to sign off on the charges, and submit them to the finance department.

There are some great products for handling this process. I particularly like Expensify, which provides an automated, networked, and mobile solution for all of this. Snapping a picture of a receipt is so much easier than saving it for a month and stapling it to a form. My younger self is jealous of how much easier this is today than it used to be.

REPAYMENT

Your default should be to reimburse your employees promptly. Preferably within a week. This will engender goodwill from the employees, and will stave off the palpable resentment that comes from their employer's having a large sum of their money for a long time. People need to actually pay these credit card bills.

The reality is that the money owed back on expenses is a giant accounting line item that can be pushed back when times are hard, in order to manage cash flow. However, resist this temptation as much as possible. Going from a week to two weeks? Okay. A month or more? No way. If a bank did this, mixed client money with institutional money, it would go to jail. It's only slightly less immoral for you to do these things.

If times *do* get hard, talk to the employees. Find out which ones care. Find out which ones hurt the most. Some will be more accommodating than others. Know who and *ask*.

REMEMBER THAT THE YOUNG ARE POOR

When I was a young tyke just getting my start in the corporate world, I worked for a company that expected me to expense everything and send in an expense report and get reimbursed. The problem was, I had no money in the bank and a credit card with a $400 credit limit on it. The company's approach was not practical. The company was so big, that it was impossible for me to find anyone to do something about this. The experience was humiliating and inefficient.

While expensing and reimbursement should be the primary expense method for most employees, take care to have an alternate loop for those who cannot use a credit card. Make it clear that it exists, and meet their needs discreetly.

TRAVEL

Travel will almost certainly be a huge part of your expenses. This needs to be carefully controlled. All travel should be approved in advance. Guidelines should be developed around appropriate airfare that can be bought. Business class and first class are out, of course. Exceptions can be made for longer flights—we allowed business class on flights over six hours once we could afford it, thus allowing it for anything longer than a transcontinental flight or a New York-London flight. Hotels should have by-city guidelines for costs. Exceptions can be made on a case-by-case basis.

A per diem for all food should be standardized—something like $50. This is exclusive from client entertaining. If the employee wants to spend the whole $50 on breakfast in bed, great. Taxis should be allowed, and car services at night, say after 10 p.m. Don't expect people to use mass transit in a foreign city. You should set up guidelines around car rentals.

You may tweak things. We made exceptions for premium economy on employees over six feet tall. We also made exceptions saying you could book the lowest nonstop fare that fit your schedule, rather than "just book the lowest fare, who cares if it has four stops and gets you in a day early."

Over time, you will feel an urge to centralize travel booking. This can save a lot of money and make employee expense reimbursement much easier. Also, you should have the company join mileage and rewards programs for hotels and cars. You can handle this in-house through a low-cost hire. There is a very good chance these services will pay for themselves and still save you money. When centralizing booking, make it very clear to everyone what the policies are, and that if there are any problems, they should come to you. Many employees will silently accept a booking of a three-stop red-eye and not say anything, but quietly seethe. Don't let this happen to you. Red-eyes and such also hamper employee productivity.

CLIENT POLICY

Be aware that many clients will have their own travel policies, and may expect you to abide by it. We had a document that we gave every client at the beginning of the job, letting them elect how they wanted to handle travel: they could book it, we could book it and expense them, or we could add a single line item for all travel to the total project bid. In all cases, we agreed to abide by their travel policy if they required it and sent the policy to us. This saved an inordinate amount of pain later.

WATCH THE BOTTOM LINE

Aside from the salaries of employees themselves, employee expenses are by far the largest budget item you will have control over month to month (since rent, etc. are fixed). Until your employee count is well into the hundreds, you should be looking at all expenses, every month. You should keep an eye on them. You should be constantly looking for ways to keep costs down, without cramping the employees' happiness or their ability to do their jobs.

Keep an eye on things like client dinners that aren't against a specific project, conference expense and trade association bloat, magazine subscriptions (it's amazing how this still happens), decoration purchases, snacks, and the like. Track individual salespeople's expenses against their sales. Look for outliers, both in sales and client service. Deal with them. Be creative. Be vigilant.

PART VII

WHAT'S NEXT?

30

EXPANDING BEYOND YOUR CORE

Inevitably in the course of your business, there will come a time when you will find yourself offering a service that you did not offer at the beginning. Often this will creep up on you—a developer might branch out to another coding language, or start accepting Photoshop documents for design, and doing some light CSS and graphic production work, whereas before you had strict guidelines on what you accepted. It might be more profound: your clients say they trust you on building websites, but it's time you also took on social media content. You may even find yourself one day with a client who trusts you and loves you, for whom you're suddenly doing print ads or a TV spot. It happens. Everything's possible in this mixed up twenty-first century. Digital agencies doing print ads. Dogs and cats, living together. Mass hysteria.

There are some businesses that stick to what they know and nothing else, and never really expand. Yet even firms known for doing a specific thing very well—IDEO and my friends at Hard Candy Shell come to mind—offer services beyond what they were initially known for. IDEO, for example, makes very nice websites these days. No point spending time debating *whether* you should expand beyond your core offering. It will inevitably happen. Let's talk about *how*.

We can break down "service expansion" into two silos. There are ancillary services that you'll grow into with any service offering—I am speaking here of things such as client service and consulting—which support your main service offering of design, technology, and what have you. These will expand naturally as your company grows, and your ability and confidence in charging for things that you once offered for free grows commensurately.

Then there is the second silo of expanded service offerings, *complementary* service offerings: design along with your development (or vice versa). Adding content. Copywriting. Viral videos. App development.

ORGANIC EXPANSION

The ideal approach here is when you've developed a great relationship with a client, and while you're doing yet another project for them, they say something along the lines of "can't you also handle the design? I have $300k for the whole thing and I'd really just like to give it to you. I know you don't handle design, but maybe you could handle the freelancing of it or something?" That doesn't sound so hard, and there are some financial incentives here for you. You know a lot more designers than your client does, and you think you can probably find someone who will do it for pretty cheap, certainly cheaper than she will be able to find, and you can either pocket the difference or (more often) take the extra resources and put it toward the part of the job you are doing. There is also the bonus, of course, that if you find the vendors and manage the process, it will be done right. You say yes. Once. Then twice. Eventually, you are saying yes routinely.

The best way to delve into a new line of business organically is to make one key hire, someone not too senior and not too expensive, but with heart and with hustle, or to train someone from within who is talented and eager. In either case, support them as they educate the company and slowly grow the workload as sales, client service, and others are brought up to speed. A lab experiment highlighting your new skill is a good way to draw attention to your new offering. And the capability should be highlighted in every subsequent pitch, even if it is not asked for. Finally, if you went the new hire route, and the hire was noteworthy enough, some PR might be possible to get the word out about your new offering. Avoid hiring seasoned executives for this type of complementary expansion. The culture and training costs will outweigh their additional experience, and you can postpone equity and partnership talks until the department blossoms.

STRATEGIC EXPANSION

As you grow, however, and the services you're expanding into are less logically linked to your core offering, you may need to think about it in a new way. At The Barbarian Group, this occurred when we decided we wanted to break into the new realms of planning and social media. We had offered both of these on an ad hoc basis to clients who requested them, but we identified these two areas as potential new growth areas for the company—because we saw demand in the marketplace increasing, because the per-hour revenue margins were higher, and because we detected increased demand for us to offer this, through conversations with our clients. However, it was clear that the manner in which we handled this in the past—taking the work, foisting it on our current employees, farming it out, or hiring new junior designers, and so forth—wasn't going to work in this case. Both required a seasoned heavyweight expert to lead the charge and stave off any criticisms by our competitors that our company wasn't qualified to be in the big leagues.

There can also be a creative benefit to expanding into complementary services. Our company organically increased our offerings because our ideas often spanned beyond a single specialty like design. When you handle all aspects of a project, your creative palette is enlarged. Design, content, and technology are very tightly wound together in the best new things that go out onto the Web. By offering these things yourself, you will find that the realm of possibility grows for your ideas and your company.

In times like these, you are going to need to make a director hire, which offers many benefits. Hiring a known expert in a field will keep competitors from plausibly claiming that your company doesn't know what it's doing or is just learning. You will be able to charge more for a senior person. On top of that, there is a massive PR potential. The switching of jobs of a known person is a newsworthy event in many cases, and you can use this to get some stories in the press about your new offering. Offer up the leadership of the company and the new hire for interviews. This will reach clients and help get the word out about your new offering. Finally, a new director hire generally comes with a strong Rolodex, which will help jump-start new business growth in this sector.

All that being said, hiring a director is fraught with risk. They may not take root in the company, eventually growing and blooming. Rather, they may wither on the vine. There will be cultural compatibility risks greater than for hiring another junior designer. Through the years, we had mixed luck here. We had some spectacular successes. But we have also had some notable failures. Extra care than normal must be taken to make sure the new director is a compatible fit.

There are also potential equity and partnership considerations, as directors who can potentially bring a large amount of new business may feel that they should be a partner. This is fine, if you and your partners all agree. Definitely work it out in advance, and take heed about the vesting and cliff tactics. This is especially important if the director turns out to be a poor fit. You can't have them walking out the door after six months with 5 percent of the company.

LOGISTICS

When adding a new department, be sure to revamp your org chart, *before you hire the new director*, making sure all personnel—old and new—are on board with the new reporting structures.

Charge the new director with getting the rest of the company up to speed through internal training sessions. This is vital. Focus especially on the client services, new business, and strategy groups—those who may recommend these new services to the client.

This will be challenging, as the director is also simultaneously trying to get the lay of the land of the new company, and trying to drum up business. Another practice is to have the new director define a 30-, 60-, and 90-day plan that addresses all of these competing challenges on their time. Everyone should agree upon this plan prior to the start of the employee's working, preferably, or within, say, two weeks. Any new director worth their salt should come in talking and learning. Beware of any new potential hire who tells you your company is screwed up and they are going to change this and this and this. It's rarely true, hugely disruptive, wastes a ton of time, and fosters resentment. It's another thing if they come back 30 days in and say that, with much of the company backing them up.

This process takes a little practice, but over time, you should get quite good at it. Adding whole lines to your business can be hugely beneficial for the rapid expansion of your bottom line, if you find the right partner.

31

HOW MUCH IS
MY COMPANY WORTH?

Given that any time for the next several years of your life much, if not all, of your net worth will be tied up in the value of your company, it is not an unreasonable question to ask, "how much is my company worth?" If you are in this business to eventually get rich, this means you will need to sell your company in due course. And you'll need to sell it for an amount that will hit your personal financial goals, which, again, means that you need to know how much your company is worth.

CONSULTING VERSUS PRODUCT COMPANY VALUATIONS

Let's talk about valuations of services businesses. Wall Street views services businesses as less valuable, per dollar of revenues, than "products" businesses. In the old days, this made sense. The classic example was the factory versus the law firm. If you bought a factory, and every person working at the factory walked out, you could put a bunch of new people into the factory without much hassle, and the factory would still keep making things and selling things. Even if you *couldn't* rehire everyone, the factory itself was worth some money. This is not the case with a law firm. If you bought a law firm, and all the employees got up and walked out, you'd be left with nothing but a bunch of lease obligations. Therefore, the factory is worth more per dollar of revenue than the law firm. This is known as the *revenue multiplier*. When people talk about businesses, they talk about the revenue multiplier you can get when selling the business. For consulting businesses (read: yours), the revenue multiplier is 1–2x total annual revenue. It's been my experience that 2x is pretty high, and that it usually falls somewhere around 1.5x.

Now, this is not the case for Internet "product" businesses, or "start-ups" (both industries—services and tech—have coalesced around the term "start-up," referring solely to product start-ups, and we will do the same here). The logic here goes that an Internet "product" is something that can keep being sold even if everyone leaves. Thus Internet product companies can be valued at exponentially higher multipliers. Often comically so. As of this writing, Google's P/E ratio is over 29. Apple's is 15. Facebook's is over 80. Amazon's P/E ratio is over 480.

Right off the bat, if you have a company doing $20 million of business, and if it is a consulting company, the company is worth maybe $30–40 million. If you have a $20 million tech start-up, it could be well worth $100–200 million. It's easy to see why getting *rich rich* is so much harder with services companies than start-ups.

Is this fair? The proposition that Internet product companies have much higher multipliers than services companies is dubious assertion these days. I can't help but ask myself which company would be more screwed if everyone got up and walked out the door—Google, where every person there is supposedly a meticulously vetted irreplaceable, magical unicorn, or WPP, an advertising holding company filled with a bunch of people identical to the people at the other advertising holding companies, from which they could pretty easily refill their ranks.

Dan Yanofsky, writing in *Quartz*, summed it up perfectly: "The reality is that calling a business a 'tech company' is a ploy to make it sound exciting to potential consumers and investors, not a method of assigning greater meaning."[1]

Google, at least, has a physical infrastructure of data centers that have some nominal value on their own, without the people. But this, too, is becoming increasingly rare, as most start-ups in the 21st century have moved their operations to the cloud. Indeed, if everyone got up and walked out of most tech start-ups these days, the purchaser would generally be left with some lease obligations, a lot of code, and a big Amazon Web Services bill. What's the code worth? It depends, but it's a very different, more subjective calculation than if they owned a factory.

Finally, let's not forget that a large chunk of these supposed product-oriented tech start-ups now must employ thousands, if not tens of thousands, of salespeople, along with legions of engineers. Now, I may be belittling my own profession here, but it's hard to imagine that it's any easier to replace 10,000 salespeople than it is to replace 10,000 art directors, copywriters, planners, and account guys.

The difference in valuations between tech-savvy service firms and tech start-ups is bunk, or at least seriously misguided. But that is an argument for another time. The point here is that is the lay of the land. These revenue multiples are the immutable hand we have been dealt.

This reality colors much of what we talk about here. It colors how much you can sell your company for. It colors your hiring practices. It colors how you approach new business.

SERVICE FIRM VALUATION MECHANICS

So, then. For professional services firms, *a company is worth about 1.5 to 2 times its annual revenue.* For example, a $10MM design shop is probably worth $15 million to, tops, $20 million. Yes, there are times that the multiple maybe slightly higher than 2x. These tend to be around highly specialized shops selling to tech companies, not holding companies. But even then—and I have assisted in several of these deals—you're generally looking at about 2x revenue.

That's it. I'm sorry if that sounds depressing. I feel your pain.

A note here. I use revenue multiple for simplicity throughout this book. Buyers often talk in terms of EBITA (earnings before interest, taxes, and amortization, or as we like to call it, profit). EBITA makes more sense when your primary reason for buying a company is pure profit, but I find in these deals that's not usually the case. Also, the sad fact of the matter is all professional services have around the same profit margins, so really it comes down to revenue levels. Either way, the concept is the same. Revenue's a bit easier for us to discuss here, and the math is easier.

DO THE MATH

A useful exercise is to do the math backwards. How much money do you want out of this? Let's say $5 million, the high end of how much it would take to be rich from the Gallup poll results we talked about earlier in the book. Let's say that means half upfront and half in three years, so it's the total payout you're going to get from the sale. Let's ignore the salary bump you may get during the years you work for a holding company, since you'll probably blow all that anyway. Let's assume you have three partners (a not unreasonable assumption), with 10 percent more for the rest of the employees. Debt's probably lower at this range, as are closing costs. Let's say $5 million total. Don't forget capital gains taxes. A $30 million sale should cover everything. This means you'll need to get your sales to about $20 million a year.

We should also say that in this scenario you're getting $2.5 million up front and $2.5 million in three years. What if you don't make it? Is $2.5 million enough? Perhaps it's better to grow the shop to where you get $5 million upfront? That could double the revenue target.

If you're one of those plotting people who look at every penny, I suspect right now you are doing furious math in your head on how to trim all of those numbers. Some of them are easier to trim than others. It's quite difficult to get the acquisition costs of a major transaction like this down, and you're not paying for that anyway. In fact, you'll have almost no say over those costs. But let's give you the benefit of the doubt and say you can shave a million off. My company managed to get to that size with only a $1million line of credit, so let's say you can too. Any less is probably possible, but do remember it will make it take significantly longer to get to these numbers, so we can only cut it to a million. Let's say you screw your partners every step of the way (and somehow they magically stay—they won't). Let's say all of that means you keep control of your firm with 51 percent of the stock outstanding. And let's say you move out of New York and only have to pay 18 percent capital gains.

To get to $5 million in this scenario, you will need to sell your company for just under $15 million.

For comparison, I know people in Silicon Valley who have brought home bigger paychecks in three years. Don't even get me started on WhatsApp.

There is an upper end to all this. Typically, it's near impossible to get your company up to, say, $100 million in value without bringing on some serious investment. And even then, this will take well over a decade. You might net $15–20 million from such a sale.

Yes, there have been bigger sales—the ad world went gaga when Ed Meyer sold his Grey Global group to WPP in 2005 for $1.75 billion, netting himself a payday of approximately $500 million.[2] It took him 50 years to build Grey to that level.

In the old days, you could take an agency public—David Ogilvy took Ogilvy public in 1966, claiming Warren Buffet as an early investor and making a fortune. But this does not happen anymore. Agencies don't go public anymore. These days, you're going to get acquired.

Furthermore, the potential acquirers are going to come knocking long, long before you get anywhere near $100 million in revenue. More likely, the whole deal will go down at about one-tenth of these levels.

We should also pause for a moment here and acknowledge that yes, $48.3 million, or even $5 million, is a lot of money, and we should all not be whining. Money doesn't matter. Yes, yes, we get that. Never forget. $5 million is a lot of money. This isn't a chapter about trying to get more money. It is a chapter to help you think about how much money you are shooting for, how long it may take to get it, and whether you are operating in the most efficient manner possible. This is about financial planning.

32

CREATING A PRODUCT IN YOUR SERVICE FIRM

By now, you may be thinking that a start-up sounds like a potentially vastly more pleasant endeavor than a services company. You're sitting there on a treadmill of endless pitches, billing, payroll, and cash flow management. Meanwhile, you're looking over at your friend at some start-up with $10 million of venture capital in the bank, head down, building something awesome. You might start to wonder why you shouldn't build one of those start-ups as well. Never mind that a start-up might be insanely more lucrative as a business. They also seem a lot more fun and, well, maybe even easier.

You may love start-ups deep down. You may be one of those people who is just dying to make a product. You *love* the tech industry, and you have a great idea, but you can't get anyone to fund it. You're not really connected to venture capitalists (VCs). You might not live in New York or San Francisco. You just *know* your idea is great, but you can't get anyone to give you any money to build it. But you're a hustler. You have mad skills.

On the face of it, this isn't as unreasonable as it sounds. Start a services firm, and use the proceeds to fund your product. Screw the venture capitalists. I'll make my own money, build my own stuff. You work with what you have. Not everyone has easy access to venture capitalists. If you don't know people, you don't know people. It can be hard to find people if you're not in the right part of the country. Sometimes we just have to hustle and get things done. Sometimes hustle is all we have.

It seems eminently logical, then, to consider getting into the start-up game with your company.

I seek not to dissuade you from this approach. But you need to know what you're getting into. For what you're contemplating is a nearly impossible task—attempted by thousands of entrepreneurs through the years and accomplished by very few. I'll also admit that, despite herculean efforts, we were not among the successful.

So as to not completely pulverize your morale, we'll also bring into the story two companies that succeeded in this endeavor—a San Francisco-based UX consultancy called Seabright Studios, and a full-service digital agency based in Blacksburg, Virginia, called Modea. Both of these shops have pulled off the near-impossible: they have successfully incubated a tech start-up out of their agency. They did so by utilizing two very different approaches, which are representative of the two broad paths of how this can get done.

But again, these are the exceptions to the rule. The vast majority of attempts to incubate products out of services firms fail. In my travels and conversations, I've met dozens of services firms that have endeavored to go down this path. Few have accomplished this. The successes that have existed prove that this path is not impossible, but such victories are rare. Extreme care and strength of heart are required.

ALL PRODUCTS ARE NOT THE SAME

One thing I find that is often underanalyzed at services companies that make products is the question of *what type* of product. To some of you, this will seem incredible, but many service company founders don't think much about which product they want to build. This is, of course, a larger issue in the tech community these days—many people are so desperate to found a start-up, any start-up, that they launch one around a ridiculous or useless product. The same holds true for many services company CEOs. They see the higher revenue multipliers at product companies and want in on that action—they aren't overly concerned with what product they actually choose.

And in this case, it's actually useful, because different types of products have different chances of succeeding in being launched from consultancies. I break them down into four types:

1. products that are useful in your industry
2. products that are useful to your clients
3. products that your firm holds some advantage in building
4. products that anyone else can build

It should come as no surprise that building products that fall into the first three categories has a higher chance of success than products that fall into the latter category. That being said, many services firm CEOs don't think about this, and are trying to build products to which their firm provides no special advantage.

Successfully incubating a start-up within a services firm does happen, of course—Vine is perhaps the most notable exception to this rule. Born out of a New York-based digital agency called Big Human, Vine was eventually acquired by Twitter, and is one of the most popular mobile video sites today.

But companies like Vine are the exception. The vast majority of successful start-ups that I have found in the services company world fall into the first three categories.

Think about what your company can bring to the table. Think about the advantages your company conveys. If you have a client that is desperately in need of a product solution, there may be an opportunity there. If your consultancy provides specialized services that give you a skill set that makes it easier for you to build certain types of products than any Joe off of the street, this may be an area where your product can succeed.

Think of your company's contacts and skill set as a potential means of overcoming barriers to entry. It's easy for two kids in Topeka to make a small social or dating app. Why does your company have an advantage over these kids? Conversely, it's more difficult for those selfsame two kids to make an enterprise app for a major telecommunications company or a complex app around secure payments and entrenched incumbent players, whereas your company may have an advantage.

Take time to think about this, because if you're going to build an app that anyone else can build, what's the point of even having the services firm? Having the company needs to be an advantage, not an encumbrance.

DOES YOUR SERVICES FIRM HELP YOU IN THIS QUEST?

The first thing you should ask yourself is whether you really need your whole company to build a start-up. Has the environment around you changed? Perhaps, earlier, when you started your shop, you had no access to capital. That may not be the case anymore. Additionally, the people at your company may not be the right people to create a technology product: you hired them for specific tasks, and they are expecting a specific lifestyle and career path, and your services shop may provide that, while a start-up may not. The hours are long, and the pay is lower at start-ups. Did you hire these people previously, knowing that eventually you'd all be transitioning to a different model? Do they know that? It's worth thinking about, and talking to them. If you're just getting started launching a services company right now with an eye toward migrating to a start-up business model later, its best to take these things into consideration as you do hire. Make sure people know what they're getting into. Take a moment and ask yourself if the services firm you have will actually help in your quest to start a successful start-up.

CROSS PURPOSE GOALS

The biggest challenge in the services-firm—to the start-up path is an existential one: the two businesses serve a very different set of goals, and they're almost always at odds. The biggest challenge is actually a subset of that: services companies and start-ups provide two different potential paths to personal wealth, but they are very different. We have talked about the importance of continuously growing your company. You will need to flow all other decisions and actions of the firm through the prism of continuous growth. To do so, you will need to pump every extra dollar you have into growing more—specifically, hiring more people ahead of the work to come later, so that you can take on more work. While on this path, there will be no extra time and resources. It'll be a challenge just to get your own company website built.

TWO PATHS: ZERO GROWTH OR WAITING

There are, then, really only two ways to go about this: don't grow at all, or grow so big that you have enough extra resources to incubate a product.

The first path, of course, is pretty clear. Don't grow. Take that extra money you make and spend it on developing a product. Don't take on long-term contracts. Don't get a line of credit. And, most importantly, don't hire people. If you are 100 percent sure you want to create a sellable product, you want to do it very soon, and you are willing to risk everything, then my advice is to go for it. Do it right now. Don't grow beyond three or four, and pump your extra funds into the start-up. Hire only for the start-up. Don't take other people's lives into your hands.

But I cannot stress this enough: be relentless in your nongrowth. Hire as few people as possible, and be upfront with your employees about your plans. Don't sign a long-term lease. Don't do anything that will incur regular expenses that will force you to take more work than you need to live on.

The next option is to wait until you're large enough to tackle a product out of your surplus revenue. Imagine if your business makes 20 percent returns on its services work, and 15 percent of that is pumped back into the company to fuel growth. This includes hiring more people, getting a larger office, doing better self-promotion, and incrementally increasing the partners' salary bit by bit over time so you don't crazy (there will never be a time to give yourself one large raise).

Now, the good thing these days is that start-up funding is in a pretty predictable place: most start-ups are funded by an initial investment in a *seed round* of $250,000 to $1 million, depending on the complexity of the idea. The concept here is to give the company just enough money to build an initial prototype, run it a while, and see if it works.

When your shop is making $1 million a year, the 5 percent you have left over is, if you're lucky, $50k. This is obviously not enough to build a prototype, and besides, that $50k probably will disappear into growth anyway. However, once your company is doing, say, $10 million a year, with that 5 percent surplus you might have some some spare capital equaling about $500k. Now we're getting somewhere. A services firm that has grown enough—taking years to do it—will, with extraordinary diligence and care, eventually be able to incubate a single start-up, seeding the company with $500k or so.

These, really, are the strongest two options for building a viable start-up incubated within your company. If you're patient, the latter choice is, of course, less risky. If your start-up fails, you still have a profitable services firm. But this takes time. And if you want to get going, fail fast, and try again, the time frames can be painful. You may see good ideas you have get built and sold while you are still working at your services firm. It's a classic risk-reward scenario.

In the end, the choice is yours. I will caution you, however: there's no splitting the difference. It's either/or. Choose now and make your peace with it.

THE START-UP TEAM VERSUS THE SERVICES FIRM TEAM

Here we come to another challenge. Yes, your company may have art directors, designers, developers, and the like. These roles may well align to similar roles at a start-up. But not all of them. *There are skills needed to bring a product to market that don't exist within a services firm. And some of the roles that you do have, are not the same.* One of the easiest examples is the CFO. An agency CFO provides tremendous value to the company—they deal with the misery of procurement hell and ensure that your company gets paid. These are vital roles within a services shop. They are also completely different from the tasks that confront a start-up CFO. A start-up CFO is vitally important in ensuring that the money you do raise doesn't run out. They are important in helping raise money, and they are an absolutely essential team member when it comes to figuring out your business model and how much to charge. None of these are really concerns that services firm CFOs have to worry about—the business model is generally pretty set (you get paid for your time), services shops don't generally need to raise money, and they generally fund themselves from their receipts.

"Okay," you're thinking. "I need a different CFO." Yes, yes, you do. But that's not all.

You will also need business development people of a different ilk, who do complex, mutually beneficial deals with other businesses, often for no money. This is very different from what your internal planners and strategists are used to, who usually do deals in which your company is brokering an agreement between a brand and a media property, in which the brand is usually footing the bill. It's an entirely different sort of affair to broker tit-for-tat arrangements.

You will need scalability engineers if your product takes off. Even the largest brand sites are a drop in the bucket compared to Facebook or Twitter, and often scalability is a nonissue in services land. Certainly no agency person ever had to contemplate building their own data center someday.

PRODUCT MANAGERS

Then there's product.

A strange and mythical beast, the product manager at a start-up. There is perhaps no other job that is so talked about, and considered so essential, that has no real means for learning to become one. What is a "product manager?"

The product manager holds immense power in a start-up. They are, quite simply, in charge of the thing the start-up is building. Now, technically, this isn't correct: the chief technology officer (CTO) is in charge of the technology behind it, and the product manager is in charge of how the product works, acts, and feels. To the consumer, the product often *is* the start-up.

In some ways, the product manager might seem to be analogous to the traditional role of the planner in an agency: being the representative of the people within the organization. But it is more. Agile development, and scrum expert Aaron Sanders describes the product manager as the "CEO of the product." They represent the customer's interest, and are "responsible for market, business case and competitive analysis" as well as the "long term and short term vision."[1]

This is a whole lot to put on one person. More pressingly, for you, as services company owner, it's not someone who is really on your team. It's not the planner, as planners have never had to deal with finances. It's not the producer, as the producer doesn't traditionally build anything and often doesn't have to think anything up. It's not an art director or designer. Chances are there is no one at your firm who is fully qualified for this role. That's not 100 percent terrible—great product mangers come from all walks of life. There is no set path. But this is likely going to pose a short-term challenge.

THE RESOURCE CURSE

One of the largest challenges in getting a start-up off the ground within your company is a simple matter of resources. Who's going to work on the start-up? The fact is that at services firms, people are usually busy, all the time. Yes, there are moments of downtime, and, yes, it's good to have something to work on in the downtime to keep everyone busy, but this will not lead to a success-ful start-up. You may get a product out here and there, as we did at TBG, but you'll not get a business out the door in this manner.

You don't need to hire people for years on end doing nothing but start-up work—maybe it's a three-month sprint to a minimum viable product. But for the time they're working on it, if you want it ever to become a real business, they'll need to be dedicated.

You may think you can avoid this by having people work some fixed per-centage of their time, every week, on the product. This will not work. Client work will get in the way. There may be some screwup that requires extra hours to fix things in time for a client launch (there *always* will be a screwup that requires extra hours—it is the nature of service companies). There may be a client who wants to pay you, who *happily* wants to pay you cold hard cash right now, to cram a few more features in before a launch. What are you going to do? Piss off your client and say, "no, no, we can't take your money, we are also working on a product on the side"? That won't fly.

Even when one *does* successfully find a way to make dedicated resources work, the temptation of taking that person off of the nonpaying work and putting them on paying work will be strong. Because it'll only be temporary. We just have to get through this little crunch. Honest.

Dedicated resources are your only hope. After all, this is what your competitor will be doing. Imagine you have a competitor. Imagine the competitor is four scrappy kids who just received a half million dollars funding from a venture capitalist. Those kids are going to live, breathe, eat, and sleep their start-up. They may well live at the office. They will put everything into this start-up like it is their one chance in the world to make something of themselves. How can you compete with this "in-between gigs" with a few part-timers? You can't. It won't work. And if you don't have a competitor now, you will eventually.

You've been warned.

THE CHALLENGES WE FACED IN BUILDING START-UPS

What went wrong with The Barbarian Group's trying to do start-ups within the company?

NO CLEAR VISION

This shouldn't need to be said, but in my days, now, of listening to pitches from budding entrepreneurs with new start-up ideas, it is still often true that many start-up ideas lack a clear product vision. This is doubly true of start-up ideas coming out of agencies. If you look at our four products that were launched out of TBG, none of them had a clear business model: A browser, a food truck app, a music visualizer, and a coding framework. All of them being software, each one of them could well have been sold, but instead, without much thought, we gave them away for free.

We justified this by saying that these were products that were promoting the company. And indeed, they did wonderful promotion for us. But that's exactly the catch: *a product you are shipping as promotion for your company is not a start-up.* It's a piece of marketing in product form. If we were serious about any of these as potential businesses, we should have figured out how we were, eventually, going to make money from them. The fact that we sold one of them to another company was mainly luck—it wasn't our plan to begin with.

With the other start-up ideas we had, that we pitched to real investors, every single time, we completely flubbed the business model portion of the proposal: we literally had no idea how they would make money. And with most start-ups I hear pitched out of agencies, this is still the case. A vague assertion that "we'll make money off of advertising" is not enough.

FIND QUALIFIED INVESTORS

When looking for VCs to fund our start-up ideas, we had no idea how to find them. This is not that surprising, given that half the reason tech-savvy, talented people start agencies is that their access to the venture capital world is sort of limited. It's more surprising to think that seven years later, as one of the most s successful digital agencies in America, we still didn't know that many VCs. We knew some rich people, but the worlds of advertising and venture capital are actually surprisingly separate, at least at the lower levels. We never once in our travels met any of the higher-level tech VCs, even though we moved in the same circles. Knowing many more VCs now, it's clear to me that most agency people really aren't that connected to the investment world.

Now, of course, this doesn't stop your shop from building your new product. But it does make it very hard to find the capital to grow the product beyond the initial prototype you got out into the wild. You'll also need talented VCs with access to the press, early adopters, and other investors. All of this is very hard to find in agency land, and if you're anything like most services firm owners, you've spent the past few years with your head down growing your company, so you probably haven't run into too many random other friends.

If you live in the Bay Area, of course, there's a bit of a different calculus going on. It's relatively easy to find these people. One has to stop and think at this moment, however: if you live in the Bay Area and have all of this talent and these great people under your wing, and you dream of making a start-up, why are you thinking of starting a services firm at all? For the rest of us, it can take a long time to make these connections.

PITCH DECKS

And there are pitch decks.

We learned the hard way that an agency pitch is not the same thing as a pitch for funding. There's actually a fairly standard way to present a tech business to top-tier venture capitalists. It is maybe 20 slides long. At first blush, that sounds a good bit like a pitch deck that agencies make for potential clients. And if there's one thing a great agency can do well, it is make a kick-ass pitch deck. Should be a no brainer. But looking at the matter more closely, the two decks are actually very different. A good agency pitch deck talks about the customers, and how well you know them, and finds insights that are actionable for the brand to inspire the consumer to buy something that already exists. The relative merit of the business itself is not under discussion, because, most of the time, it is already a business making revenue. Of course, there are times you're launching a new product, but even then, a good pitch deck doesn't debate the quality of the business or product. It plans how to act. It's a roadmap to getting a customer to buy something that already exists. A VC pitch deck, however, is a completely different beast. It is an abbreviated business plan. It has to identify a real market opportunity, of significant size, and explain how that market opportunity can be capitalized upon.

Find some help from someone who has been before the almighty VC before and get your pitch in order. Don't rely on your amazing success getting clients to create this pitch.

THE MYSTERY OF THE FINANCIALS

Then there are the financial projections. There's a whole financial component to VC pitch decks that is not present in agency pitch decks. Prior to trying to get funding, we were not familiar with these, as we never had to do them, really, for our clients. After all, their businesses were already up and running.

The financials in a VC pitch deck have two parts: the "use of funds," which explains how you are going to spend the money you are asking for, and the "projections," which lay out how you envision the business growing over the years toward profitability.

The use of funds portion of the financials can feel like something we understand and have done before as a marketer. In an agency pitch deck, you often have to explain how much the idea will cost. You say to your potential client, "Here's the idea, it'll cost this much, and this is what we'll do with the money." That part can feel a lot like the use of funds section of a VC pitch deck, except you ALSO have to say, "and from there, we will be at this point, at which point, we will now be selling this much, or have this many registered users, and we will be on the path to profitability like this."

For most agency people, this becomes the entirety of the financials. This makes sense, because it's the part they've been doing forever.

Except there's a whole additional part: the projections.

The psychology behind financial projections section of the VC pitch deck is something that is virtually unknown for agencies. In advertising, we hide behind the fact that our work may not be successful at all. We're not selling guarantees. We know that there are a million factors involved in what makes a consumer decide to buy a product, and we are but one of them. More relevantly, our clients know this too. We know that advertising works, and this can be mathematically proven. The point is, we operate in a realm of mutually understood relativity.

A financial projection, however, is a very different thing. As agency folk, we assume that it is more akin to a production budget or a media plan—for those are the only places where we see a bunch of numbers that are lined up to make a concrete plan. So when an agency person tries to make financial projections for a VC pitch deck, we try and couch our financial projections in the definitive. We try and hedge our bets. We are consumed with making the numbers 100 percent real and accurate.

This is a fallacy. All good VCs know that the financial projections are, more than anything, a proxy for showing how big the market *could* be, and how ambitiously you are thinking, and how rigorous your logic is. They need to be realistic in the sense that they have accounted for all the potential costs, and there are some real variables upon which your thinking is based, but they do not need to be a 100 percent perfect prediction of the future. They are a model, not a promise.

But most importantly, you need to actually have these financials in your deck. Almost every product pitch deck for funding I have seen from agency people forget to include real financial projections in their first deck draft. And the very few that do, are so used to underpromising and overdelivering, as they so often do in the marketing world, that their projections are so tepid as to be uninspiring. Investors are not looking to invest in blasé.

This leads to another important point about the financials: as agency people, we are used to pitching against other agencies. In all probability, these agencies probably have fee structures roughly the same as ours. There IS a tradition of pitching on price and competing on price in the agency world, but it is far, far more rare than pitching on the quality of your ideas.

With a VC pitch deck, however, this is totally a different situation. You are not pitching against five other potential entrepreneurs who have the exact same idea as you. You are pitching against other potential investments, in potentially any industry, that this particular VC has heard pitched. Ask yourself: regardless of industry, which idea looks better? The one that thinks it can get to $500 million in sales in year three, or $50 million? In which would you rather invest your money, all else being equal? It's astonishing how often agency folk forget this.

For our part, we made all of these mistakes in our decks. They had beautiful comps. They were filled with gorgeous ideas that we really wanted to build and that we knew would get a ton of traffic. They were comically light on how they would actually make money, and indeed in many of them we barely touched upon the topic at all. Because we did nothing to project to them how big the market could be. We didn't mention traffic driving, e-commerce, or affiliate deals at all. Okay, we may have mentioned them briefly, in passing, but it was clear we hadn't modeled anything out and had no idea of the real numbers behind them.

PRODUCT FOLLOW-THROUGH

Perhaps the biggest challenge for services firms when they begin making products is learning to think about the product as something that *always exists now and forever more*. This is very different from the advertising world, where typically all marketing is thought of in seasons and campaigns. The advertising world is getting better at sustained marketing initiatives, thanks to the pressures and rigors of social media, but we are still a long way from implementing solid community management, agile development cycles, a/b testing, and lean start-up methodologies. We are, generally speaking, conditioned to build a thing and then move on.

We experienced this pain very acutely with our food truck application. It was a great app, and some really sweet technology was implemented to glean the locations of food trucks through their Twitter accounts. We even built functionality for the trucks themselves, should they desire, to login to a site and keep the app updated. We did *not*, however, make any plans at all for getting the word out to food trucks, helping them use the site, or handling a situation where a food truck changed their Twitter handle, for example. Nor did we plan any personnel to handle customer support requests, bug fixes, feature requests, and the like. We just built it and shipped it. The quality of the app at first was very high, but over time the experience slowly degraded to become unusable.

We were not unaware of this situation—in fact, we spent great amounts of time thinking about how to solve it. In the end, however, we realized that the only solution was a dedicated staff member, and since we had previously made zero effort in trying to think of an actual business model for our food truck app, it was impossible to justify adding a body to the product full time (everyone else was working on the project in-between paying projects).

This is an inevitable situation if you don't have a clear business plan and a sense of what kind of revenue the project might lead to. It becomes impossible to justify spending more money on it. Moreover, even if you do have clear financial goals, our agency was not well experienced in hiring community outreach people, business-to-business (B2B) outreach evangelists to food trucks, or customer support rep.

CONTINUOUSLY ITERATE ON YOUR PRODUCT

Related to follow through is the repeated "iteration" of the product itself. There are various approaches to this, and I strongly encourage you to familiarize yourself with them—waterfall, agile, scrum, lean. If you're a web shop, you may have some good experience with agile methodologies, but even then, it's hard to apply those to a hobby project on the side. And without continuous development, your application will most likely die.

This proved to be the case with Plainview, The Barbarian Group's well-regarded browser. Feature requests and bug requests came in fast and furious as the user base grew, but it was months between updates—once it was even a year. This frustrated our users, who often only needed a single small bug fix in order to use the browser. And it allowed the more mainstream browsers, such as Google's Chrome, to build in features that made them potential replacements (Chrome now allows for full-screen browsing). In theory, the presentation and site queuing features of Plainview could have helped protect its market share from this encroachment, but it took us forever to ship those features.

WHAT WE DID RIGHT

Let's go a little easier on The Barbarian Group. What did we do right when it came to building products?

SHIP CODE

This one is easy: we got products out the door. This is something I am still incredibly proud of. We shipped many products at The Barbarian Group, and some of them were successful in their own way. We built a music visualizer that we eventually sold to Apple, and that is now part of iTunes, installed on over 20 million computers throughout the world. Did we make much money? No, probably less than we spent on building it. But we got the code out, and we got it into people's hands.

We built a browser. It was called Plainview, and it became a widely used browser for presentations and kiosks (its chief feature was that it ran in full-screen mode by default, and you could load multiple web pages in advance).

We built an open source framework called Cinder that allowed creative people to code in an easier way. It is still widely used to this day, and has been used in installations, museums, at rock concerts, and more. (To find out more about Cinder, if you're interested in such things, please visit libcinder.org).

We built a fun little app called BeTheMayor that let you see how far away you were from becoming the mayor of a Foursquare venue. We built another little app that allowed you to find and follow the food trucks that might be near you.

This is an impressive accomplishment. In my time at TBG, we built and shipped over five different products.

I know what you're thinking. "That's *it?*" Yes. That's it. But trust me when I say this is far, far better than most agencies.

PROMOTE

We did a great job—sometimes—of promoting our products. This is something that marketing services firms are, of course, very good at. There will be less money to promote your product than you have had promoting a brand, of course, but all ad budgets are headed into the shitter anyway, and by this point you've probably gotten pretty good at being scrappy on behalf of your client and their marketing needs.

33

CASE STUDIES OF
START-UPS WITHIN AN AGENCY

CASE STUDY: MODEA

Throughout my travels and conversations in advertising, when talking about building product within services firms, and who has done it right, I invariably point to Modea. Odds are that you have never heard of the shop. Despite its founder, David Catalano, sitting with First Lady Michelle Obama at the State of the Union as a symbol of job creation throughout the recession, Modea has by and large stayed under the radar of most of the pundits and students of digital advertising. Its relatively remote location in Blacksburg, Virginia, has helped with this, but so has the attitude of the founders. "Modea has always been outside the industry," says CEO Catalano.[1]

Modea, cofounded by Catalano and Aaron Herrington, got its start as a digital development shop. As a practitioner of the crafts and tactics laid out in this book, Catalano has been first rate. Frequently through the years, he and I would trade notes, tips, and techniques for agency management. In recent years, both of us have turned our attention to the world of tech start-ups, and have wrestled, in our own ways, with the question of how best to utilize the resources of our agencies toward the goal of achieving higher value through the increased multipliers of product companies. "Aaron and I are entrepreneurs more than we're 'ad guys,'" says Catalano. In fact—and here is where Modea truly stands alone—Modea has, at the time of this writing, birthed two successful product start-ups, and is well on its way with its third.

What is it that has allowed them to achieve this success?

At a top level, placing Modea's success within the framework we've already laid out, Modea approached the start-up world by choosing to get big enough. First, it waited until it was large enough to spare resources for its product endeavors. Secondly, the products it created were products with which it had a special advantage. In this case, these were products that their clients could use or love. Additionally, it applied relentless discipline and best practices toward the creation of its products: it applied dedicated resources. It created separate legal entities for the products, and brought in excellent co-investors, advisers, and board members. It maintained strict financial discipline. It stayed focused.

Modea's first product, Moveline, is a mobile-first, incredibly simple tool for helping people move. It allows for the easy acceptance of bids from multiple moving companies, with multiple options, all from your smartphone. The user no longer needs to invite over to their house the estimator from multiple moving companies to obtain multiple bids. Rather, the user films their house on their smartphone, guided by Moveline's personnel. Moveline then facilitates multiple bids and pricing options for the customer, ranging from full service packing and moving, to pack-it-yourself street pods, to renting a truck and driving it yourself (with an optional, additional packing crew).

Moveline was birthed of a client need. Roanoke, Virginia-based van line Lawrence Transportation Systems (LTS) came to Modea looking to expand its market. Founded in 1932, LTS has been one of the principal shipping companies behind United Van Lines since 1942. It is, by any definition, a legacy incumbent in the transportation business. LTS enlisted Modea to look for ways to expand its shipping opportunities. Through the work of Modea, Moveline was born. It was developed in house, conceived originally as a web-based moving tool for consumers.

Modea knew that eventually, however, Moveline would need to fly the coop, so to speak. Thus it was launched as a separate legal company. A CEO was found who could dedicate himself to the product and the company, the exceptionally talented Frederick Cook, whom Catalano had met during his sideline hobby as an angel investor. Moveline also requisitioned some of Modea's personnel—most notably Modea strategist Kelly Edison, who served as Frederick's cofounder and head of product. Because Modea had reached a stable size, with sufficient resources above the necessary life-sustaining, growth-funding minimum, it could afford to apply Edison's efforts, along with developers, and so on, to Moveline in its infancy.

Catalano, Cook, and Edison then applied to, and were accepted to, TechStars New York, a tech accelerator program. This allowed the company to work, refine, and receive the wisdom of additional, outside mentors, ultimately culminating in a round of investment from outside parties (the fund at which I work was one of the investors). Modea, and the original moving lines company, retained equity portions in the new start-up, and board representation, but the company was, at this point, an independent company with Cook as the CEO.

Since then, Moveline has grown and prospered. Revenues are growing, and it has received a second round of investment from some of the country's best venture firms, including Zappo's CEO Tony Hseih's investment group, Chris Dixon's Lowercase Capital, and TechStars' own David Cohen.

The birth of Moveline could easily have been a catastrophe. Moveline was birthed at Modea in partnership with an established, legacy van line company looking to expand its market through new tools. Such a remit given to another agency may well have resulted in a simple tool, or a faux start-up that was, really, just a marketing campaign.

Because Modea was launched as a separate business, it did not continue to take too much time and energy from Catalano and his partner. This freed them up to continually manage Modea, and look for additional opportunities.

Creating this product in this fashion gave Modea the confidence to plunge into completely reorganizing Modea as a shop that seeks to repeat this success for its clients. We see this in its recent second, as yet unnamed, product. But don't let the lack of a name fool you. This product, borne of the needs of one of Modea's telecommunication clients, has already reached revenues into the seven figures, for multiple clients. It is a going company, almost instantly profitable. Modea is now seeking to complete a hat trick with a third product for a health-care concern.

Like many services firms, Modea started out with something approaching blind growth. It began with digital development, and then expanded into more marketing-related areas such as design, art direction, planning, and copywriting. The company grew from website development to display advertising, mobile app development, and social media—like many digital shops do. "We were even doing television ads," Catalano recalls, with something approaching disgust.

With the success of Moveline, however, Catalano sensed other opportunities. He has since refocused his business. He laid out for me a three-stage model that outlines the process with which Modea assists its clients in not just their marketing needs, but in all aspects of digital innovation, culminating, with the best-suited clients, in the development of new lines of business. "We incubate product/market fit. We find a founding team, and we use the agency as an accelerator."

Superficial lines of business were discontinued, and Modea reorganized along this process. They retrenched in the areas more focused on innovation, strategy, and technology, and pulled back in the more marketing and advertising-related functions.

This has necessitated some ("a few," Catalano stresses) layoffs, but more importantly has changed the sort of people Modea hires. "It's a different ilk of people who do start-ups....At Modea when I think about doing start-ups within the agency, I'm thinking about finding a set of people who will be deemed 'cofounders,'" Catalano explains. "Then I will leverage Modea's expertise to support the founding team." He is sanguine about eventually losing these people to the start-ups they create. "As we refine our model we'll continue to recruit people who are only at Modea in an interim manner."

Catalano describes this as the repositioning of his agency as "a fundamental shift in the raison d'être for the consultancy." He goes on to say, "It exists not only to solve gnarly problems for clients, but to dive deep into various verticals to evaluate market opportunities." He adds, "We are more of an accelerator in that way."

"Our model is set on decreasing the risk profile," Catalano says. Because the client and Modea have extensive knowledge of the markets they seek to enter, they bring an advantage that an outside competitor cannot have. They use the agency as an accelerator, speeding up production and connecting, but also insulating the start-up from the incumbent client, who may unintentionally smother it.

Modea did not come by this process out of the blue, and there were bumps along the way. "We've tried the small start-up stuff. I've been to Y Combinator and TechStars [demo days] and seen how those programs work. I love the model but it doesn't make sense for an agency. We've even tried soliciting start-up ideas from people." This is something we, too, tried at The Barbarian Group with limited success. Catalano's experiences mirror my own. "We got a ton of great ideas. Ideas are worthless. What matters is having the right people committed to realizing an idea." Catalano qualifies this by saying that there have been outliers, but that he believes, "Generally speaking, if they were the right people they would quit my agency and start their own venture."

Can you replicate this success? While Catalano may be able to repeat his success more quickly the second time around, it should be noted that Modea was founded in 2006, and Moveline entered TechStars in 2013—seven years later. Regardless of whether Modea needed time to experiment or not, Modea needed time to *grow,* to give Catalano and Herrington time to build up the cash to handle these endeavors. Due to the benefits of building products for clients, some of this was funded by their clients, but much was not: clients do not fund reorganizations and CEOs-in-waiting.

I find that many people in the services game who are dreaming of building products are not this patient. Seven years of growing a product company that is not their ultimate dream is painful for them. This approach is not for everyone. That is okay. But to even *attempt* this approach, I stress again, your company has to have grown to a certain size.

CASE STUDY: SEABRIGHT

If Modea's patient approach is not for you, perhaps the experience of a small UX consultancy in the Bay Area is of interest. They are, or were, called Seabright, formerly based in San Francisco. Cofounders Gino Zahnd and John Bragg met at a previous job, a tech start-up called Kosmix. Kosmix was then acquired by Walmart, becoming @WalmartLabs. From that, Seabright was born.

I met Zahnd and Bragg in New York when we all sat on the same panel. The panel was meant to share stories, tips and tricks from the world of start-ups. At the panel, Zahnd mentioned that their new start-up, Cozy, was spun out of their previous services company, Seabright. This immediately piqued my interest. Cozy—a rental payments and management company—seemed like it was doing well, and any successful start-up spawned from a services company was of interest to me.

What struck me about Seabright and Cozy was how quickly Cozy launched out of Seabright. This was, to put it simply, the opposite approach of Modea. The services firm, Seabright, was always intended to be temporary. "We actually founded Seabright to build our own products,"[2] Zahnd says. "We were going to fund everything ourselves, with part of that funding coming from what we viewed as a part-time UX consultancy."

To this end, resources were kept minimal. This is important. Knowing, in advance, that Seabright was going to be a temporary thing, Zahnd and Bragg made it a point to keep overhead—especially employees—low. "We've been extremely conservative in how we've built the team, how we've approached launching products, and how we viewed ourselves in the market." When, eventually, the time came to make the transition from Seabright to Cozy, there was only one full-time employee to deal with. "We had one full-time employee at Seabright, and he left shortly before we started making the transition. We had a number of contractors as well." Contractors, of course, can be let go with far less disruption to their lives than full-time employees.

Choosing a product, for Seabright, took some work, and Zahnd and Bragg did not hit on Cozy right away. They started out with a product called Doneski, which was "a little web app to-do list." They knew, however, that Doneski was never going to be their "big" product. Doneski was a stepping-stone. "We created Doneski to test heavy gesture use and offline capabilities in mobile browsers." However, they knew, even then, that their main product would be one of two ideas, Cozy being one of them. The other was a product called Drivetrain, which was in the commerce space—essentially a "cash register in a box that works everywhere." They had started work on Drivetrain, only to watch payments company Square "erode most of our ideas in a spectacular fashion."

The experiences with Doneski and Drivetrain drove their approach to Cozy. "Failing on Drivetrain in that manner taught us some key lessons," Zahnd says. One of those lessons was that in this product space—involving payments—attention was key. "We also came away armed with the knowledge that first and foremost we were building a type of financial service. Because of that, we knew it wasn't the kind of thing we could just build and see if people like it. When you're moving people's housing payments, the product has to be air tight." This made Zahnd and Bragg realize that perhaps their approach of self-funding products through their consultancy wasn't the best approach, and that focus was needed. "Knowing these things, we swallowed our pride, and knew it was time to go raise money from VCs, build a team, operate a proper beta, and launch a company around our idea," Zahnd says. Upon raising that round of funding, they shut down Seabright.

It might be tempting to say that Seabright was never really a proper agency. But it was, for a time. Zahnd states that revenues were "a couple million dollars, so we didn't just want to walk away from it." They had clients and an employee. That being said, "we clearly knew we were going to shut it down" from the start, and "start a company, and not look back." Zahnd and Bragg took care to wind things down in an orderly manner. Once they had arrived at the idea for Cozy and wanted to focus on research and prototyping, they began to wind down Seabright even before they went out to raise their round. "We didn't take on any more work. We ended up bootstrapping Cozy for about eight months before we closed our seed round. That allowed for a smooth transition."

On first blush, it might appear that the choice of Cozy as a product for Seabright does not appear to play to the consultancy's strength in any way. It wasn't built for a client, and it wasn't something that was useful to the company as a creative tool. However, Cozy's success could well be argued to rely on a useful, intuitive user interface, and, being a UX consultancy, this is an area in which Seabright excelled. Additionally, Seabright was a UX consultancy that could build product. "We saw that the old UX consulting model of handing off deliverables simply doesn't apply in today's world," Zahnd says. "So we wanted skin in the game for everything we worked on." Seabright focused on running miniproducts for its clients, showing them "that it's possible to operate like a start-up inside a big company." These experiences gave Seabright an edge in building a great product, rapidly iterating on it, and understanding how to fit that product into a larger economic context. Was this enough? It is hard to say. I do believe Seabright had better chances of success with Cozy than with, say, a photo sharing app, which anyone can build. The level of complexity for a rental and management tool is high—and Seabright's enterprise product experience doubtlessly proved quite useful.

34

WORKING FOR START-UPS

When working for a tech start-up—that is, a venture backed start-up—there is the opportunity to work for equity, or ownership in their company, in addition to, or in lieu of payment in cash. This can be tempting. You could do the work, for some money, and then on top of that also get some equity in the start-up for which you are working. It might be the next Facebook, and who knows how much that equity might be worth one day. Some words of caution, though.

EQUITY ONLY VERSUS CASH AND EQUITY

There is a difference between working for equity, and working for cash *and* equity. It's one thing to get your full rate, and an equity sweetener on top of that. It is another to get no payment, or less payment, and some equity to make up the difference. These are two very different scenarios. You'll notice I lumped no payment and less payment together, rather than payment of any amount and no payment as two separate groups. That was intentional. *Getting paid anything less than your regular rate requires you to place some valuation on the equity.* If you got your full rate, great, it's all upside. But if you've discounted, the equity is, in theory, making up part of the equation.

EQUITY VALUATION

Valuing that equity is tricky. It's a hotly debated item in the best of circumstances, the valuation of a new start-up. When you're thinking of owning a chunk of a new start-up, it's tempting to think of how much it could be worth if everything went great. You own 2 percent of a company that may one day be worth billions! Heck, even if it's only worth *one* billion, that's $20 million for you! Amazing!

The reality of it is that there is a very, very slim chance that this will come to pass. Saying there's a 1 percent chance is generous, but it's a good starting point to reset expectations. If the best outcome is that you will get $20 million on a $1 billion sale, applying a statistical likelihood of 1 percent brings that number down to a concrete value of $200,000. Personally, I use the 1 in 1,000 figure, since that seems to be closer to reality, which brings us, in this example, to $20,000. Did you discount more than $20,000 for this? If so, you may have done yourself a disservice.

I probably did 20 of these deals in my time at TBG. Only one of them ever worked out, and it took four years. The profits from this one success offset the discount *on that one client*, but came nowhere near to making all the for-equity work we did, in total, profitable. It was, absolutely and unequivocally, a financial disaster, despite the one win, many years later.

I should also qualify this by saying that I did find, long after, an email from one of the founders of one of New York's most successful, high-profile start-ups, inquiring about our doing work for them for a substantial stake in the company. We declined. That share would have been worth a good chunk of money—perhaps $10 million. But if anything, it proves my point—you have to know how to pick them, on top of everything else. Furthermore, I firmly and absolutely believe the company would not be as successful today had they hired us to do that work.

THE START-UP TEAM AND HOW SERVICES FIRMS FIT INTO IT

This leads me to the next problem with doing work for start-ups: the team.

A start-up that has the full team together is one of the most important criteria that savvy investors look for in investing in a company—to make sure it has people covering business, product, tech, and design. By the very nature of outsourcing tech and/or design to your shop, this is a company that doesn't have all the checkboxes checked off. Now, maybe it's going to get there someday, but who knows. It could well have a great prototype after working with you, but that won't matter if it still doesn't have a full team.

Nowadays, in my job as a venture capitalist, when I evaluate potential start-ups, a company's having a service firm partner, rather than having dedicated team members on staff, is a warning sign. It can be overcome—especially if the same people are planning on coming to the start-up full time once the start-up is funded—but it's always viewed with some concern.

The very nature of your relationship with the start-up may adversely affect its probability of success.

To be sure, there are times when a very talented, very smart start-up founder uses a service shop for something and it works out spectacularly. But by and large, if a founder is coming to your company to do some work, it's because he can't find anyone else to do the work, and that is a warning sign either for the founder's personality, or the start-up's vision. Which means, by and large, the equity deals that will be available to your firm are, on the whole, less likely to succeed. So, again, why take the equity?

SHOULD YOU JUST JOIN THE START-UP?

There is, occasionally, that rare, wonderful moment when a start-up comes to a services firm and needs exactly the things your shop is great at, and you hit it off so completely with the founder and their vision that the two of you become peas in a pod, and you just can't believe how awesome it would be to work with this person. If that's the case, you should leave your company and join her. You could also merge your shop with the start-up, if your company is small and everyone there would work well on the start-up. Or you could close up shop and rehire the right people to the start-up. These are all viable options. You'll notice, though, that none of them involves your firm actually working for that start-up. Find another way, and join forces more permanently. The VCs will look much more kindly upon it.

35

GETTING ACQUIRED

Let's start this chapter with more than the usual caveats. Ignore this chapter completely if you don't want to sell. Good for you. Whether to sell your company or not is a deeply personal decision. It is up to you and your partners. We've had an arc through this book of a certain type of company plan—one in which you create and grow a great company in order to sell it one day so that you may reap the reward of your years of effort. I don't think there is anything immoral about this plan, but it is not for everyone. Your company will change after a sale. Selling your company does not come without a cost.

Luckily you have some control over how much your company changes, through the actions you take and the words you speak *throughout the lifetime of your company*. If everyone in the company is a shareholder or on a profit sharing plan, for example, and you have always been upfront that one day the company will get acquired and you will all get some money, your company will naturally attract people who find such a prospect attractive. The big day will probably be a relatively joyous one. However, if you live in denial of this forever, and then one day, out of the blue, sell the company, it may be less of one.

WHO'S BUYING

Generally speaking, you are almost certainly looking at getting acquired by a larger agency or, more likely, the agency holding companies that own them. Advertising, like many industries, is dominated by a small number of big players. In this case, they are Japan's Dentsu, London's WPP Group, Paris' Publicis, and two New York holding companies, Omnicom and Interpublic. Bubbling below them are a handful of smaller holding companies that also acquire agencies: Hakuhodo, Havas, Aegis, MDC Partners, and Cheil, the Samsung-affiliated Korean holding company to whom we sold our company. There are other potential agency acquirers—some of the larger agencies within these holding companies still perform their own mergers and acquisitions (M&A), and some of the larger digital conglomerates such as Sapient acquire some digital firms. But these smaller firms may well eventually find themselves being acquired by the big five, so you may as well resign yourself to being in one of these networks. Possibly better to just choose, rather than having a future acquisition choose for you.

There are other avenues, of course. You could find a way to sell your shop to Google, Apple, Facebook, or Twitter. If you are specialized in a specific niche, understand that market intimately and know what you're doing. This is increasingly becoming a potential path for you.

You may think that these tech companies are a bit more aggressive on the acquisition side, and that because they are tech companies they may pay more for your company. In advising several of these deals, I have not found this to be especially true. They may move more quickly, and they may offer more lucrative employment contracts, but by and large, they stick to the 2x multiplier.

WHEN

When is the right time to consider selling? The first immutable truth is that there's really not much you can or should do to sell your company until people start asking about whether you are interested in selling. Repeatedly. Investment banks will start calling and introducing themselves. Out of the blue, client agencies will ask you out for coffee or ask you if you are interested in selling. One of the holding company CEOs may pop by for a visit. For our part, a visit from John Wren, the CEO of Omnicom, in 2006, five years into our company, told us that if we wanted to, we could now probably sell. We still waited three more years.

After that, the math kicks in. You want to be sure the company is big enough to get the valuation you desire, minus all the fees, other people, and whatnot. Broadly speaking, you should also consider how you'd feel if half the money is three years away. When you shop your company, you'll eventually find the best partner. It may even have the highest bid. But that particular bid may not be exactly the right payment dynamics—it may be a five-year employment deal rather than three. It may be loaded with most of the compensation on the back of the deal, and be heavy on salary rather than equity. And there is a risk might you get fired before that. The last thing in the world you want is to get to the finish line and realize that your decade of hard work is not going to achieve your goals. It's easy when doing these calculations to get optimistic—I can get a 2x bid. I can get it all up front, and so forth. Do the math, assume the worst, and go from there.

STARTING THE PROCESS

When it's time to sell, the key is to do it quickly, build up a buyer's frenzy, and get it done. Staying on the market for a long period of time is death. Don't do it halfway. Do it all in one fell swoop. Don't be always for sale. You can "talk" to people casually all the time—and you should. But don't let any of those conversations get too far unless you're ready to go full throttle. When you're ready to sell, and the math works out, start talking to everyone. Engineer some hype.

If it doesn't work, you're going to have to take a year off. More people know about these deals than you can ever imagine. Assume once this starts that employees will know. It is possible to avoid this, but it is largely luck. A company that goes on the market is hot gossip. A company that stays on the market and fails to sell is juicy gossip. The key is to put yourself on the market only when you know there is enough interest from multiple people, and get it done fast—six months is a good goal. Three months of shopping, three months to close the deal with your chosen partner.

There is the common situation in which one specific suitor has gotten your goat, and suddenly you find yourself contemplating selling to this specific company, without including other bidders. On the one hand, there is a level of trust by both parties in these situations that can be damaged by taking the deal to the larger market. You may also feel, in your heart, that this company is where you belong. I cannot tell you, in absolute terms, not to pursue this kind of deal. I find that in these instances, the acquiring company, about 50 percent of the time, makes a more than fair offer. The other 50 percent of the time, they are flat out lowballing. It's not always easy to tell which is going on without having some outside market validation. Unless the money is absurdly good—blowing away all the math you've done—and you've worshipped this company since you were a child, you should shop the deal, but in the end, it's a personal decision. If you decide to pursue it, however, know this: if the deal falls through, you'll be as tainted as you would be if you had gone onto the open market, and you probably won't be able to try to sell your company again for a year.

LAWYERS

You're going to need a specialized lawyer. There are so many innumerable insane complications to selling your company that it is impossible to do it yourself. It's impossible to do it with a family lawyer. This stuff is hard core. There were some things our lawyers did where the rewording of a single clause literally saved millions of dollars.

The acquirer will pay the legal bills when the acquisition goes through, but you will be stuck with them if it doesn't. The goal is to include the lawyers as late as possible, but practically speaking, this is basically impossible. The first thing any serious party will want is a ton of due diligence arriving at a term sheet, neither of which you can easily do without your lawyer. It is going to cost a lot of money to sell yourself. Your company needs to be big enough to undertake this endeavor and be able to easily pay all the bills if it fails.

Your law firm should have substantial M&A experience, preferably with selling to the type of company you are selling to (presumably other agencies, holding companies, or tech companies).

ADVISERS

You will also need an adviser. There are basically three types. Your lawyers, if you are using a big firm, probably have a good M&A arm. They can be useful. We relied on them heavily. It's good they are in your corner, definitively, whereas other types of advisers may not be. But they are expensive—you pay them whether you sell or not. They also don't always love giving flat-out practical advice. Lawyers tend to hedge and focus unduly on mitigating risk. You will need someone else in your corner with whom you can speak more philosophically.

The second type is your company's advisers, if you have them, or other trusted colleagues who have been through this. They are good because they may personally know many of the players. They may have sold or been courted by your suitors. They know where they got burned. They are more or less free. If you have these, use them. But remember, they have no skin in the game, may have only been through this once, and may even have multiple motivations—especially if they are currently working for one of your suitors. Still, they can be invaluable.

INVESTMENT BANKS

The third type of adviser is an investment bank. These are worth talking about in some detail.

Investment banks aid individuals or organizations with making investments. For our purposes, this means assisting in the buying and selling of companies. An investment bank can be hired by either party—the buyer or the seller. Each party may hire its own investment bank. An investment bank may not be simultaneously hired by both the buyer and the seller, though the bank may know both parties. Indeed, part of the reason for hiring an investment bank is to gain access to its deep knowledge and network of potential buyers or sellers. There is a good chance that whoever buys you will be represented by an investment bank.

There is also the opportunity and possibility that you can hire an investment bank to help sell your company. This is a decision you will have to make.

Working with an investment bank has several advantages. They will know buyers that you may not be aware of. They will have a good sense of how much money you can make with the sale of your company. They'll coach you and help you learn how to put your best foot forward to potential buyers. They will assist you in the maddening, tedious, painful process of due diligence. You will still need lawyers for the deal, but you will be able to lean on your investment bank for many of the negotiations, term sheets, and advice.

Investment banks are not without cost. They are paid as a percentage of the deal—typically 10 percent or more. This can be hugely expensive. The plus side of this is that you will generally not have to pay them if you don't sell your company, once they have agreed to take you on as a client, provided you're not secretly cooking the books or something like that. As an alternative to lawyers as advisers, at least you don't have to pay the bank unless you sell.

A word of caution here. When you're looking to sell, it's easy to discount these costs. "I'll be rich then. Ten percent won't matter," you may well think. Once the deal is done, however, it's almost certain you will be singing a different tune. The money will add up. It's not funny money. It's your money, and you're spending it the moment you're making it.

The best time to use an investment bank, then, is when you have a good feeling that they can help you get a higher price for your company than you would on your own. Don't forget—these banks aren't doing you any favors, and they are pitching you for the work. Just because they say they can get you more money doesn't mean they will. Tread with caution. If you are being heavily pursued by multiple large holding companies, these banks will be less useful. It you don't know anyone, and no one has reached out to you directly, it may well not be time to sell your company. An investment bank may be able to help you unload it, but it won't necessarily be for a great price.

Two places where an investment banks network can be valuable is if one holding company is courting you, but you have no contacts with the other ones, or if you think Google, Facebook, and so forth might make a viable acquirer as opposed to a holding company, as they calculate valuations somewhat differently—especially if you have a lot of developers.

When selecting an investment bank, you want one that has a proven track record of selling companies to the companies you are looking to sell to—specifically either agency holding companies or tech companies. Look at the press releases around past acquisitions. They will usually say who did the deal. Try and ascertain whether they were assisting the buyer or the seller. Ask colleagues who have sold their services firms. If things are going well, one or two of these may have already contacted you.

The size of your company and the potential sale price are a factor in whether or not to hire an investment bank. I've assisted several friends in the sale of their companies in the $1–2 million range. That is a very different project than a sale in the $10 million or $100 million range. For our part, we did not use an investment banker to broker our sale—though our acquirer did. We found ourselves in the enviable position of having several potential suitors and good contacts within them. This meant that we leaned heavily on our lawyers for our acquisition advice. In the end, this worked out, as the sale went through and the acquirer covered the legal bills. Had the sale not gone through, we would have been stuck with this bill. Though the bill would have hurt, we could have covered it. It was a calculated risk. We also did not lean too heavily on the lawyers until we had a broad outline of a deal in place, and had decided on our preference of sellers. This limited our potential exposure. It did, however, cause some complications in the deal as our lawyers advised of additional terms that we then asked to be included in the deal. Our acquirers were accommodating, but not all will be.

TALKING THE TALK

Once you've decided you're for sale, either in partnership with an investment bank or not, you're going to start pitching your company to people.

Pitching your company isn't that different from the pitches you've been doing as part of your job for years now, except you are pitching the entire company. Remember that different potential acquirers have different motivations and needs in potentially acquiring you. Find out what these are—the investment bank can help here. Cater your pitch to the clients. If your potential acquirer is thinking of buying you because they are flat-out terrible at digital marketing, for example, and you spend your whole pitch talking academically about making television spots, they may feel like things are a mismatch. If you spend the whole meeting talking about money, but they are buying you because they know they need better creative chops, your pitch may be off (though, hey—in that scenario I've met few buyers who aren't pleasantly surprised to learn that a creative shop also knows how to manage its money).

A word here about "the talk." It's acceptable—ideal, even—to strike the pose of a creative genius, or an outsider, or a maverick to the holding companies. This is fine, because you'll probably have been doing this in front of your clients all along. You presumably will have mastered it by the time you get to selling. However, it is vital that when you sit down at the business table with them, you have to flow all of that into the concept of continuing to grow your company. You can say that you "want a bigger canvas" or that you "yearn for your work to reach more people." All of these are codes for growth, and a seasoned holding company M&A guy knows this.

DISCUSSIONS AND NEGOTIATIONS

In all cases, whatever the reason the company is considering buying you, there will be a part where the talk turns to money. The company will want to know your margins, your balance sheet. This is where the tactics we laid out earlier in this book come into play. Your balance sheet should show your margins and how much of that profit then went into refinancing growth. If you have an experimental lab that you use to acquire business, it should be marked accordingly. This is one place we really messed up at first. We just showed profit and loss, and it was difficult for their accountant to see we were actually a perfectly profitable company, that we just spent all the money on growth. They could see the growth numbers, but that wasn't enough. We later reworked our accounting to make these various endeavors more transparent. That helped a lot.

There will also be many philosophical talks about what you want to achieve, where you want to see the company go, and what issues the potential acquirer will face. While to some extent you also want to color this conversation with the topics and goals they are focused on, it does pay here to have a more open, honest, far-reaching conversation. You are seeing whether there is a cultural fit. You are seeing whether you can work with these people. There will be several people involved in this process whom you will never, ever see again once it's done. You want to find the people to whom you will be talking to day to day, and focus on them.

Early on, there will be some top-level conversations about money. If you have a banker, they may well have handled such talks behind the scenes. Potential buyers will want to know top level what range you are looking for, both as a straight number and as a revenue multiple. As the conversations proceed, the field will narrow. Money will be talked about in more detail. What would a deal look like? How much upfront? How long is the deal? Is it a full purchase or a majority purchase? What would the employment contracts look like? There is still plenty of room to negotiate, but slowly the deal will take shape. You, and each of your potential acquirers, will have some issues you're flexible on, and some you are not flexible on. This is the point at which all parties should show their cards about anything they're firm on. Some companies will fall out of the process through some intractable items.

This may go on a couple rounds, with increasing fidelity. Eventually, you'll narrow the field to one or two companies, and eventually to one. At this point, you will want to either come to a term sheet, a bulleted list of top-level points about the deal that both parties can agree upon, or a letter of intent, which states both companies are interested in making the acquisition work and agree to work on it to the exclusion of other potential offers for a certain amount of time. A term sheet is preferable because a letter of intent can lock you up from talking to other potential interested suitors, and in the end, the buyer can walk away at the end of the term. Sometimes a letter of intent is unavoidable. It should have a short term to it—potentially a couple of weeks (this is rare, but you should shoot for it). You can also try to have it include some payment to you covering legal costs if the deal falls apart. The fact is, you are poor and the burden of risk of this part of the process is borne more by you than them. There may be instances where it needs to come down to trust, but by and large, look for these protections here.

This is by no means an exhaustive list, but it is vital you try and think of everything that matters, and make sure you and the acquirer agree about things. Some areas that we found were vital to discuss were whether or not the acquirer would pay off our bank debt in addition to the purchase price or part of it, how the company would be recapitalized for growth after the acquisition, whether or not the acquirer could merge us with other companies in its network without our permission, whether or not it could open offices without our permission. Remember, the acquirer will own your company or the majority of it after this deal. Anything that is not explicitly denied them is allowed. For our part, we drew up a large matrix of a couple dozen scenarios and worked out who how many board votes would be required to execute each scenario.

Once the term sheet is signed, the nitty-gritty work begins. The idea here is that after the term sheet, the whole thing can be turned over to the lawyers and they can magically turn it into legalese, but it doesn't work that way in reality. Invariably, dozens of smaller issues will crop up, and you will need to be vigilant. You can't win them all. But you can't lose them all, either. Most issues will be of clear importance to one party or the other, and a swift nego-tiation involves a trustful tit for tat—that matters to you, so sure, but this matters to me, so let's change this. Invariably it'll come down to one or two issues that may scuttle the deal. Each party is going to have to give here. You need to stay vigilant and work through them all with your lawyer. There will be times you'll need to tell your lawyers to chill. There will be times you'll need to pick up the phone, call your main contact at the acquiring company, work it out, and then both go inform your lawyers. It will take a while. But you'll get through it.

Or not. One of the most painful things you'll hear—over and over—throughout this process, is that the deal ain't done till it's done. It can go wrong at any time. And it's true. It can. I find that this is where the personal touch matters. Choose your acquiring partner wisely. They need to be sane, competent, and trustworthy. And so do you. This is the greatest protection against the deal going south.

But sometimes, the acquisition will implode, and you will have to aban-don the whole thing. Take your licks. Walk away. Get back to running your business. Make it better. Fight another day. If your company is awesome, and you keep on keepin' on, more opportunities will come.

SALES TERMS VERSUS EMPLOYMENT CONTRACTS

Broadly speaking, any acquisition deal will have two parts: how much the acquirer is paying for the company and what the terms of your employment are afterward.

The purchase of the company will either be a complete purchase or a majority purchase. Buying anything less than 51 percent of the company is an investment, not an acquisition, as the other party will not be in charge. Buying the company outright is common, but so is buying a controlling interest, with the rest being left with the founders. In such cases, it's also common, though not always, to work out a deal in advance for the subsequent purchase of the remainder of the company. This may be after a set amount of time—say three to five years—or when the various founders are ready to retire.

There are some purchasing agents that work in other ways for reasons specific to them—tax legislation in their home country, binding agreements they have made with their own shareholders or bankers, and so forth. these companies generally understand they are operating outside the norm, and will attempt to compensate in some manner.

When doing early negotiations with a company, it's important to get a sense of the type of deal it is thinking of and where its primary interests lie in order to ensure they jibe with yours. If you are only interested in a full 100 percent sale, and the potential acquirer only purchases 51 percent stakes early on, you may be at irreconcilable odds.

Whether or not it is buying 100 percent of the company or 51 percent, the odds are that in the vast majority of deals, the acquirer will want you to agree to stay with the company for a set number of years. This is generally accomplished by having you negotiate and sign a new employment agreement with the new company.

The interplay between the employment agreement and the purchase of the company is vital. You may not have ever signed an employment agreement with the company before. Additionally, this area deserves additional attention if the various founding partners are in different boats, or have different plans for the future. For example, it may be understood that some partners are to stay, and some are not. Banks and acquiring companies are very sophisticated about this. Various strategies are employed, loading up more cash in the acquisition or employee contract as circumstances warrant. If they really just want one partner, for example, they may keep the purchase price low and top up the employment contract. This can foster resentment with the other parties.

Broadly speaking, in this case, an effective strategy may be to negotiate the purchase price to all the partners' liking, and then move on to the employment contracts, understanding that some partners may not be retained. It's less of a sting to be out of a job when you are happy with the $2 million you just got for your shares. In reality, however, this is rarely practical in the real world. Excessive communication and honesty by all parties, at all times, is of course the best approach. Find out early whether the acquirer is interested in keeping everyone onboard and whether that aligns with your plans. Great caution must be taken here.

It's easy to look at the acquisition price, and the look at your employment contract, add it all together and think, "This is how much I made." But the two monies are very different. And remember, they can always fire you, even if you have an employment contract. Don't count your chickens before they hatch.

Every partner negotiating an employment contract should have a personal lawyer, separate from the lawyer who does the sale deal. Think about the employment agreement as a separate document from the acquisition. Though all the employment contracts will need to be signed before the deal is done, this agreement is specific to you as an employee.

This contract will cover your salary, benefits, bonuses, rights, and the like. There will be a noncompete section and a section dealing with what happens if you are fired prematurely. Even if you are completely convinced these sections are unnecessary, focus on them and keep them as much to your benefit as possible. Get a lawyer who has experience with the M&A of creative services firms. There will be times when an individual partner can scuttle the deal during their individual employment contract negotiation, especially in (but not limited to) situations where they don't have a good lawyer. This can be a monstrously trying ordeal—all your hard work hanging by a thread, your fate in their hands. There's not much you can do here except not be that person, and apply great tact, at exactly the right moments. Don't panic.

In addition to the founders, there will be other employees whom the acquirer has identified as important, quite possibly because you told them this in the course of your talks. If they are already under employment contracts, great. If not, you and the potential acquirer are going to need to fix this, with great tact and discretion. It will not be fun.

If it is understood among you and your partners that one partner does not want to, or will not, stay with the new organization, it's probably good to not paint them as irreplaceable. Turning to clients, this is a trickier matter. Lawyers will pore over your contracts. They may freak out because there are or are not certain clauses about the sale of the company in these contracts. There's not much you can do here. Savvy buyers understand this is a risk. Resist pressure, in all but extreme cases, to go to the clients in advance.

That being said, your company may be beholden to one specific client, and that client may care very much about who owns you. Relationships will vary. If this is an issue in your business, you may have to talk to your acquirer in advance. A banker can help you identify precisely the best time to do so, but so can the employee closest to the client. Timing matters. Clients talk. Client disclosure (or consent, if necessary) should be as close to the end as possible, and confined to one or two high-level people at the client.

DUE DILIGENCE

In your initial conversations, potential acquirers may take your word for it when it comes to reporting things like revenue, clients, and margins. They may simply be happy to look at a top-level financial report you supplied them. It will all seem very trustworthy.

To some extent it is, but in the words of the Russian proverb, "trust but verify" will be their motto. There will come a time, before the deal is done, when an army of lawyers will confirm that what you say is true. This is called "due diligence."

This is, to be blunt, a miserable process. You'll be asked to open your books. The other company will want to examine your contracts. They may want to talk to a couple clients. They will almost certainly require an outside auditing firm to verify your books. They'll ask you about your dog. Your parents. Your college boyfriend.

If you're serious about the deal, start working on this right away. Getting an outside audit of your books early in the process will speed things up later. It's worth it. Do it. Start gathering (signed!) copies of all your major contracts. Gather all your employment agreements and partnership agreements. Signed versions. Get a list from a potential acquirer early (they will generally be happy to offer it) or your lawyers or investment bank, and start working on it. ASAP.

Next, there will be a risk that the acquirer will use what is being found in due diligence to adjust the purchase price. Don't put up with this. Your lawyers or investment bank can guide you through the potential pitfalls in the actual documents. But even if this risk has been mitigated, some acquirers will use discrepancies in due diligence to lower the purchase price. The normal negotiating tactics of being willing to walk away from any deal you balk at apply here, but that being said, my advice is to not put up with this. It signifies mistrust, and in these instances there is a good chance the company is buying you for your clients, reputation, or personnel, and billing is only a part of it. You will have to make your own call here. After all, the change may be minor. The buyers may not be the actual people with whom you're working day to day, so they might not get your long-term working relationships. It should also be said that the more honest you are, the less this will be an issue. Record keeping matters, but beware the buyer who tries to dock you for not finding a single signed contract.

Finally, remember that there is some room to push back. This is especially the case if you are trying to keep the acquisition secret, or there is intense competition to buy your company. They're all probably going to want you to open the books, and it will look highly suspicious if you're against an outside audit. However, disclosing things like employee contracts and, particularly, client contact are items you can often push back against. The bankers doing this deal often hand over all due diligence to an army of lawyers who are, generally speaking, working off of a template. If any one or two things specifically raise your ire, you can often escalate the issue back to your main contact and explain your concerns. It's rare that any one piece is mission critical, save the audited books.

INCLUDING THE EMPLOYEES

How much to discuss with employees will be a personal decision, and one that goes to your core vision. It goes deep into their hopes and aims of the company why they joined. How well they will be personally rewarded for it. The general culture and mood of the company. What you've said before.

Even if you want to, you will not be able to tell them much. The most you can practically tell them is "we are talking to some people." A poker face will be needed here.

When they do learn, some will be indifferent. Some will be disappointed. Some will be excited. But it will change the dynamic. Once you announce, you are going to have to earn their trust back. This is doubly true if you have promised in the past never to sell.

THE BIG DAY

Eventually, you will find yourself at the big day. It will be highly orchestrated. There is much to do. You'll need to sign the documents, of course—a scary, life-changing, and surreal experience. Handshakes. Photographs. Maybe even some champagne popped. But you're not done yet.

You'll need to inform your employees, your clients, and the press, in that order. Plan the timing of everything out in advance. Announce a mandatory company meeting. This will be one of the most important company meetings of your life. You will need to sell this deal to the employees. You'll need to make them understand why this is a good idea. How it affects their jobs. Where we're going now. They will have questions. Answer all of the ones you can. Promise to follow up on the others. From here on out for the next few months, keeping the employees happy is going to be a big part of your job. It starts now. Get them excited about this deal.

You'll also need to tell your clients. If you've had some key major clients that the buyer insisted on telling, they may already know. You'll need to tell the rest. Generally, I found this to be a pretty pleasant experience. Most of my clients were congratulatory and happy for us. The odds are, you'll know if you have a problem client, and the path will have been worked out in detail with your potential acquirer. But with all clients, it's important you tell them before the news breaks.

Only once your employees and clients have been told should you tell the press. Your acquirer may be eager for press from this deal. Make sure it's understood you need time to get your ducks in a row prior to it. There may be some interviews set up, but they should be embargoed until a specific day and hour, giving you time for your company meeting and client calls. Working with a PR company that knows what it's doing here helps immensely. It's also possible that your acquirer doesn't want to make a big deal about this deal. If so, good. It'll make your life easier.

GROWTH DOESN'T STOP AT THE SALE

In the end, regardless of what *other* reasons they have, the holding companies will expect you to continue growing even after you have been acquired. It may be a race to the finish line, but the finish line is not the day you've been acquired, it's the day your contract period is up. Unless you have already grown your company so much that you are getting more than enough money for your whole life in your initial payment from the first part of the sale, but if you pulled that off, you have presumably already learned the lessons of growth.

AFTERWARD

The sale does not have to mean the end of greatness for a company, and if you navigate the waters well, it can be an immensely empowering thing for your company. That being said, most acquisitions fail. Succeeding is the exception, rather than the rule. Your reputation as a businessperson doesn't end with the sale—it ends with proving you can negotiate these treacherous waters and lead your company to success and prosperity after the sale.

The sale of a company is not the end of your obligation. And while the financial reward may be obtained, your work is not done. It is my hope that this is your belief too. People who flip a company and disappear right after the sale are part of the reason, as you are entering this life-changing moment in your life, some people may think it is a sad ending. Never forget that what happens after the sale matters as much as what happens beforehand. Every time someone out there flips a company, cynicism about M&A is given purchase.

Mergers and acquisitions have, at their heart, a level of trust not found in many other places in American business. The buyer is trusting that the seller will continue to work hard to ensure the company's success, even if it is no longer financially motivated to do so. Yes, there are often follow-up contracts, promises made, and so forth. But when someone's just made a life-changing amount of money, the promise of additional money may or may not motivate them any longer. Every buyer trusts that the seller will not screw them over. That they won't abandon ship, that they won't bail or flame out. The reality is, however, that every buyer is making a leap of faith.

TAKE CARE OF YOURSELF

Your life will change with the sale—you may well be financially stable and even well-off for the first time in your life. The lives of others in the company may change as well, if you have partners and/or you have given employees some substantial equity. Take care that these lifestyle changes do not impact the company. Great companies work hard to maintain their culture after a sale, and you should too. Be aware of the discrepancies in people's net worth. Don't flaunt it. Don't buy a yacht or a start driving a Ferrari to work. Don't get distracted by the weirdo cold-calling investment advisers and private banks that are now courting you (by and large, you should literally not talk to any of these people). Famed tech investor Brad Feld and his wife, Amy Batchelor, advise two things: make no major personal financial decisions for at least three months. And take 10 percent of your money, after taxes, and buy yourself something nice. This seems like sound advice.[1]

In the first years after a sale, it's important not to rock the boat. Later on, if you have successfully managed the transition to your new owners, changes may take place, but right now, at this moment, the culture of your company has taken a body blow, and you need to work as hard as possible to nurture the culture back to health. This is important.

And, hey. Congratulations.

THE FEAR

So. There you have it. Go forth, be fruitful and multiply.

I leave you with one last warning.

Don't panic.

There will be times you freak out. There will be times when you want to give up. Many, many times. There will be times you want to curl up in a ball and cry. There will probably be times that you do.

There will be some devastating days. Layoff days will be particularly brutal. There will be weeks, months, even whole years that you will feel like giving up. David Ogilvy summed up the fear that all agency owners feel: "Every day for years I thought [the agency] was going to fail. I was always scared sick. I remember saying one day: if this is success, God deliver me from failure.[1]"

The fear will age you. Excuse this stretch of a metaphor, but I often think of how much our presidents age. Clinton, George W., Obama. It's amazing how much the pressures of office age them. We have nothing on them, but the pressure exists nonetheless. For my part, I emerged from a decade of running an agency 60 pounds heavier, a cholesterol-overdosed near alcoholic with a bad back. It's taken me years to recover.

On top of this, if you keep creativity as part of your job, there is another fear that Ogilvy speaks of. In his book *Ogilvy On Advertising*, he wrote, "The copywriter lives with fear. Will he have a big idea before Tuesday morning? Will the client buy it? Will it get a high test score? Will it sell the product? I never sit down to write an advertisement without thinking THIS TIME I AM GOING TO FAIL."[2]

This is the fear that all creatives know. Of being able to come up with something brilliant, on command, again and again, for your whole life. There are some who believe that all ad creatives burn out eventually. That the only ones who succeed are the ones who learn to replace their own inner brilliance with a process and a team. This is cold comfort. If anything, it makes matters worse. Not only is the pressure of coming up with a great idea relentless and eternal, but you will get worse at it, and the solution is even more work. Of an entirely different kind.

You read about other agencies in interviews. You see them at conferences, and they seem indomitable. Confident. Fearless. "How can they be that way?" you might think. "Why can't I be that way?"

Yet I've also heard what those same people have told me, and I them, at 3 a.m. at the bar later that night, ten drinks in. In my years since, when I meet people who were once my most worthy competitors, founders of companies that I viewed as near perfect, as we got to know each other and talked about the past, I realized they were feeling the same insecurities and stresses that I was. They are not so different from us. Everyone gets the fear. Nigel Bogle confides, "A lot of what drives me on is fear of failure, it makes you want to go on trying very hard to be successful."[3]

Perhaps you are of hardier stock than us. Perhaps you're blessed—or cursed—with an ability to compartmentalize. An ability to not let the sufferings and fears of others get to you too much. Perhaps you're not one to get too freaked out with the livelihoods of so many people in your hands. If so, part of me—but only a part—envies you.

For the rest, I can offer some underutilized advice: find someone to talk to. It's no coincidence that those in the business with a spouse seem more well adjusted. But it is not always feasible for those of us who are single to go out and find one, especially when the pressures of the job are so unrelenting. Ogilvy was driven to therapy, Freudian analysis in his case, as was the fashion at the time.[4] I can sympathize. I was too. It helps. Do what you need to do. Try and stay healthy.

One other thing to watch out for: measuring progress in your career. It took me ten years to accumulate my wealth from an ad agency career. In that time, my job title didn't change once. I didn't get a single promotion. Graeme Wood in *The Atlantic* comments that "Career advancement is the standard yardstick by which most people measure success, and without that yardstick, it's not easy to assess whether one's time is well spent."[5] If you need this kind of day-to-day yardstick for your progress, find alternatives. Make a list of dream clients and track against that. Measure progress of the company through annual revenues or number of employees. Find these alternatives because as you grow your company, your peers in traditional agencies will be getting promotions, switching jobs accompanied by front page *Advertising Age* articles, and winning awards, while you will be doing none of these things.

I can also offer you some consolation. I can tell you that you are not alone. Because these feelings are absolutely, completely normal.

I can also tell you that it will absolutely be worth it. Fail or succeed, you will be a better person. I look upon my years running The Barbarian Group as some of the best and most exciting of my life. I am confident you will too. Good luck.

NOTES

INTRODUCTION

1. Bill Bernbach, DDB.com, http://www.ddb.com/BillBernbachSaid/Slideshow/we
-forget.html, retrieved September 19, 2014.

2 THE VISION

1. Nike.com, *Nike Mission Statement*, http://help-en-us.nike.com/app/answers/detail/a
_id/113/p/3897 (September 8, 2014).
2. Quora.com, *What Is a Brand?*, http://www.quora.com/What-is-a-brand (March 6,
2013).
3. Tony Hsieh, *Delivering Happiness: A Path to Profits, Passion, and Purpose* (New York:
Hachette Book Group, Kindle Edition, 2010), p. 151.
4. Ibid. p. 154.
5. Ibid. p. 152.
6. John Hegarty, *Hegarty on Advertising* (London: Thames & Hudson, Kindle Edition,
2010), Kindle Locations 874–875.
7. Scott Goodson, "How to Start a Successful Ad Agency," *Fortune*, December 5, 2010
(http://www.forbes.com/sites/marketshare/2010/12/05/how-to-start-a-successful
-ad-agency/2/).

3 THE VALUE PROPOSITION OF CULTURE

1. Kenneth Roman, *The King of Madison Avenue: David Ogilvy and the Making of
Modern Advertising* (New York: Palgrave Macmillan Kindle Edition, 2010), Kindle
Locations 3318–3320.
2. Sean Silvertone, "The Profit Power of Corporate Culture," *Harvard Business School*,
September 28, 2011 (http://hbswk.hbs.edu/item/6818.html).
3. Rob Goffee and Gareth Jones, "Creating the Best Workplace on Earth," *Harvard
Business Review*, May 2013 (http://hbr.org/2013/05/creating-the-best-workplace
-on-earth/ar/pr).
4. Leo Burnett, *Communications of an Advertising Man: Selections from the Speeches,
Articles, Memoranda, and Miscellaneous Writings of Leo Burnett* (Chicago: Leo
Burnett Privately Printed, 1961), p. 81

4 CULTURE AND VISION

1. Rob Goffee and Gareth Jones, "Creating the Best Workplace on Earth," *Harvard
Business Review*, May 2013 (http://hbr.org/2013/05/creating-the-best-workplace-on
-earth/ar/pr).
2. Brett Martin, "Postmortem of an Internet Backed Startup," medium.com, September
17, 2003 (https://medium.com/p/72c6f8bec7df).

5 COMMUNICATION

1. Brett Martin, "Postmortem of an Internet Backed Startup," medium.com, September 17, 2003 (https://medium.com/p/72c6f8bec7df).
2. Tony Hsieh, *Delivering Happiness: A Path to Profits, Passion, and Purpose* (New York: Hachette Book Group, Kindle Edition, 2010), Kindle Locations 2247–2250.

7 IDEAS

1. Steve Jobs, as quoted in Philip Elmer-DeWitt, "Steve Jobs: The Parable of the Stones," in *The Triumph of the Nerds: The Rise of Accidental Empires*. dir. Robert X. Cringely. PBS, 1996. Film; Neil Gaiman, journal.Neilgaiman.com http://journal.neilgaiman.com/2009/01/journeys-end.html, January 16, 2009; Johann Wolfgang von Goethe, as quoted in goodreads.com, https://www.goodreads.com/quotes/24395-a-really-great-talent-finds-its-happiness-in-execution, September 14, 2014; Thomas Edison, as quoted in wikiquote.com, http://en.wikiquote.org/wiki/Thomas_Edison, September 14, 2014; Voltaire, as quoted in goodreads.com, https://www.goodreads.com/quotes/230582-originality-is-nothing-but-judicious-imitation-the-most-original-writers, September 14, 2014; Nancy Prager, Protect and Leverage, http://nancyprager.wordpress.com/2007/05/08/good-poets-borrow-great-poets-steal/, May 8, 2007, Quote Investigator, http://quoteinvestigator.com/2014/06/01/creative/, June 1, 2014.
2. google.com, retrieved May 28, 2013.
3. Gregory Solman, *Hilton Reignites Debate over the Value of Ideas,* http://www.adweek.com/news/advertising/hilton-reignites-debate-over-value-ideas-79800, May 30, 2005.

8 PROCESS

1. James Webb Young, *A Technique for Producing Ideas* (CreateSpace Independent Publishing Platform, Kindle Edition, 2014), Kindle Location 71.
2. A good overview can be found in Stephen Fox, *Mirror Makers* (Champaign, IL: University of Illinois Press, 1997), pp. 180–187.
3. W. Glenn Griffin and Deborah Morrison, *The Creative Process Illustrated: How Advertising's Big Ideas Are Born (HOW Books,* F+W Media, Inc. Kindle Edition, *2010),* Kindle Locations 367–371.
4. David Kiley. *Getting the Bugs Out: The Rise, Fall, & Comeback of Volkswagen in America* (An Adweek Book, John Wiley and Sons, Kindle Edition, 2002), Kindle Locations 2665–2668.
5. John Hegarty. *Hegarty on Advertising,* (Thames & Hudson. Kindle Edition, 2010), Kindle Location 878.
6. John Coleman, *Six Components of Great Corporate Culture,* http://blogs.hbr.org/cs/2013/05/six_components_of_culture.html, May 6, 2013.
7. Wikipedia, "Process Is Important," http://en.wikipedia.org/wiki/Wikipedia:Process_is_important, retrieved September 14, 2014.
8. Ralf Herbrich, *Research at Facebook: "Nothing Is Riskier Than Not Taking Risks,"* https://www.facebook.com/notes/facebook-engineering/research-at-facebook-nothing-is-riskier-than-not-taking-risks/10150604394583920, March 7, 2012.
9. Hegarty, Kindle Location 891.
10. Rob Goffee and Gareth Jones, "Creating the Best Workplaces On Earth," *Harvard Business Review,* May 2013, http://hbr.org/2013/05/creating-the-best-workplace-on-earth/.
11. Young, Kindle Location 149.
12. Griffin and Morrison, Kindle Locations 2793–2798.
13. Hegarty, Kindle Locations 856–861.

14. Timothy Dolan. (2010). "Revisiting Adhocracy: From Rhetorical Revisionism to Smart Mobs." *Journal of Future Studies* 2: 33–50, p. 8.
15. *Harvard Business Review*, May 2013.
16. Fox, p. 300.
17. I suppose you may be the chairman of a large, moribund agency desperately in need of new ideas who is reading this book for some reason. In that case, I advise you to change the climate before you bring in the orchids.
18. *Harvard Business Review*, May 2013.

9   WORKING FOR OTHER AGENCIES

1. "Crispin Acquires Texturemedia", *Adweek,* June 18, 2008, http://www.adweek.com /news/technology/crispin-acquires-texturemedia-96123.
2. LinkedIn, http://www.linkedin.com/in/andrewbdavison, retrieved September 14, 2014.
3. Dentsu, Summary of First Half of Fiscal 2013 and Management Strategy, November 15, 2013, http://www.dentsu.com/ir/data/pdf/20142QEAPREE2.pdf, retrieved September 14, 2014.
4. "Publicis Groupe Acquires Indigo Consulting in India," *The Economic Times,* April 24, 2012, http://articles.economictimes.indiatimes.com/2012-04-24/news/31392619_1 _jarek-ziebinski-leo-burnett-india-arvind-sharma; "Publicis Groupe Acquires Flip Media, Leading Middle Eastern Digital Agency," flipcorp.com February 2, 2012; "JWT to Acquire Majority Stake in Hungama Digital," JWT.com, June 13, 2012, https:// www.jwt.com/en/asiapacific/news/jwttoacquiremajoritystakeinhungamadigital/, campaignbrief.com; "TBWA India Acquires Digital Company Magnon," January 9, 2013, http://www.campaignbrief.com/asia/2013/01/tbwa-acquires-magnon -indias-le.html, WPP.com; "Y&R acquires majority stake in Turkish creative digital agency C-Section," February 28, 2013, http://www.wpp.com/wpp/investor /financialnews/2013/feb/28/yr-acquires-majority-stake-in-turkish-creative-digital -agency-c-section/; "Aegis Group PLC AGS Acquisition of Roundarch," February 22, 2012, bloomberg.com, http://www.bloomberg.com/bb/newsarchive /ahoHIww9bnlo.html; Rachel Strugatz, "Create the Group Buys Morpheus Media," *Women's Wear Daily,* June 20, 2011, http://www.wwd.com/media-news/digital /createthe-group-buys-morpheus-media-3669132.
5. "What Exactly is a Frenemy? Sir Martin Sorrell, Chief Executive of WPP Thinks Google Is One," *Social Business Thinking,* http://londoncalling.co/2008/03/what-exactly-is-a-frenemy/, retrieved September 14, 2014.

11   THE BASICS

1. John Hegarty, *Hegarty on Advertising* (Thames & Hudson. Kindle Edition, 2010), Kindle Location 1342–1343.
2. Cosima Marriner, "We're Only Three Phone Calls from Disaster," *The Guardian*, November 30, 2005, http://www.guardian.co.uk/media/2005/nov/30/business. advertising.
3. Rae Ann Fera, "10 Ways to Fix the Agency Pitch Process," *Fast Company*, March 7, 2002, http://www.fastcocreate.com/1680035/10-ways-to-fix-the-agency-pitch-process.

12   THE EMOTIONAL

1. Simon Sinek, "Why Don't Agencies Advertise?" *Brandweek,* April 17, 2006, http:// sinekpartners.typepad.com/refocus/2006/05/why_dont_ad_age.html.
2. John Hegarty, *Hegarty on Advertising* (Thames & Hudson. Kindle Edition, 2010), Kindle Locations 554–555.

3. Ibid.
4. Scott Goodson, "How to Start A Successful Ad Agency," *Forbes*, December 5, 2010, http://www.forbes.com/sites/marketshare/2010/12/05/how-to-start-a-successful -ad-agency/2/.

13   THE PITCH

1. John Hegarty, *Hegarty on Advertising* (Thames & Hudson. Kindle Edition, 2010), Kindle Locations 1236–1244.
2. Rae Ann Fera, "10 Ways to Fix the Agency Pitch Process," *Fast Company*, March 7, 2002, http://www.fastcocreate.com/1680035/10-waysto-fix-the-agency-pitch-process.
3. Ibid.
4. Hegarty, Kindle Locations 1136–1138.
5. *Fast Company*, March 7, 2012.
6. Peter Coughter, *The Art of the Pitch: Persuasion and Presentation Skills That Win Business* (New York: Palgrave MacMillan, Kindle Edition, 2012), Kindle Locations 2699–2701.
7. Hegarty, Kindle Locations 1272–1273.
8. Ibid.
9. Coughter, Kindle Locations 1011–1017.
10. Ibid.
11. James P. Othmer. *Adland: Searching for the Meaning of Life on a Branded Planet* (New York: Knopf Doubleday Publishing Group. Kindle Edition, 2009) Kindle Locations 82–83.
12. *Fast Company*, March 7, 2012.
13. Hegarty, Kindle Locations 1364–1368.
14. Gregory Solman, "Hilton Reignites Debate over the Value of Ideas," *Adweek*, May 30, 2005, http://www.adweek.com/news/advertising/hilton-reignites-debate-over -value-ideas-79800.
15. Ibid.

14   THE RATIONAL

1. The confidentiality notice is generally useless, and many RFPs explicitly say that they will own your ideas and do with them what they may—a topic for another section— but I find a copyright and confidentiality notice here are useful anyhow, and no one's ever complained.
2. Brian Morrissey, "Do Agencies Need Chief Digital Officers?", *Digiday*, May 9, 2012. http://www.digiday.com/agencies/do-agencies-need-chief-digital-officers/.
3. Michael Bush, "Procurement: We're about Value, Not Price," *Advertising Age*, April 26, 2010. http://adage.com/article/agency-news/procurement-price/143473/.
4. Brian Morrissey, "The Age of Procurement," *Digiday*, May 10, 2012, http://www .digiday.com/agencies/the-age-of-procurement/.
5. Digiday, May 10, 2012

15   ON PARTNERS AND PARTNERSHIP

1. Paul Graham, *Want to Start a Startup?*, Y Combinator, http://www.paulgraham.com /start.html (March 2005).
2. "BBDO Worldwide (Batten, Barton, Durstine & Osborn)," *Advertising Age*, November 15, 2003, (http://adage.com/article/adage-encyclopedia/bbdo-worldwide-batten -barton-durstine-osborn/98341/).
3. "DDB Worldwide," *Advertising Age*, September 15, 2003, http://adage.com/article/ adage-encyclopedia/ddb-worldwide/98431/.

16   THE TEAM

1. Sheryl Sandberg, *Lean In: Women, Work, and the Will to Lead* (New York: Knopf Doubleday Publishing Group. Kindle Edition, 2013), Kindle Locations 866–867.

17   EMPLOYEE RETENTION

1. John Lax, *The Story of Our Company,* Teehan and Lax, http://www.teehanlax.com /story/teehan-lax/ (retrieved September 16, 2014).
2. http://www.ogilvydma.com/

18   EMPLOYEE DEPARTURES

1. Guy Kawasaki, "The Art of Laying People Off," *American Express Open Forum,* November 18, 2008, https://www.openforum.com/articles/the-art-of-laying-people -off-1/.
2. Paul Smalera and Ben Horowitz, "The Right Way to Lay People Off," *Fortune,* September 20, 2010, http://tech.fortune.cnn.com/2010/09/20/six-steps-to-how-startups-can -survive-layoffs/.
3. Ibid.

19   BOOTSTRAPPING

1. Chris Brook, *The K Foundation Burn a Million Quid*, (London: Elipsis London PR Ltd, 1998), p. 5.
2. Lord Rock and Time Boy, AKA The Timelords, AKA Rockman Rock and Kingboy D, AKA The Justified Ancients of Mu Mu, AKA The Jams, AKA The KLF, AKA The Fall, AKA The Forever Ancients Liberation Loophole: *The Manual (How to Have a Number One The Easy Way)* (London: KLF Publications, 1988), pp. 20–21.
3. Richard Webb to The Barbarian Group, Memorandum, "[Announcements] TBG and MONEY," May 30, 2008.
4. David Catalano, personal interview, March 9, 2014.

20   "I WANT TO GET RICH"

1. Belinda Luscombe, "Do We Need $75,000 a Year to Be Happy?", *Time,* September 6, 2010, http://www.time.com/time/magazine/article/0,9171,2019628,00. html#ixzz2MsjjJO6q.
2. Robert Frank, "Super-Rich People Happy with Basically Everything in Their Lives, Infuriating Survey Finds," *Huffington Post,* February 27, 2013, (http://www .huffingtonpost.com/2013/02/27/super-rich-people-happy-w_n_2774495.html).
3. Catherine Rampell, "Who Counts as 'Rich'?", *The New York Times Economix Blog,* December 9, 2011, http://economix.blogs.nytimes.com/2011/12/09/who-counts-as -rich/.
4. Christine Hsu, "What Is Rich? Survey Reveals Income Aspirations," *Medical Daily,* December 2011, http://www.medicaldaily.com/articles/8179/20111209 /annual-income-net-worth-150-000-1-million-rich-wealthy-demographics .htm#dTOhLtBYZsDiRp1Y.99.
5. Graeme Wood, "Secret Fears of the Super-Rich," *The Atlantic,* February 24 2011, http://www.theatlantic.com/magazine/archive/2011/04/secret-fears-of-the-super -rich/308419/?single_page=true.
6. Ibid.
7. Ellen Cushing, "The Bacon-Wrapped Economy," *East Bay Express,* March 20, 2013, http://www.eastbayexpress.com/oakland/the-bacon-wrapped-economy/Content ?oid=3494301&showFullText=true.
8. Stephen Fox, *Mirror Makers* (Champaign, IL: University of Illinois Press, 1997), p. 209.

22 BANKS AND FUNDING

1. Ami Kassar, "Why Small Business Lending Is Such a Confusing Mess," *The New York Times,* June 5 2012, http://boss.blogs.nytimes.com/2012/06/05/why-small-business -lending-is-such-a-confusing-mess/.
2. Matt Taibbi, "Yes Virginia, This Is Obama's JOBS Act," *Rolling Stone*, April 12, 1012, http://www.rollingstone.com/politics/news/yes-virginia-this-is-obama-s-jobs -act-20120412.
3. National Federation of Independent Business (NFIB) Research Foundation, *Small Business Credit in a Deep Recession,* http://www.nfib.com/Portals/0/PDF/AllUsers /research/studies/Small-Business-Credit-In-a-Deep-Recession-February-2010 -NFIB.pdf, February 2010, p. 6.
4. NFIB Research Foundation, *Small Business, Credit Access and a Lingering Recession,* http://www.nfib.com/Portals/0/PDF/AllUsers/research/studies/small-business -credit-study-nfib-2012.pdf, January 2012, p. 8.
5. NFIB Research Foundation, January 2012, p. 12.
6. NFIB Research Foundation, February 2010, p. 12.
7. NFIB Research Foundation, January 2012, p. 18.
8. Some lines of credit may have some restrictions on how you spend the money, but in our world this is generally rare.
9. Catharine P. Taylor, "M-word Is Back," *Advertising* Age, May 27, 2002, http://adage .com/article/news/m-word-back/52079/.
10. Small Business Administration, *U.S. Small Business Administration Final Plan for Retroactive Analysis of Existing Rules*, January 23, 2012, http://www.sba.gov/sites /default/files/SBAFinalPlanRestropectiveAnalysisofExistingRules23Jan12.pdf, January 23, 2012.
11. Kassar, June 5, 2012.
12. David Catalano, personal interview, March 9, 2014
13. Ian Mount, "When Banks Won't Lend, There Are Alternatives, Though Often Expensive," *The New York Times,* Aug 1, 2012 (http://www.nytimes.com/2012/08 /02/business/smallbusiness/for-small-businesses-bank-loan-alternatives.html? _r=0).
14. Ami Kassar, "The State of Small-Business Lending," *The New York Times,* January 8, 2013, http://boss.blogs.nytimes.com/2013/01/08/the-state-of-small-business -lending/.
15. Mount, August 1, 2012.
16. Ibid.
17. Ibid.
18. NFIB Research Institute, February 2010, p. 6.
19. NFIB Research Institute, January 2012, p. 15.
20. NFIB Research Institute, February 2010, p. 18.
21. Ibid. p. 7.
22. NFIB Research Institute, January 2012, p. iv.
23. Ibid. p. 21.
24. Ibid.
25. David Catalano, personal interview, March 9, 2014.

24 HOW MUCH TO CHARGE?

1. Betsey Sharke, "Fixing the Bottom Line," *Adweek*, April 12, 1993, http://www.adweek .com/news/advertising/fixing-bottom-line-bby-betsy-sharkebbr-clearnonebr -clearnonewhile-politicians-debat.

31   HOW MUCH IS MY COMPANY WORTH?

1. David Yanofsky, "There's No Such Thing as a Tech Company Anymore," *Quartz*, March 30, 2013, http://qz.com/64934/theres-no-such-thing-as-a-tech-company-anymore/.
2. Bradley Johnson, "After Just 50 Years, Ed Meyer Exits," *Advertising Age*, December 4, 2006, http://adage.com/article/print-edition/50-years-ed-meyer-exits/113589/.

32   CREATING A PRODUCT IN YOUR SERVICE FIRM

1. Aaron Sanders, "Scrum Product Manager / Product Owner Roles and Responsibilities," *The Product Management Hut*, January 23, 2009, http://www.pmhut.com/scrum-product-manager-product-owner-roles-and-responsibilities.

33   CASE STUDIES OF START-UPS WITHIN AN AGENCY

1. All quotes from personal interview, March 2014.
2. All quotes from personal interview, March 2014.

35   GETTING ACQUIRED

1. Brad Feld and Amy Batchelor, *Startup Life: Surviving and Thriving in a Relationship with an Entrepreneur* (Hoboken, NJ: Wiley. Kindle Edition, 2013), Kindle Location 2866.

36   THE FEAR

1. Kenneth Roman, *The King of Madison Avenue: David Ogilvy and the Making of Modern Advertising* (New York: Palgrave Macmillan. Kindle Edition, 2010), Kindle Locations 1712–1715.
2. Ibid.
3. Cosima Marriner, "'We're Only Three Phone Calls from Disaster,'" *The Guardian*, November 30, 2005, http://www.theguardian.com/media/2005/nov/30/business.advertising.
4. Roman, Kindle Locations 1712–1715.
5. Graeme Wood, "Secret Fears of the Super-Rich," *The Atlantic Monthly*, April 2011, http://www.theatlantic.com/magazine/archive/2011/04/secret-fears-of-the-super-rich/308419/.

INDEX